DARK

DARK MATTERS

Exploring the Realm of
Psychic Devastation

Ira Brenner

KARNAC

First published in 2014 by
Karnac Books Ltd
118 Finchley Road, London NW3 5HT

British Library Cataloguing in Publication Data

A C.I.P. for this book is available from the British Library

ISBN 978 1 78049 163 9

Edited, designed and produced by The Studio Publishing Services Ltd
www.publishingservicesuk.co.uk
e-mail: studio@publishingservicesuk.co.uk

Printed in Great Britain

www.karnacbooks.com

CONTENTS

PART III: SOCIETAL REALM

PART IV: TECHNICAL REALM

PART V: EPILOGUE

ACKNOWLEDGEMENTS

The creation of this book could not have taken place without the ongoing inspiration from my patients and the meaningful exchanges with many colleagues, among which I can only name a few: Salman Akhtar, Helen Epstein, Richard Kluft, Ilany Kogan, Dori Laub, Marc Lipschutz, Dominic Mazza, Michael McCarthy, Vera Paisner, Nadia Ramzy, along with the members of her Palestinian–Israeli Work Group, Eric Stake, J. Anderson Thomson, and Vamik Volkan. I also wish to recognise the encouraging support of this project by Oliver Rathbone of Karnac Books, the expert attention to detail in the preparation of this manuscript by Deborah Szumachowski, and my wife Roberta Brenner's deep appreciation of my need to keep writing.

Permissions

I am grateful to the following for permission to reprint material that appears in this book.

Chapter Two: "Splitting of the ego" was previously published as "On splitting of the ego: a history of the concept", in *On Freud's "Splitting of the Ego in the Process of Defence"*, edited by T. Bokanowski and S. Lewkowicz (Karnac, 2009) and reprinted by kind permission of Karnac.

Chapter Four: "Seeing and not seeing" was previously published in *On Freud's "The unconscious"*, edited by S. Akhtar and M. K. O'Neil (Karnac, 2013) and reprinted by kind permission of Karnac.

Chapter Five: "The intergenerational transmission". The three poems in this chapter ("Things my Father Won't Do"; "A Daughter Dreams"; "How to Spot One of Us") originally appeared in *How to Spot One of Us*, by Janet Kirchheimer (CLAL, 2007) and are reprinted by kind permission of CLAL: The National Jewish Center for Learning and Leadership.

Chapter Six: (1) "Playing and survival" was previously published as "Playing for survival during the Holocaust", in *Play and Playfulness: Developmental, Cultural, and Clinical Aspects*, edited by M. C. Akhtar, (Lexington Books, a member of the Rowman & Littlefield Publishing Group, 2011) and is reprinted by kind permission of the publisher.

Chapter Six: (2) "The Butterfly", "Homesick", and "The Little Mouse" were originally published in *I Never Saw Another Butterfly: Children's Drawings and Poems from Terezin Concentration Camp, 1942–1944*, by H. Volakova (Artia, Prague, 1978, 1993). Compilation published by Schocken Books (an imprint of the Knopf Doubleday Publishing Group, a division of Random House LLC), 1993, and reprinted by kind permission of Schocken Books.

Chapter Seven: "Geopolitical identity disorder" was previously published as "The Palestinian/Israeli conflict: a geopolitical identity disorder" in *American Journal of Psychoanalysis*, 69: 62–71.

Chapter Ten: "Handling the compulsion to repeat" was previously published as "An unusual manifestation of repetition compulsion", in *On Freud's "Beyond the Pleasure Principle"*, edited by S. Akhtar and M. K. O'Neil (Karnac, 2011), and reprinted by kind permission of Karnac.

Ira Brenner, MD, is Clinical Professor of Psychiatry at Jefferson Medical College in Philadelphia and Training and Supervising Analyst at the Psychoanalytic Center of Philadelphia, where is he also Director Emeritus of the Adult Psychotherapy Training Program. He has developed a special interest in the area of psychological trauma and is the author of over eighty publications. He has co-edited two special issues of the *International Journal of Applied Psychoanalytic Studies* where he is Associate Editor of the section on Trauma. He has written four books: *The Last Witness: The Child Survivor of the Holocaust*, co-authored with Judith Kestenberg (1996); *Dissociation of Trauma: Theory, Phenomenology, and Technique* (2001), *Psychic Trauma: Dynamics, Symptoms, and Treatment* (2004), *Injured Men: Trauma, Healing, and the Masculine Self* (2009).

A member of Phi Beta Kappa and the Alpha Omega Alpha medical honour society, he has received a number of awards for his work, including the Gratz Research Prize from Jefferson for work on the Holocaust in 2000, the Piaget Writing Award for his 2001 book, and the Gradiva Award for his 2009 book. He has also received the Bruno Lima Award from the American Psychiatric Association for his work in disaster psychiatry and the Practitioner of the Year Award from the

Philadelphia Psychiatric Society. In 2008, Dr Brenner received the President's Award from the Psychoanalytic Center of Philadelphia for extraordinary service. He lectures nationally and internationally and co-chairs two discussion groups at the winter meetings of the American Psychoanalytic Association, one on the Holocaust and the other on dissociative disorders. He maintains a private practice of adult and child analysis in the greater Philadelphia area.

Introduction

After a turbulent, three-month attempt at treatment of a traumatised young woman whom he named Dora, Sigmund Freud concluded that "No one who, like me, conjures up the most evil of those half-tamed demons that inhabit the human breast, and seeks to wrestle with them, can expect to come through the struggle unscathed" (Freud, 1905e, p. 109). Before this declaration, the psychological perils of working with those with very troubled minds became quite clear to his mentor and erstwhile collaborator, Josef Breuer. Breuer had had a disastrous experience with his famous patient, Anna O, whose profound erotic transference, florid symptomatology, and iatrogenic morphine addiction culminated in her forced institutionalisation. After this ordeal, ". . . Breuer had vowed never to treat a case of hysteria again, and he eagerly referred new cases to his junior colleague" (Makari, 2008, p. 41).

More than a century later, there have been significant advances in psychopharmacology of the severely traumatised mind, but the challenges in the human encounter remain essentially unchanged. The inevitable collision of psyches continues to drive clinicians away and deter many others from even trying. After all, those who have endured overwhelmingly cruel and, at times, life-threatening treatment at the hands of others, especially family members, have internalised such relationships, which inevitably become enacted to some degree in therapy.

The fate of this internalisation is essentially the topic of this book. In the ever-expanding universe of the human mind, much more is being understood about how the trillions of connections in the brain can create the elusive state we call consciousness. However, we still are a long way off before we can integrate these findings with the wealth of clinical knowledge derived from psychoanalytic exploration. In addition, just as the universe itself has been determined to be held together by invisible forces and contains huge amounts of a mysterious substance known as "dark matter", so, too, we see that the psyche is largely held together by invisible, unconscious forces and mental content. This realm has been referred to with a variety of terms with overlapping meanings, including primal repression (Freud, 1915d), beta-elements (Bion, 1962a), the unrememberable and the unforgettable (Frank, 1969), the unthought known (Bollas, 1987), multi-sensory bridges (I. Brenner, 1988), unformulated experience (D. B. Stern, 1997), presymbolic representations (Beebe, Lachmann, & Jaffe, 1997), and zero process (Fernando, 2009). This domain is especially important when there is "alteration of the ego" (Freud, 1937c) that occurs as a result of psychic trauma in which both neurobiological changes as well as major disturbances in character formation may be seen.

The notion of "dark matter" of the mind is explored in Part I, the Prologue.

The rest of the book addresses three different realms of "dark matter": Chapters Two through Four deal with the "Conceptual realm", in which theoretical and historical perspectives are illustrated with clinical material. Starting with an elaboration and review of Freud's paper on "Splitting of the ego in the process of defence" (Freud, 1940e) in Chapter Two, I further discuss the implications of the concept of dissociation and its controversies as well as its "chequered history" (Glover, 1943) in the psychoanalytic movement in Chapter Three. Chapter Four is an elaboration of Freud's paper on "The unconscious" (Freud, 1915e), with an emphasis on disturbances of perception that may be seen in those who have been traumatised and who employ powerful, elusive defences.

Chapters Five through Eight address the "Societal realm", social and large-group trauma spanning the gap between clinical and applied psychoanalysis. The phenomenon of intergenerational transmission of trauma associated with genocidal persecution is explored in Chapter Five. Chapter Six reports on the rather neglected topic of children's play during the Holocaust. Chapter Seven applies the model of a traumatised, dissociated mind to the Palestinian–Israeli situation, and Chapter Eight offers some insights into the traumatised American psyche following the attacks on September 11.

The third section, the "Technical realm", features three chapters that focus on the technical challenges and modifications of technique that the analyst might need to consider when working with a traumatised patient who employs defensive, altered states of consciousness. Chapter Nine addresses the importance of containment. Chapter Ten examines an unusual manifestation of the repetition compulsion associated with dreams, and Chapter Eleven emphasises the idea that such treatment in and of itself is quite "psychoactive" and a powerful agent of change in patients previously thought to be unanalysable.

I invite you, the reader, to explore this book in any way. Each chapter stands on its own and can be read in any order. If you are not familiar with my earlier writings, I have tried to provide enough background throughout for you to get a sense of some basic ideas, such as the dissociative character and its organising influences.

This book is dedicated to the controversial nineteenth-century Austrian astronomer known as Leo Brenner (no relation to the author). Through his own lens, he explored the terrain and the craters near the dark side of the moon.

PART I
PROLOGUE

CHAPTER ONE

Why dark matter?

"Deep into that darkness peering, long I stood there
   wondering, fearing.
Doubting, dreaming dreams no mortals ever dared to
   dream before . . ."

(Poe, 1845)

Junior year. Circa 1970. Urban campus a few blocks from the White House. I was walking to organic chemistry class, the do-or-die course for pre-med students. You might say I was a bit preoccupied with my future. After rounding the corner from my dormitory, heavy textbook in hand, I got caught up in an impromptu antiwar rally. Hurriedly weaving my way through the crowd, the chants, the bullhorns, and the placards, I came face to face with an approaching phalanx of the District of Columbia police department. They clearly were not going to be interested in my plight. Armoured in their riot gear of helmets, shields, and batons, they literally ploughed through the crowd. Quickly following those more prepared than I who knew where to run for cover, I scurried into the lobby of another dormitory. Just as I got through the door, the guy behind me was pulled back out by an officer, was smashed in the head with a club, and then pushed back in nearly on top of me. The image of this fellow student's bloodied face and glazed look haunted me for a very long time. However, I am a bit hazy about getting to class that day.

Without realising it at the time, I had a first-hand experience of the marvels of traumatic memory. Sometimes, it can be indelible and intrusive. Other times, as Freud said, ". . . nothing of the forgotten traumas shall be remembered and nothing repeated" (Freud 1939a, p. 75).

Several decades later, I was sitting with a patient who had survived a dramatic pier collapse along the riverfront that had taken a number of lives. Negligent construction was at fault. He was enjoying the two-for-one drink special that evening and was, as the expression goes, feeling no pain. He was flirting with a woman when, suddenly and unexpectedly, the wooden structure gave way, trapping him underneath the black water amid the shattered timbers and shredded awning. The more he struggled to break free, the more he became straitjacketed by the canvas. Were he not such a strong swimmer who could hold his breath, calm himself down, and just happened to swim in the right direction to the surface, away from the watery chaos, he, too, would have drowned. He made his way to the shore many minutes later downstream, completely exhausted, and dragged himself to dry land, while paramedics were trying to resuscitate someone. It was the woman with whom he had just been flirting, but he was too horrified and depleted to react. He thought he saw her looking at him knowingly and helplessly as her life ebbed away. He was haunted by the memory of her eyes, which kept him awake at night, followed him everywhere, and persecuted him. I was able to draw on my own mini-trauma as an erstwhile antiwar dissident to help me understand, tolerate, and empathise with the horror, blocked grief, and survivor guilt of this young man. What enabled me to do so was the result of an ongoing process dealing with the dark matters of my own mind and the minds of others.

It is this simple, everyday word in the English language that usually evokes an aura of mystery, hiddenness, and possible danger—"dark". We are all familiar with many expressions that use this word, such as the "dark side of the moon", "going to the dark side", "dark places", or being in a "dark mood". Someone may have "dark humour", or be doing something "under the cover of darkness", or is "afraid of the dark". The word "dark" itself—"this is very dark"—is quite evocative. When it comes to racial politics, those of darker skin are usually more subject to prejudice and oppression. Someone also could have "dark motives": "Who knows what evil lurks in the hearts of men? The Shadow knows!" Furthermore, it is always "darkest before the dawn". Also, there are "dark years" and the "Dark Ages" themselves. In contrast, there seem to be many fewer positive uses of the word "dark": rich, dark coffee, dark chocolate, and those people who prefer dark meat over white meat. Also, when we refer to the dark side of human nature, it is associated with the Latin word for left-handed, or sinister, which, interestingly, is controlled by the right side of the brain. It is in this right hemisphere, in the hidden, non-verbal, mysterious corners of the mind, where it is likely that we will find the realm in which the legacy of severe trauma leaves its dark shadows on the psyche.

Freud confidently stated that "The effects of traumas are of two kinds, positive and negative" (Freud, 1939a p. 75). While we are generally more familiar with these positive symptoms of remembering and re-experiencing, the so-called negative symptoms inhabit a murky space in our theories and in our minds. It is a realm which, as noted above, Freud insisted ". . . follow[s] the opposite aim: that nothing of the forgotten traumas shall be remembered and nothing repeated" (Freud 1939a, p. 75). Such a pronouncement would have these symptoms as being "beyond the pleasure principle" (Freud, 1920g), but are they really exempt from the repetition compulsion? Are they banished to some dark corner of the mind, trapped and unable to exert any influence? Gone without a trace? Almost, but not exactly. Indirect evidence of these ". . . defensive reactions" was to be inferred by certain ". . . 'avoidances', which may be intensified into 'inhibitions' and 'phobias'" (Freud, 1939a, p. 76). Contemporary thinking would also consign dissociative phenomena to the realm of negative symptoms.

Curiously, modern scientists are grappling with a comparable and more complex challenge—understanding a mysterious force of astronomical proportions that is essentially also invisible. It does not reflect, emit, or absorb light, and has no electrical charge. Yet, it is so important that it comprises about twenty-five per cent of the entire universe and appears to be the glue that holds the galaxies together as they hurtle through space at unimaginable speed. Thought to comprise infinitesimally small, subatomic particles that have yet to be fully proved and identified, this phenomenon is known as "dark matter". It is inferred to be present mathematically, due to unaccounted-for substances in the cosmos and by studying the subtle differences in the movement of heavenly bodies that cannot be explained by gravitational forces and other known influences. Like the excessive amnesia of childhood and adolescence that might be a clue that one has sustained severe early trauma, the presence of something extremely important might be suspected by the absence of something equally important. In this case, it is coherent narrative owned by the patient.

In the current revision of the criteria for post traumatic stress disorder in the *Diagnostic and Statistical Manual of Mental Disorders, Fifth Edition (DSM-5)* (American Psychiatric Association, 2013), the evolution of the concept of negative symptoms can be seen as greatly expanded from Freud's original idea of two categories:

C. Persistent avoidance of stimuli associated with the traumatic events(s), beginning after the traumatic event(s) occurred, as evidenced by avoidance or efforts to avoid one or more of the following:

   1. distressing memories, thoughts, or feelings about or closely associated with the traumatic event(s).

   2. external reminders (i.e., people, places, conversations, activities, objects, situations) that arouse distressing memories, thoughts, or feelings about, or that are closely associated with, the traumatic event(s).

D. Negative alterations in cognitions and mood associated with the traumatic event(s), beginning or worsening after the traumatic event(s) occurred, as evidenced by two or more of the following:

   1. inability to remember an important aspect of the traumatic event(s) (typically due to *dissociative amnesia [author's italics]* that is not due to head injury, alcohol, or drugs).

   2. persistent and exaggerated negative beliefs or expectations about oneself, others, or the world (e.g., "I am bad", "No one can be trusted", "The world is completely dangerous"). (Alternatively, this might be expressed as, e.g., "I've lost my soul forever", or "My whole nervous system is permanently ruined").

   3. persistent, distorted blame of self or others about the cause or consequences of the traumatic event(s).

4. persistent negative emotional state (e.g., fear, horror, anger, guilt, or shame).

5. markedly diminished interest or participation in significant activities.

6. feelings of detachment or estrangement from others.

7. persistent inability to experience positive emotions (e.g., unable to have loving feelings, psychic numbing). (American Psychiatric Association, 2013, pp. 143–145)

Here, we can see the growing recognition of the role of dissociative symptoms not only in the well-known intrusion phenomena of recurrent flashbacks and total absorption in the trauma, which are listed under "positive" symptoms, but also in the peritraumatic amnesia, depersonalisation, and derealisation in the negative symptoms.

The role of the psychoanalyst in the treatment of those who have sustained significant trauma in many ways parallels the history of the psychoanalytic movement itself. From its inception and early research into hysteria to its overvaluing of psychic reality, to its current recognition of the importance of the relationship, there are a multitude of models to fit all occasions and all temperaments of analysts.

I never imagined that my own career would have evolved the way that it has with a special interest in the area of psychic trauma—at least consciously. Looking back, however, I can see how certain experiences, events, relationships, and circumstances have facilitated my taking this path. I grew up in a state of confusion about heavenly and earthly matters. I could not understand how anything worked and especially why people behaved the way they did. As a very curious young boy, I wondered about everything, but most of the grown-ups around me did little to satisfy my quest for answers. My questions were either met with a shoulder shrug, a pat answer, or the sense that I should not have asked in the first place. My childish preoccupations might have been met with derision, impatience, disinterest, or worse. A little boy does not ask about a "land" far, far away called Auschwitz. Therefore, I spent a lot of time in quiet contemplation, trying to figure things out on my own and creating silly theories to explain the world around me. As fascinated as I was and still am about nature, I was particularly drawn to the human condition, especially the darker side of human nature. How could people do unimaginably cruel things to others and, more remarkably, how could anyone survive?

One of my most emblematic recollections of trying to understand motivation involved my irascible Hebrew schoolteacher, who became enraged when a fellow classmate asked something about the existence of God. Such a basic question in a parochial learning institution must have been heard as blasphemy. Our instructor, a mercurial Holocaust survivor of a very famous ghetto uprising, whose scars were quite prominent, burst forth with a thunderous retort and declared, with a menacing, pointing finger, "DON'T ASK QVESTIONS!" I thought to myself even back then that his reaction seemed a bit extreme, even downright absurd, for a supposed educator, but it was an attitude with which I was familiar, none the less. I realised years later that one of his favourite questions was a mildly humorous attempt to control his thinly veiled contempt for us well-fed and spoiled American children through his familiar refrain: "Are you thirsty for knowledge or thirsty for Coke?" My school-age formulation back then was that he was still affected by bad memories of the Holocaust and took it out on us. That someone could continue to be deeply affected by terrible experiences in the past was axiomatic for me. I lived it every day in my family, and one might say that the connection was "baked" into my mind.

I was bolstered from being too squelched in my curiosity about God because I thought I had already acquired that coveted information from the wisest man I knew—my great-grandfather. Perhaps I was even a bit smug about it. He was the most likely person in my little world to have any real answers, but he was terrifying to a four-year-old. Blind, bearded, forbidding, and lost in prayer whenever I saw him, I was not even sure he knew I existed, let alone knew who I was. Nevertheless, I somehow knew I must overcome my reticence and seek a private audience with him. I just did not know quite how to do it. Whenever I would see him at his usual spot at my grandmother's house, where I visited weekly, he would either be standing and rocking in his silent devotion or sitting down and reading Braille with his gnarled fingers. He always seemed busy, and I could never muster up the courage to approach him on my own. I would take a step forward and then retreat to the sanctuary of an adjacent small room to watch the television that was always on, which was more "white noise" than sound and always out of focus. The "rabbit ears" on the top of their TV never worked as well as the fancier antennas on the roofs, and I always wondered why they did not have that kind. I guess I figured that since my grandmother was always too busy in the kitchen to watch and my grandfather was always working at his little corner grocery store, then the most likely person to watch was a sightless old man, so what difference did it really make if there was lousy reception. Nobody could answer that question either, so I had to come to that conclusion on my own.

I had a more important question on my mind than the state of their television, though, so when the time came to talk to him, I did not want to squander my precious moments with him. After many weeks of pondering the challenge, I told my mother I had a very important question to ask her grandfather. She did not ask what it was, and I did not specifically tell her, but I think she sensed it was of cosmic significance. To my relief and gratitude, she somehow arranged it, perhaps something as obvious as telling him I wanted to speak to him. I wondered how she did it, but did not dare ask such a foolish question. So, I dutifully approached the family sage, sat very near him, and whispered in his ear. He quietly and respectfully listened to my burning question: "Zayde, who made God?" There, I did it! He paused for a moment and matter of factly said to me, "The thunder and lightning!" I cherished that secret knowledge, an answer that only two people in the world knew for as long as my preoperational mind would allow me to do so. I could not have asked him the obvious follow-up question, which would come to me when I had a slightly more developed mind, which was, "Then who made the thunder and lightning??" By that time, I realised that if God were truly the creator of the universe, then He would have created the thunder and lightning, not *vice versa*, but by the time I realised all this, my great-grandfather had died. He took his mystical knowledge with him, and I was left to ponder the meaning of his response ever since. Did he truly believe what he had told me himself, or did he think that he would mollify me enough so that I would leave him alone so he could resume his silent communion with his maker? Or did he imagine that some day I would realise the circularity of his response and ponder on it and struggle with it as one would with a Buddhist koan? I would like to think the latter was the case.

I continued to struggle with deep questions and was especially drawn to the seemingly unanswerable mysteries of the mind. That I, among other things, might have become known for having expertise in the psychoanalytic treatment of dissociative identity disorder

(DID), that is, providing what many consider an obsolete treatment of a condition that even many of my psychoanalytic colleagues doubt exists, fills me with both an enormous sense of pride and a sense of ironic amusement. While other devoted specialists have spent their lives in the study or pursuit of a cause they believe to be valid and worthy only to discover much later on that they were misguided at best, or had totally wasted their time at worst, the sense of disillusionment and despair from realising that one's life work has been for naught must be overwhelming. Working in splendid isolation or with a group of over-zealous believers who reinforce each other's views because of their like-mindedness, or blind allegiance to a charismatic leader, are prescriptions for such a disaster. Because of my own circumstances and relationships, however, I feel fairly assured that, despite the controversy surrounding this aspect of my work, I am on the right track. Moreover, having had some success in my clinical work has been validating. Taking this particular path, however, has, at times, been quite lonely and uncertain, with very few signposts along the way. It has, therefore, been essential to have had my own network of mentors and colleagues with whom to confer.

It has been shown that expansion and innovation in different fields often come from the periphery (Bos & Groenendijk, 2007), and the field of psychoanalysis is no exception. From the beginning of the movement, Freud's list of ousted members of his inner circle are, for the most part, still remembered today, for example, Adler, Rank, Jung, and Stekel, not to mention other dissidents such as Ferenczi, Klein, and Horney. Those who continue to maintain their affiliations seem to have the most influence on the mainstream. Drawing on the work of McLaughlin, a sociologist who studied so-called "positive marginalists", Bos and Groenendijk have concluded that ". . . optimal marginal intellectuals have access to the creative core of an intellectual tradition, but are not bound by institutional restrictions. They are therefore in an ideal position to transfer novel ideas from the margin to the core" (p. 4). They add: "When marginal ideas become consecrated they may change dominant opinion, but in themselves these ideas also change during this process because they now acquire a new status, and with that—a new meaning" (Bos & Groenendijk, 2007, p. 3).

Until recently, I did not have the perspective possessed by my two main mentors, Vamik Volkan and Judith Kestenberg, who, fairly probably, could be considered "positive marginalists". Prominent members of the analytic community in their own right, each had a special area of interest, expertise, and creativity that was a bit off to the side of the mainstream, which mutually influenced the other. Volkan, a Turkish Cypriot, grew up on an island torn apart by ethnic violence between Greeks and Turks, and has made important contributions in many areas, such as pathological grief and applying psychoanalytic thinking to international conflict resolution. He is a brilliant clinician, superb teacher, and prolific writer, and I first met him during my psychiatric residency when his ground-breaking text on object relations theory in the 1970s was published at the same time as Kernberg's. He offered seminars on trauma that included group disasters, both of man-made and natural origin, in which the suddenness and the enormity of the losses made it impossible for the survivors to mourn. He convincingly taught us that such individuals might manifest psychotic-like symptoms, such as hallucinations of a lost loved one and almost delusional preoccupation with inanimate objects that were their possessions, which he called linking objects. So, for dynamic reasons due to traumatic loss, I learnt that people might develop serious symptoms that are best treated by intensive, analytically orientated therapy, not medication. It was a fascinating idea that intrigued and inspired me, but was a bit ahead of my clinical experience, as I spent much time on the inpatient unit with acutely psychotic patients where medication was necessarily prescribed. Fortunately, my first attending psychiatrist on this unit was another unusually gifted individual, Salman Akhtar. Among other things, he encouraged me to write. Interestingly, the one article I did co-author with him was during that time and on the topic of the differential diagnosis of fugue-like states (Akhtar & Brenner, 1979). That paper, in a sense, foreshadowed my work with fugues of dissociative origins and dissociative psychopathology.

Interestingly, Akhtar, my muse, whose mammoth contributions to the analytic literature rival those of any other analyst past or present, has written possibly the only paper on mentorship (Akhtar, 2003a). He describes the role of the mentor as being equidistant among parent, teacher, lover, and analyst. There is no doubt that I formed lifelong bonds with both Volkan and Kestenberg, as they have been phenomenally influential throughout my professional life.

For her part, Judith Kestenberg was like my psychoanalytic mother. Born in Poland and fortuitously being here in the USA when the Nazis invaded Poland, she could not return to her family because they were murdered in the Holocaust. She characterised herself in a darkly humorous way as "a child of non-survivors". She was an early collaborator with Margaret Mahler, and I first met her in New York at the American Psychoanalytic Association meetings when, as a candidate, I started attending discussion groups. Her group on the Holocaust, GPSEHSG (Group for the Study of Effects of the Holocaust on the Second Generation), co-chaired with Martin Bergmann and Milton Jucovy, was of pivotal importance to me for many personal and professional reasons. Here it was, back in the early 1980s, and this distinguished group of analysts was saying such things as that the real person of the analyst was important. Sometimes, even personal disclosure was necessary. Moreover, while psychic reality was no doubt essential to the analytic enterprise, the fact of external reality, and especially massive psychic trauma, was essential to take into consideration in certain cases. Specifically, with such trauma due to genocidal persecution, not only were the survivors profoundly affected but also, through some not fully understood mechanism, there could be transmission of this trauma to their offspring. Something that went deeper than identification, and before the burgeoning research on attachment describing the transmission of fear from mother to infant, this intergenerational transmission was described by Kestenberg as a "time tunnel" (Kestenberg, 1982a), a transposition. Some children of survivors could unconsciously be living out their parents' Holocaust experience that was interwoven into their developmental course. Marion Oliner was close when she described "hysterical features" to this double book-keeping, which today we might consider to be in the dissociative realm. Kestenberg also stressed the importance of survivors not being able to mourn their incalculable losses of loved ones, of possessions, of community, of personal health, and of the possibilities that one might have had in life. Interestingly, she was not familiar with Volkan's work on pathological grief, which dovetailed beautifully with her thinking. I remember how important it was for me to facilitate a meeting between the two of them to ensure that each could become familiar with the other's work. Another very important aspect of my apprenticeship with Kestenberg was learning from her about the importance of finding ego strength in even the most traumatised individual. In fact, it is quite easy to find the pathology and the symptomatology, but much more difficult to tease out the resilience, the ego strengths, and the capacity for mastery.

Becoming a research interviewer for Kestenberg's Child Survivor Project while I was still a candidate deepened my relationship with her, as I became a much closer collaborator with her. Not only did I have the opportunity to learn about intergenerational transmission by joining their monthly study group in New York, but I also interviewed over one hundred child survivors who were under the age of thirteen during their persecution. With the help of a semi-structured analytically and developmentally orientated interview protocol, these meetings were recorded, transcribed, coded, and then analysed for recurrent themes, along with over 1,200 other interviews throughout the world. Selma Kramer was extremely supportive of my work in this realm and, together with Kestenberg, had encouraged me to do child analytic training. It took me two more decades to get ready for that step, however.

I authored and co-authored a number of papers with Kestenberg until ageing and ill health sapped her vigour. She was a dynamo of curiosity and perfectionism whose contributions ranged from infant development, female sexuality, and movement therapy to probing the minds of both Holocaust perpetrators and their victims. When it became evident that she was on an irreversible decline, Salman Akhtar suggested that I assemble a collection of papers that she and I had written into a book before it was too late. Kestenberg heartily endorsed this idea, and in 1996 we got the American Psychiatric Press to publish *The Last Witness: The Child Survivor of the Holocaust*. Every week I went to her hospital bedside, which was set up in her house, to review the latest revisions and editorial suggestions of the manuscript. She would remove her oxygen mask and, for brief moments, her fiery intellect and uncompromising vision would burst forth. To almost her last dying breath, she argued with the publishers about their wanting to omit a passage so as not to offend German readers: it was about the Nazis' displaced, unconscious wish to murder their own children as a factor in their genocidal blood lust. What I learnt about mourning from her, Volkan, and, of course, the termination of my own analysis, all came to bear when she died not long after the publication of the book.

While I was thoroughly involved with the Holocaust research, my day job as a Unit Director at the Institute of Pennsylvania Hospital took a fateful turn when a new attending psychiatrist started admitting his patients to my floor. Although still a candidate who was not appreciated by many analysts at the time, Richard Kluft was already an internationally acclaimed expert of what was to be called multiple personality disorder (MPD) at the time. He had left Reading Hospital and started flooding 49th Street (the location of the hospital) with his legendary "multiples". At times, this population could be so out of control that what we described as "borderline" behaviour would have been a welcome relief. Dr Kluft brought with him a new set of terms, techniques, and understanding of the mind fractured by severe, early, and persistent trauma, which was both daunting and, at times, dubious. He had many detractors and sceptics who might have deterred a less single-minded individual, and I was immediately impressed by his uncommon brilliance. The only problem was that I had no idea what he was talking about, and his patients were regularly destroying the fabric of my inpatient milieu. Therefore, it became an administrative imperative to find out as quickly and as thoroughly as possible what was going on.

Sitting with some of these patients, who frequently switched personalities and told the most lurid tales of being victims of satanic ritual abuse, CIA mind-control experiments, and child prostitution rings, I thought their credibility was often in question. In fact, it was this form of splitting of staff, that is, whether they were believable or not, that often distinguished them from borderline patients. Yet, I had a similar intersubjective experience of being with them as I did when talking with Holocaust survivors. I felt as though I were in the presence of a severely traumatised individual. Dr Kluft was clearly on to something, but it was not until I finally recognised that same trance-like, quasi-psychotic symptomatology associated with amnesia in one of my outpatients who had never had any contact with him that I became a "believer". Then a dissociative disorders unit opened up and subsequently expanded, and I had the opportunity for daily immersion in this world as I became an Associate Director, along with David Fink, under Dr Kluft's leadership. There, we took turns interviewing all the patients and comparing notes on our diagnostic and therapeutic impressions. It was an unparalleled opportunity to observe Dr Kluft's hypnoanalytic technique as I developed my own style of evaluating this chameleon-like adaptation in this patient group. It left me with a definite impression that dissociation is widely misunderstood, often unrecognised, and more prevalent in various forms than we ever imagined. I can even say that it underlies both negative and positive symptoms of post traumatic stress disorder (PTSD). While it is not difficult to conceptualise how the amnesia and total avoidance of traumatic material that characterises the negative symptoms could have a dissociative basis, it may be that the positive signs of intrusion phenomena—flashbacks, nightmares, and enactments—also employ dissociation, but in a different way. Kitty Hart, an Auschwitz survivor, recounted how, upon her return to the death camp many years later, she simply concluded: "I never left!" (Hart, 1981). Her mind, trapped in the traumatic experience, could not fully process the passage of time or perception in the here and now. A splitting of the mind, as per Breuer and Freud (1895d), occurred and, in order to be able to function at all, a dissociation occurred to allow some healthy ego to go on with life.

In addition to my mentors, certain clinical experiences have been nodal points in my appreciation of the myriad ways in which the effects of trauma may manifest in the mind. For example, during my psychiatric residency, we had a rotation through the spinal cord unit that was usually populated by a number of young quadriplegics who had sustained paralysing injuries. These patients received consultations with neurosurgery, neurology, orthopaedics, and psychiatry. In addition to assessing their psychological reaction to their new status, in this population we were taught to take a dynamic history of what was going on in the patient's mind prior to their accidents. Not surprisingly, we often discovered familiar psychoanalytic themes supporting Freud's contention of unconscious factors in accident proneness. To consider that even catastrophic accidents might follow some principles described in *The Psychopathology of Everyday Life* (Freud, 1901b) was absolutely astounding as we recognised, for example, unconscious guilt, a wish for punishment for unacceptable impulses, castration anxiety, etc. Then, in the aftermath of this tragic new condition, we could see the ways in which they defended against their anxiety and grief. Disbelief, denial, disavowal, and forgetting, which, in retrospect, could all be subsumed under a dissociative banner, were evident. Here, I could see the interplay of unconscious motivation, external factors, and irreparable bodily problems resulting in a very traumatised mind.

Then, when I worked at the Veterans Hospital with Vietnam veterans, I had a patient who was one of the most feared men in the building. I think it was part of my initiation as a newly minted psychiatrist to be assigned to this unit. A huge, muscular man, whom I discovered was misdiagnosed with schizophrenia, was on a massive dose of antipsychotics but periodically would go berserk when he was in town on a pass. At those times he would become agitated and destructive and would throw bricks through the plate glass windows of stores, get arrested, and require a team of officers to subdue him. He would then be dragged back to the hospital in shackles and be in seclusion for weeks at a time. When I finally had a chance to meet him, the first thing I noticed was how flamboyantly he was dressed. We were in the middle of winter, and he was wearing a Hawaiian pineapple shirt and a straw hat with a jaunty feather. Moreover, he was talking a mile a minute. This was in an era when lithium was barely known at this VA hospital. The patient responded beautifully to lithium carbonate, since he was actively manic. It was a classic presentation. His antipsychotics were drastically reduced, and he could then begin to slow down and talk. What I learnt was that he was overwhelmed by his combat experience in Vietnam and, at times, thought that he was still there throwing grenades at the Vietcong when he threw bricks in the town. This patient taught me about co-morbidity. His trauma and flashbacks obscured the diagnosis of mania with bizarre symptoms and complicated his treatment. Yet, his symptoms had meaning and could be worked with psychotherapeutically when treated for his affective disorder.

When I left the VA and started work at a private hospital, I had a patient who was suicidally depressed and unresponsive to medication. As an incidental part of his history, he happened to mention that he was a Holocaust survivor and was terrified of being in a mental hospital, as it revived memories of him being a prisoner in a concentration camp. He was not sure where he was at times; he was not sure if he could trust his doctor and demanded to know if I were Jewish. I had great compassion for him and did family therapy as well, meeting his Holocaust-survivor wife and his massively obese son. Two starving camp survivors in a well-intentioned effort to prevent such a disaster in their offspring overfed him constantly, and it became a way of life for their son. What seemed so obvious to me was, of course, totally unconscious to everyone in this family system, and when I discovered the Holocaust discussion group around this time, my understanding of intergenerational transmission deepened. I worked with this man for several years after his discharge and was struck by a certain concreteness in his thinking, nicely described by Grubrich-Simitis (1984), which often accompanies massive psychic trauma. He needed to see a neurologist at one point, and discovered that there was one in town whose last name was the same as that of a Polish city, Lublin, that had once been a refuge for him. So, for him, "going to Lublin" was a literal experience. His profound sadness and unresolved grief seemed indelible as he would drift off into a reverie about what was no more and how unspeakable atrocities could never be put into words. These states of mind had a dissociative quality to them, I later realised.

When I left that hospital, I then worked at a community hospital where volumes of inpatients were diverted from the state hospital to my unit and, like a huge fishing net, we never knew what the daily census would be. One of these patients was a young woman admitted in a suicidal crisis due to homosexual panic. With a family history of alcoholism, she was drinking herself to death and had destroyed a promising career as a medical illustrator. Surprisingly, she was eager for psychotherapy and I accepted her into my growing private practice. About ten years later, after several more hospitalisations and serious suicidal regressions, she decided to become sober. Around that time, it became clear that her fluctuations in mood and ways of relating were due to serious dissociative psychopathology and not schizophrenia or borderline states. One day on the unit, she told me how overwhelmed she was by a painting of a Native American mother braiding her daughter's hair. The mother was straddling the young girl, lovingly engulfing her while grooming her. This tender scene brought back the nightmare of the patient's relationship with her own mother's sadistic sexual abuse, which, incredibly, had persisted until the present. Over the next fifteen years, we worked to uncover, reconstruct, and contain the disjointed, brutal story of near drowning into sexual submission and soul murder, which she survived (see Chapter Two). Needless to say, the management of her complex "mosaic" transferences and my countertransference was an essential feature of this heart-breaking and ultimately important case. Working with cases like this sharpened my senses and alerted me to the subtle manifestations of defensive altered states occurring in much less disturbed patients, including many who use the couch in analysis.

So, as I look back at my career, which began almost forty years ago, I realise that I have been working largely in the shadows that have surrounded the Freudian spotlight, which has illuminated the psyche in a certain way. As Freud himself famously described psychoanalysis as ". . . our one beacon-light in the darkness of depth-psychology" (Freud, 1923b, p. 18), his use of darkness as a metaphor for the unknown and unknowable is quite prevalent throughout his writing. From ". . . the sexual life of adult women is a 'dark continent' for psychology" (Freud, 1926e, p. 212) to ". . . [prehistoric] pictures [which] are situated in the darkest and most inaccessible parts of the caves . . ." (Freud, 1912–1913, p. 90), the implication was that such realms were beyond the reach of psychoanalysis. More recently, authors making reference to the astrophysical phenomenon of black holes (Eshel, 1998), from which no light or knowledge could escape, have further reinforced the view of many classically trained analysts that attempts at exploration were either futile or "not psychoanalysis" and, therefore, not likely to yield much benefit for the patient. In my view, a revisiting of the earliest insights of psychoanalysis needs to be integrated with the latest theoretical developments and discoveries in the neurosciences in order to better appreciate the myriad effects of psychic trauma.

Psychic trauma could be thought of as the reaction to overwhelming stimuli and affects, such as helplessness and fear, resulting in a rupture of the mental representation of the space–time continuum. The separation of the psyche described by Janet as dissociation (Janet, 1889), and Breuer and Freud as splitting of the mind (Freud, 1895d), is based on a spatial model of the mind. Since we now know that, according to modern physics, space and time are interchangeable and on a continuum that constitutes the fabric of our existence, this relationship needs to be taken into consideration when it comes to mental processes and their disruptions. Depending on one's level of development and the form and dynamic significance of the experience, as well as the nature of one's object relations, there might be major disturbances of mental functioning, alterations of consciousness, disorientation, and disturbances of memory, perception, processing, and identity. The continued impact of this rupture, as well as the compensatory measures that have been taken, would make up the dark matters of the mind. Just as dark matter, invisible to the human eye, comprises much of the universe and can be inferred only by studying its gravitational effects, so, too, can the devastating effects of trauma and the resulting dissociation sometimes only be recognised by the absences, deletions, and indirect manifestations in the patient.

PART II
CONCEPTUAL REALM

CHAPTER TWO

Splitting of the ego

"If each, I told myself, could but be housed in separate identities, life would be relieved of all that was unbearable . . ."

(Stevenson, 1886, p. 109)

Introduction

Human thought leads us to wonder about the origin and nature of things. While such curiosity is not the exclusive domain of our species, our primate cousins appear to be more concerned with more basic issues of finding food, finding a suitable mate, and surviving. We, too, concern ourselves with such instinctual demands as well as more sublime themes. Our wonderment about matters such as human nature, our existence, and the origin of the universe have occupied us for millennia and promise to vex us for many more. Such ineffable questions spawn not only scientific enquiry but also challenge our imagination, activate primary-process thinking, and provide a canvas on to which projective phenomena may be painted. As these mental processes converge, resulting in richly textured ideas, theories, and belief systems, it

21

cannot help be noted that certain patterns keep appearing in our attempts to understand and organise our world. One of these patterns is that a thing can change by becoming divided, separated, or split into two or more parts. For example, the division of cells—mitosis— is a basic pattern of life. It is a spatial model, which seems to be more readily understood than a model based on the more abstract, but more comprehensive, space–time continuum, which is less readily apparent to our minds (I. Brenner, 2002a).

This principle of division may be invoked in many situations rang- ing from the mundane to the most supreme. For example, sacred texts and ancient traditions addressing the "big questions" inevitably espouse a creation myth utilising a variation of this notion. In the Western world, for example, where the Judeo-Christian influence has prevailed, the all-familiar first chapter of the Hebrew Bible, Genesis, describes how God said, "Let there be light!" and thereby created day and night by splitting the primordial darkness. As creation continues, God then splits the water above and below the heavens as well as on the earth by creating land masses that divide up the seas. Compara- tive studies of creation, such as those done by Neumann (1954), a dis- ciple of Jung (whose own "split" with Freud, incidentally, is one of the more well-known stories in the creation of the psychoanalytic move- ment), reveal the universality of this formulation: ". . . in all peoples and in all religions, creation appears as the creation of light. Thus the coming of consciousness, manifesting itself as light in contrast to the darkness of the unconscious, is the real 'object' of creation mythology" (Neumann, citing E. Cassirer, 1954, p. 6). He, therefore, sees "creation" as a metaphor for the topographic theory of the mind.

Despite Freud's being a "godless Jew" (Gay, 1987; Rizzuto, 1998), the impact of his own religious heritage has been the topic of consid- erable interest (Halpern, 1999; Ostow, 1989; Yerushalmi, 1991). It has even been speculated that the tradition of keeping things separate, such as those in the Jewish dietary laws, might have subtly influenced Freud's thinking about mental organisation (I. Brenner, 2003–2004). He found the notion of a split in the psyche so compelling that in addi- tion to splitting of consciousness and splitting of the mind (Freud, 1895d), he applied it in his formulations about neurosis (1940a), perversion (1923b), and psychosis (1940e). Although Janet predated Freud with his theory of disaggregation, or dissociation, being caused by a fracture of the psyche (Janet, 1889), his model posited a passive disintegration based on trauma and constitutional factors as opposed to Freud's dynamic model based on conflict, anxiety, and unconscious motivation. As Pruyser (1975) notes, "The lure of the split in the psyche . . ." has tempted many and has stood the test of time.

The evolution of Freud's ideas

In Freud's early writings, he and Breuer describe "splitting of consciousness" (Freud, 1895d, pp. 12, 67, 69, 123) in which there was a separation of mental contents from the dominant mass of ideas. It was a precursor to the "cornerstone" concept of repression. They also referred to "splitting of a personality" (p. 45), where opposite behavioural states occurred. In addition, they wrote about "splitting of the mind" (pp. 225, 234), characterised by the simultaneous existence of conscious and unconscious ideation. This observation was particularly vexing because the patient could alternate between different states of mind, carrying on conversations, behaving in a volitional way, and having relationships one moment and then switching to another state and having amnesia for all of the above. Breuer described this phenomenon very well in the case of Anna O, whose "clouds", surly, agitated moods, and hysterical symptoms would fluctuate as she amnestically shifted from her very disturbed self to her usual self. Utterly devastated by the physical deterioration and death of her beloved father, this very ill, grief-stricken young woman required both high doses of chloral hydrate and the "talking cure"—a term she herself coined. When it was determined that "the motive for splitting of consciousness . . . was that of defence" (p. 166), psychoanalysis was truly born. (However, it would take almost another century for serious discussion to occur about combining psychoanalysis with pharmacotherapy, which Anna O also pioneered.)

In contrast to Janet's contention of constitutional weakness and an inability to maintain a synthesis of the mind, Freud recognised that dividedness of the mind could be understood "dynamically" from the conflict of opposing mental forces (Freud, 1910a, pp. 25–26). However, his turning away from the study of altered states of consciousness, dissociation, and hysteria to repression, the structural model, and splitting of the ego was a decisive turn of events in the history of psychoanalysis, leaving much still to be learnt from his earlier work.

A re-reading of his collaboration with Breuer suggests that he never fully embraced the latter's notion of the hypnoid state, even back then. His own individual contributions to their volume—his case reports and his section on the psychotherapy of hysteria—seemed from the start to reflect their theoretical differences. Breuer emphasised "hypnoid" hysteria and "retention" hysteria, whereas Freud preferred "defence" hysteria, which he believed was at the root of the other two subtypes. Moreover, Freud did not feel as proficient in hypnosis as Breuer did and perhaps was a bit eager to replace hypnotism with his own method. In so doing, he seemed to overlook his own observation that spontaneous, autohypnotic states might occur (Freud, 1891d) which might, in fact, be quite refractory to free association unless the analyst is aware it is happening and can work with the patient while in the trance (I. Brenner, 1994). As a result, much of Breuer's work was never fully integrated into the mainstream or "dominant mass of ideas" of psychoanalytic thinking. However, the idea of a split in the psyche persisted and was reworked throughout Freud's lifetime. Splitting of the ego came to be seen as an alternative defence to repression and a form of psychological damage control to possibly stave off total disintegration

> . . . by deforming itself . . . and even perhaps by effecting the cleavage or division of itself. In this way the inconsistency, eccentricities and follies of men would appear in a similar light to their sexual perversions, through acceptance of which they spare themselves repressions. (Freud, 1924b, pp. 152–153)

In his last writings about the study of the mind that he created, Freud's final written thoughts on splitting of the ego are summarised in Chapter VIII, "The psychical apparatus and the external world", of *An Outline of Psycho-Analysis*:

> Two psychical attitudes have been formed instead of a single one – one, the normal one, which takes account of reality, and another which under the influence of the instincts detaches the ego from reality. The two exist alongside of each other. The issue depends on their relative strength. If the second is or becomes stronger, the necessary precondition for a psychosis is present. If the relation is reversed, then there is an apparent cure of the delusional disorder. Actually it has only retreated into the unconscious – just as numerous observations lead us

to believe that the delusion existed ready-made for a long time before its manifest irruption. (Freud, 1940a, p. 202)

Alluding to a case of chronic paranoia in which the patient's dream was more based in reality than his daytime delusions, Freud (1922b) contended that splitting of the ego was operative in all cases of psychosis as well. Federn elaborated upon and extended these ideas as they pertained to psychotic illness, describing ego states and intro-ducing the concept of ego boundaries (Federn, 1952). Then, seeing the applicability of the notion of ego states, Watkins elaborated upon Federn's ideas and linked them back to the all-but-forgotten realm of dissociative psychopathology (Watkins & Watkins, 1997). While Freud was less sanguine about the efficacy of analysis in treating very disturbed patients, he thought, nevertheless, that they illustrated this phenomenon well. However, he felt that the condition of fetishism was even more illustrative and was ". . . a particularly favourable subject for studying the question" (Freud, 1940a, p. 203). In such cases, he contended that the dread of castration was so overwhelming that the young boy

> . . . disavows his own sense-perception which showed him that the female genitals lack a penis and holds fast to the contrary conviction. The disavowed perception does not, however, remain entirely without influence for, in spite of everything, he has not the courage to assert that he actually saw a penis. He takes hold of something else instead – a part of the body or some other object – and assigns it the role of the penis which he cannot do without. . . . Their behaviour is therefore simultaneously expressing two contrary premises. On the one hand they are disavowing the fact of their perception – the fact that they saw no penis in the female genitals; and on the other hand they are recog-nizing the fact that females have no penis and are drawing the correct conclusions from it. The two attitudes persist side by side throughout their lives without influencing each other. Here is what may rightly be called a splitting of the ego. . . . In fetishists, therefore, the detachment of the ego from the reality of the external world has never succeeded completely. (Freud, 1940a, pp. 202–203)

This phenomenon was also recognised by Freud to be operative in the dream state:

> . . . the dreamer's ego can appear two or more times in the manifest dream, once as himself and again disguised behind the figures of other

people. . . . In itself, this multiplicity is no more remarkable than the multiple appearance of the ego in a waking thought . . . [Freud, 1923c, pp. 120–121]

. . . this splitting of the ego . . . neither so new nor so strange . . . is indeed a universal characteristic of neuroses . . . as regards some particular behaviour, two different attitudes, contrary to each other and independent of each other. In the case of neuroses, however, one of these attitudes belongs to the ego and the contrary one, which is repressed, belongs to the id. (Freud, 1940e, p. 275)

Given the evolution of Freud's theorising over time, he invoked the concept of splitting to describe a dividedness of consciousness between the id and the ego, the ego and the superego, and within the ego itself. It fell upon his followers to apply this mechanism to virtually all of their own models of the mind, such as the normative split in the ego between observing and participating ego (Sterba, 1934), splitting in object relations theory (Klein, 1946), and the vertical split in self psychology (Kohut, 1971). Lacan also emphasised the dividedness of the ego (Lacan, 1953). However, there was a missing link that seemed to bridge Freud's frustrated wish to connect dream psychology with psychology (Lewin, 1954) as well as integrate hypnoid hysteria with "mainstream" analytic thinking (I. Brenner, 1999). Moving in this direction are the contributions of Fliess (1953a), who described "hypnotic evasion", Dickes (1965), who redefined the hypnoid state as a defensive alteration of alertness to ward off instinctual pressure, and Shengold (1989), who delineated the facilitating and vigilance-enhancing aspects of the "autohypnotic defense".

Clinical report

Perhaps the best way to illustrate the history of the concept of splitting of the ego and to elucidate this missing link is through a clinical report in which my appreciation of the nature of the division of a patient's mind evolved and deepened over two decades of analytic therapy.

There would be times during a session when Mary (I. Brenner, 2004) would suddenly take off her glasses. Since the magnification of her lenses accentuated the deadness of her eyes and the blankness of her expression, the contrast of seeing her eyes ablaze with rage after this abrupt gesture was even more dramatic. At these times, the patient's voice, syntax, body language, and overall demeanour changed. It was as though a mildly sinister prisoner who had been blindfolded and shackled had just broken out of his restraints, ripped off his eyeshades, and mockingly declared to his startled captors, "I'm free! Try to stop me!" Preferring the stealth value of being unknown, this aspect of the patient's mind functioned like an ominous terrorist bent on secretly sabotaging and disrupting the daily functions of a society. Almost as though taunting me, the patient's anger seemed to feed off of being in my presence. Initially, I felt a sense of uneasiness and puzzlement as the patient just glared and sneered at me, speaking about Mary in the third person as though she were being held hostage.

Significantly, changes in her visual perception were prominent in her symptomatology. Sometimes, she would lose her peripheral vision and feel as if she were wearing blinkers. Other times, things looked very blurred to her, as though she were opening her eyes under water, while at other times her field of vision just went dark. While these disturbances were much more consistent with hysterical conversion symptoms, the more inexplicable change in her vision was apparently in the ocular refraction that enabled her, in a certain state of mind, to see as well, if not better, without her glasses. Indeed, were she to keep them on in this ego state, then her vision would have become even more blurred once again. Had I not seen this phenomenon in several other patients, where, for example, one woman used two different pairs of glasses with very different refractions prescribed by two different ophthalmologists, it would have made me question the veracity of her claim. In another such case, a woman who also wore glasses most of the time, like Mary, except when she, too, was in a certain frame of mind, made the mistake of going for laser surgery to correct her near-sightedness. Despite my urging her to postpone the surgery at least until we could learn much more about when and why she did not need her lenses, her denial of the possibility of the presence of split-off ego states was so great that she went ahead with the procedure. I was concerned that the irreversible surgery to correct her near-sightedness would be disastrous for her when she lapsed into this mysterious other state, resulting in grossly impaired vision that might not be ameliorated even with another set of glasses.

Unfortunately, I was correct, and she suffered with a very unsatisfactory result that absolutely baffled her ophthalmologist (see Chapter Four). With these clinical experiences in mind, I had to consider the possibility that the involuntary muscles that controlled the shape of Mary's eyeballs and the focal length of her lenses were being affected by her shifting mental states in an unusual manifestation of a psychophysiological disturbance.

In addition, Mary had amnesia for the time she was in her glaring, angry state. Not only did she not remember what was said during these episodes, but she also did not even remember that she had them. For many months, she was not even aware that she had lost any time. Rather, she would be astounded that the session had seemed to end so quickly and tried to mask her confusion about it lest she betray the secret about her seemingly separate selves, a secret that she was apparently trying to keep from herself most of all. Enlisting her curiosity was most difficult, as she exuded a blasé attitude about it all, an attitude that was quite consistent with the *"la belle indifférence"* (Freud, 1915e) described in hysteria.

As described in Breuer's celebrated case of Anna O, the first symptom to be relieved by the "talking cure" was her inability to drink water. Although transferential factors and deeper traumatic origins were probably operative (Britton, 1999), it was officially associated with her repulsion over seeing her governess's dog drink out of a cup, which was linked with her father's dying of complications of tuberculosis and his expectoration. Her disgust over seeing her pet dog drink out of a glass was so overwhelming to her that her mind resorted to a rather drastic and disruptive solution—a splitting of her consciousness. In their jointly authored preliminary notes, which Breuer later iterates and Freud refutes, it is observed that ". . . the splitting of consciousness which is so striking in the well-known classical cases under the form of 'double conscience' is present to a rudimentary degree in every hysteria . . ." (Freud, 1895d, p. 12). Jones was apparently impressed enough also to mention that Anna O was a case of double personality (Jones, 1953), whereas the hysterical conversion symptoms were apparently of much more interest and perhaps fit more easily into Freud's formulation than the problem of double personality. Indeed, Freud confessed that "Strangely enough, I have never in my own experience met with a genuine hypnoid hysteria" (Freud, 1895d, p. 186).

Interestingly, it was striking to learn, after a number of years of treatment with Mary, that she, too, had a deep connection with dogs. (The role of dogs in other patients' case histories has been well documented (Escoll, 2005).) Her connection, however, was much more intimate than Anna O.'s. Whereas the mere sight of seeing a dog lap up water with the use of its tongue triggered Anna O, Mary ultimately recalled that as a young teenager she had actually utilised a dog's tongue to lap up her personal fluids for sexual pleasure. While babysitting for a family with a particularly affectionate canine, she literally taught the dog to lick her vagina until she reached orgasm. She pursued this secret, shame-laden sexual practice for several years each time she babysat, but then, somehow, put it out of her mind until we began to recognise the presence of her absences. Whereas Anna O reportedly improved after the recovery of her memory, Mary continued to deteriorate as we both began to wonder how it was that such a young girl would have ever come up with the idea to enlist the dog as a sexual partner in the first place. Indeed, even early on, Freud was a bit sceptical about the cathartic method in and of itself being curative due to the complex mental organisation of traumatic memories and pathogenic ideas ". . . which is stratified in at least three different ways" (Freud, 1895d, p. 288). He described different zones with alterations of unconsciousness organised according to chronology, theme, and word connections around a nucleus of the original trauma.

For Mary, the retrieval of the memory of cunnilingus by a dog was, indeed, the tip of the proverbial iceberg, as disturbances in the family, which were alluded to early on in the treatment, took on a more ominous quality. Recovery of these memories, however, was piecemeal, painful, and over time. Mary was bent on obliterating her capacity to think and remember by drinking large amounts of alcohol quite frequently. She noted that after the "happy hour" before dinner, her job was to prepare the drinks for her father. He became so drunk that he faded from the family picture, leaving Mary and her sisters to the mercy of their dictatorial and sadistic mother. Apparently identifying with the alcoholic father who withdrew and did not "know" what was going on, so, too, did Mary enhance her own psychological wish not to know with alcohol. What was known and remembered was sequestered in the angry, glaring, altered state of consciousness as well as in a number of other eventually identifiable states.

As Breuer and Freud originally described it, there is a ". . . tendency to such dissociation, and with it the emergence of abnormal states of consciousness (which we shall bring together under the term 'hypnoid'), [which are] the basic phenomenon of hysteria (Freud, 1895d, p. 12). At this point in his theorising, however, Freud struggled with reconciling Breuer's idea of the pathogenic effects of traumatic events occurring during autohypnotic, self-hypnotic, or hypnoid states and/or traumatic events causing the hypnoid states themselves *vs.* his own idea of repressed sexual instincts as the underlying aetiology of hysteria. In Mary's case as well as Anna O's, there was growing clinical evidence of both hysterical, visual symptoms and hypnoid states associated with amnesia. The role of early trauma had not yet been delineated with Mary, but the importance of unconscious sexual urges had emerged because the precipitating event bringing her to treatment was homosexual panic associated with the seductive overtures of an older woman, which overwhelmed the patient with guilt and suicidality.

The dramatic event that brought the presence of the seemingly separate selves into clear focus occurred when Mary cut herself with a razor blade that had been hidden in the binding of a book. Unbeknown to her in her usual state of consciousness (i.e., her "dominant mass of ideas"), in a *condition seconde* (Freud, 1895d), she deliberately put the razor in an obscure place that could not be found unless one were knowingly looking there. Thus, the blade had stayed there for days until an opportune moment of desperation presented itself and her alter ego could generate enough strength to cathect and "take over" consciousness in order to execute the deed. When discovered, the patient, in an inappropriately calm voice and demeanour, identified herself as Priscilla and described the incident in the third person, insisting that "she" did the best she could to limit the bloodshed and implied that there was a separate, destructive influence inside that was barely contained. That destructive influence, eventually known as Ralph, was the one who did not need the glasses and, in "his" mind, did not need any form of therapy either.

Over time, a number of different personifications came to light. For example, there would be times when the patient would be plagued by a mysterious, auditory hallucination of a terrified young boy saying, "God is trying to kill me!" This was usually associated with agitation and confusion, and Mary would become inwardly distracted and listen to this repetitive plea for help. This voice was associated with a young boy, Timmy, trapped inside, who believed that if the patient continued to speak, then "he" would be annihilated. Another force that stopped the patient's speech was an elderly woman, Flora, who was the personification of a censor and constricted the patient's throat ever more tightly until she gasped. These two "others", representing a symptom and an inhibition, effectively prevented Mary from continuing with her associations and, as we came to realise later, served as a deterrent from revealing any secrets about her relationship with her mother. In addition, there were several young girls whose cries of sadness, fear, and pain could be heard inside and then outside, if they were to take over consciousness and express themselves directly to me. There was also the "transparent guy" who functioned like a psychological prism directing energy to either Mary or Ralph. If the latter was fuelled by the "transparent guy", then he could become even angrier and stronger and take over again.

This dazzling array of other "personalities"—and a host of many more whose appearances were fleeting and rare—seemed to populate the patient's psyche and serve a variety of functions for her. On one level, they represented her intrapsychic conflict, which she experienced in the form of an interpersonal conflict between these different parties. As a multi-purpose structure with their own biographies and cohesion, they could convey a sense of overall continuity of the self as a defence against the lack of self-constancy and object constancy, which was associated with separation and annihilation anxiety. They housed contradictory views, affects, fantasies, drives, and ego capabilities. For example, Mary was the only one who could drive, whereas both Ralph and Mary could paint equally well, but usually rather different subjects. Ralph painted bloody, graphic, violent scenes that terrorised Mary, who eventually gave up painting out of fear that whatever project she might start would be hijacked by Ralph. Then, once her deep, unconscious troubles had become represented on the canvas and externalised, the image would then "work back on her" and constantly torment her. Having the effect of an unwelcome and poorly timed interpretation that can be overwhelming and increase resistance, Mary's artistic associations then became blocked and she stopped painting for more than a decade.

In his bid to "take over the body", Ralph suffered from a quasi-delusion that if he could merely kill off Mary then he would be victorious and free to do whatever he wanted. What he wanted was a sex change. "He" believed that he was a man trapped in a woman's body and, as such, the patient experienced a transsexual conflict in the form of Mary and Ralph fighting over the fate of the sexual anatomy of the body. If Ralph had his way, he would cut off the breasts either by himself or with the help of a surgeon if he had the money, close up the vagina, and craft a penis. Arrangements were being looked into for male hormone injections to acquire facial hair and facilitate the gender transformation. The patient also joined an organisation of transgendered people to obtain support while going through this process. The patient even notified the members of her community that henceforth people should call her by the male name "Phillip", the name of a latency-age boy she believed was residing inside who went deeply underground around puberty.

When breast buds developed and menarche started, "he" could not tolerate the reality of becoming a woman, which resulted in a split in the patient's ego, analogous to the previously described mechanism Freud attributed to fetishism. Yearning for a return to a less conflictual time, the patient hoped to redo her sexual development and become a man this time. However, the patient's sexuality was even more complicated in that it appeared as though different selves had different forms of sexuality. For example, Mary was in a committed lesbian relationship where she was the more passive sexual partner to an aggressive and demanding lover. Ralph, on the other hand, hated the partner and tried to strangle her on more than one occasion. He had strong sadomasochistic erotic tendencies and would become very aroused with the transference fantasy of shattering the glass in one of my picture frames, grabbing a shard, rushing over to me, slitting my throat, cutting off my penis, and having an orgasm during the process. So, it appeared that perverse sexuality in the form of bisexual sadomasochism, transsexualism, and bestiality existed in separate ego states. Urges to stalk young children were also expressed but not actualised. In particular, the patient's profound desire to be a male was apparently the strongest and associated with so much distress, internalised aggression, and shame that much of her suicidality was organised around the struggle over the domination and sexual fate of the body. The patient dressed in men's clothing and often wore a rolled-up sock in her panties to create a penis-like bulge. In fact, she sometimes kept it there for many days at a time, not changing her underwear, which resulted in urinary tract infections from poor hygiene. In addition, the length of the hair on every part of the body became a battleground on which this war was waged, often with life-and-death implications. Having taken a massive overdose and not telling anyone until several days later following her lapsing in and out of a coma and throwing up repeatedly, resulting in aspiration pneumonia, her plight was taken very seriously. Furthermore, since she did not cry out for help but silently withdrew instead, a pattern seen during interruptions and breaks consistent with an adult version of an avoidant type of attachment disturbance, she was especially worrying. Massive regression could occur if hair on the head got too long or if underarms and legs were shaved, and over time I was able to intervene as a mediator during these very intense "territorial disputes".

The memories of childhood trauma that emerged were sparked by seeing a painting of a woman braiding a young girl's hair while straddling her with the legs wide apart. Mary contacted me and said that she had something very urgent to tell me. She revealed that her mother had required her to be a sexual partner and a source of pleasure for her as far back as she could remember and even until the present time. This astounding revelation was fleshed out over time with the help of her personifications, the resumption of her painting, and the remembering of her dreams. Not infrequently, Mary would report a dream in which she was a detached spectator witnessing an unknown child being hurt and molested in a certain way. Then, within days of the dream, she might involuntarily lapse into a "hypnoid" state and become a very young child who narrated or abreacted a traumatic experience almost identical to what was described in the dream. However, in the autohypnotic state, the patient would have no memory of the dream, and *vice versa*. This reciprocal amnesia seemed to sever the connection among memory, dream, and reliving, maintaining a split in the ego for defensive purposes (see Chapter Ten).

One major recurrent theme of her dreams was being underwater for so long that she could no longer breathe and imagined that she could fly and breathe underwater. In her dissociated child state subsequent to such a dream, she would alternate between describing being held underwater in the bathtub by her mother for so long that her mind cut off and re-experiencing a gasping, burning throat and emotional blankness after being let up from the water. Intersubjectively, I experienced the horror for her that she was too deadened from the experience to feel consciously. The hysterical symptom of blurred vision, "as though being underwater", was also linked to this torture and ameliorated after several of these abreactive episodes in treatment. During the reconstruction of her childhood, Mary recalled that her mother would undress and sit on her face, straddling her with her legs apart, as in the painting, teach her to lick her vagina until she was satisfied, and then roll over off her in exhaustion. The young child knew nothing of sexual excitement, orgasm, or menstruation and was terrified but required to perform her duty on demand at any time under any conditions or else she would be severely punished. Being thrown into the bathtub and nearly drowned into submission was apparently a diabolically effective means of breaking the child's spirit, making her into an automaton (Ferenczi, 1933) and sexually enslaving her.[1] Cloaked in religiosity and threatened with the curse of God if she were to reveal this heinous form of baptism, she was repeatedly told that "God will kill you" if she ever told anyone. Hence, the hallucination of Timmy's "God is trying to kill me!" was apparently the dissociated child's cry in response to this aspect of her brainwashing and soul murder (Shengold, 1989).

In addition to understanding the traumatic origin of the blurred vision and the auditory hallucination, it also became clear that Mary knew how to teach the dog to perform cunnilingus because she, too, was trained like an animal to perform the same act. In addition, it appeared that the near drownings resulted in an altered state of consciousness, perhaps not unlike a near-death experience, which was encapsulated and contributed to the formation of a dissociated child self (I. Brenner, 2001). As Mary grew up and tried to live a "normal" life, attending school, church, and playing with friends, she also, side by side and simultaneously, lived a secret life as her mother's sexual slave, which required the deployment of all efforts available in her psyche to keep things separate. Splitting of consciousness and splitting of the ego reached psychotic proportions when she became convinced that her mother could read her mind, know her inner thoughts, and know her whereabouts at all times. Manifested in the transference, Mary was convinced at these times that my office was bugged with recording and surveillance devices that went directly to her mother, believing that I was in a conspiracy with her to keep her daughter mentally ill and totally submissive. This tendency towards paranoia was rather intractable at times, as her permeable ego boundaries (Federn, 1952) and grossly disturbed body ego predisposed her to such periodic regressions with this additional manifestation of splitting of the ego. At these times, she simultaneously existed in one reality: that I was simply her analyst trying to help her, and in another reality: that I was a spy in league with her mother, where even the slightest movement of the chair in my office from one session to the next was a secret message that she had to decode. While she was trying to outwit her mother and be loyal to her by not revealing anything about herself, she was also trying to get help and understand the nature of the disturbance of her mind.

Obscured by the dramatic and disturbing nature of the psychopathology, the nature of Ralph's involvement with the mother remained an unsolved and crucial part of the puzzle of the patient's disturbance of identity. Over time, Ralph began to open up and assist in the following reconstruction: at some point after Mary's adolescence and the transformation that occurs during that turbulent time, the disavowal of the reality of her female gender identity required more ego-weakening dividedness of her psyche as the incestuous relationship with her mother continued. She remained "on call" twenty-four hours a day, seven days a week, for the mother's pleasure. No matter what the patient was doing, she might be interrupted by her mother's calling her name in a certain melodic way as if to say, "Oh, Mary, do you know what time it is? It's time for me!" Mary obediently stopped whatever she was doing and followed her mother to the bedroom in an entranced, obedient state. While in that state, the mother taught her a new form of sexual pleasure, commonly known as fisting. She was instructed to insert her hand, one finger at a time, make a fist, and then forcefully pump the mother's vagina, which caused her much pain. It satisfied the mother's sexual masochism and stirred up the patient's own sexual sadism. Initially repulsed by this demand and unable to perform this duty, she became overwhelmed with anxiety, lapsed further into an autohypnotic trance, and switched to her major alternative consciousness, Ralph, who took over. This opportunity to inflict pain upon the mother to further identify with the aggressor and to "fist fuck" the mother further consolidated Ralph's sense of himself as truly a "motherfucker". "He" took every opportunity to live up to such a reputation, and this erotically fuelled cruelty staved off the patient's despair over being a menstruating female with breasts and without a penis.

Literally becoming mother's phallus rather than remaining an unconscious fantasy or a symbolic derivative (Lacan, 1982), the fist was used as a penis and rage was "his" predominant affect. "He" experienced no guilt whatsoever, and it was not until many years later when, after countless cycles of the patient's expressed sadomasochistic wish to revel in a blood orgy in the transference and my containing these fantasies within my own psyche, Ralph began to acknowledge hidden, positive feelings for me. Concurrently becoming able to tolerate ambivalence for me without dissociative splitting and switching, another sign of integration of the patient's psyche, was Ralph's "feeling" Mary's guilt and horror over fisting the mother. Furthermore, when Mary was "out", she became able to recover the memories of this experience of her mother and to talk about them. This *détente* between two tortured selves was beautifully represented in a painting that depicted the merging of Mary's and Ralph's bodies, complete with breasts and a penis in which each was embracing the other.

Summary and conclusion

To help understand the complexities of Mary's psyche, which bears resemblance to the "double conscience" described by Breuer and Freud during the inception of psychoanalysis, we may apply the theoretical elaboration and metapsychological advancements in the concept of splitting of the ego and then return to the archaic concept of hypnoid hysteria in order to reconsider it in a brighter light. Under certain traumatic conditions in childhood, it may be impossible for one's mind to reconcile the contradictions necessary for psychic and, possibly, physical survival, such as the need to maintain an attachment to a murderous, sexually violating mother. Under such circumstances, there might be a coalescing of self- and object representations into seemingly separate selves maintained in autohypnotic, hypnoid states. Analytic work with such patients with his lower-level dissociative character (I. Brenner, 1994) who fulfil the diagnostic criteria for dissociative identity disorder (American Psychiatric Association, 2013) reveals the presence of organising influences that seem to contribute to the creation of these personifications, which Fairbairn (1952) considered to be a variant of the usual functioning structural units of the mind—that is, the id, the ego, and the superego. The organising influences that analytic exploration has revealed to be underlying these selves include perverse sexuality, the autosymbolic phenomena seen in dreams, hypnoid, and hypnogogic states (Silberer, 1909), near-death experiences, and the overall mentally divisive effects of aggression, as seen in Mary's case. Intergenerational transmission of trauma has also been described in other such cases (I. Brenner, 2001). This unique and idiosyncratic assemblage of representations has survival value and, despite major disturbances in relationships, could result in areas of very high ego functioning (Oxnam, 2005).

Whereas it is a generally accepted principle, originally posited by Freud, that the unpleasurable or "bad" self- and object representations tend to be externalised and the "good" self- and object representations remain internalised (Freud, 1915e), the analyst may see a pseudo-externalisation and displacement to the inside dissociated selves as an additional "ingredient" to these structures. In addition, the amnestic autohypnotic barrier adds to the unique qualities that make them more encapsulated and distinctive than the contradictory selves separated by disavowal and the vertical split described by Kohut (1971).

Because of the presence of not only various ego functions, but also drive derivatives from the id, as well as superego prohibitions and aspirations, these personifications might also be considered "pathological intersystemic suborganizations". This concept, described by Schafer (1968), has been advocated by Lichtenberg and Slap (1973), who contend that "pathological intersystemic suborganization" is a more precise designation for contradictory, psychic groupings as exemplified by fetishism than is the term "splitting of the ego" (p. 784).

In their own splitting of Freud's usage of the term "splitting" into four categories (that is, a general developmental principle, an organisation of psychic contents in infancy, as a defence, and as a way of maintaining contradictory psychic groups), Lichtenberg and Slap argue for a *restrictive* use of the term "splitting" to reduce the confusion of tongues (Ferenczi, 1933) that plagues our theorising. Their recommendation is to limit the use of the term "splitting" to "the tendency in infantile life by which an organization of memory traces of the earliest expression is based on primordial quality of pleasurable good or painful bad" (Lichtenberg & Slap, 1973, p. 784). While this effort may reduce definitional ambiguity, in so doing we might even further obscure and threaten to relegate to the dustbin of history the still not fully appreciated significance of Breuer's and early Freud's "splitting of the mind". The compelling nature of its successor, "splitting of the ego", has had so many far-reaching implications that, perhaps ironically, it has suffered from its own success. The history of this concept, reviewed through a contemporary case report resembling Anna O's, might help put this term back into historical perspective and further more understanding of some of our greatest clinical challenges.

CHAPTER THREE

On dissociation

"I write differently from what I speak. I speak differently from what I think. I think differently from the way I ought to think, and so it all proceeds into deepest darkness"

(Kafka, 1914, p. 8)

Introduction

It could be argued that psychoanalysis is a psychology of trauma that, after more than a century of fruitful elaboration and detours, is coming back to its roots. In order to do so, however, it is necessary to find a way to incorporate the way altered states of consciousness may be used as a psychological defence. From his early collaboration with Breuer, where he never quite embraced the role of hypnoid states in hysteria, Freud struggled with the myriad effects of trauma upon the psyche. Having been weighed down by the "cornerstone" of repression, we still find ourselves fitting our clinical observations into theory that does not always fit and often fails to recognise dissociative phenomena when they manifest themselves.

In this chapter, I review the evolution of psychoanalytic thinking on dissociation and related phenomena, the dissociation of everyday life, attachment and dissociation, dissociation in adult trauma, and dissociation in severe early trauma associated with dissociative identity disorder (DID), formerly known as multiple personality.

In their now legendary writings on hysteria, as noted in Chapter Two, Freud and Breuer describe "splitting of consciousness" (Freud, 1895d, pp. 12, 67, 69, 123), the separation of mental contents from the dominant mass of ideas, which was the precursor to repression. They also referred to "splitting of a personality" (p. 45), where opposite behavioural states occurred. In addition, they described "splitting of the mind" (pp. 225, 234), characterised by the simultaneous existence of conscious and unconscious ideation. This observation was particularly disturbing because of alternations to different states of mind and having conversations, having intentionality, and having relationships one moment and then switching to another state and having amnesia for all of the above. Breuer described all of this in the case of Anna O, whose dream-like "clouds", petulant moods, and hysterical symptoms could disappear suddenly as she amnestically shifted from her very disturbed self to her usual self. Traumatised by the deterioration and death of her beloved father, this very ill, grief-stricken young woman required both high doses of chloral hydrate and the "talking cure"—a term she herself coined. When it was determined that ". . . the motive for splitting of consciousness . . . was that of defence" (p. 166), psychoanalysis was truly born. (However, it would take almost another century for serious discussion to occur about combining psychoanalysis with pharmacotherapy, which Anna O also pioneered.)

As noted in the previous chapter, Freud recognised early on that conflicting mental forces could divide a mind for dynamic reasons (Freud, 1910a, pp. 25–26) and not for constitutional or biological reasons, as put forth by Janet. However, Freud left much work to be done in this realm, that is, of dissociation, hysteria, and trauma, because he then changed direction and developed further his ideas about repression, drive theory, and the structural model. Consequently, the earlier notion of "splitting of the mind" was either forgotten about or mistakenly thought to have been completely subsumed by his later, far-reaching concept of splitting of the ego.

However, Freud must not have been fully satisfied, because he revisited the topic and summarily dismissed it in a rather disingenuous way. In *Civilization and Its Discontents*, he states,

> There are cases in which parts of a person's own body, even portions of his own mental life – his perceptions, thoughts, and feelings – appear alien to him and as not belonging to his ego . . .

> Moreover, in the case of the most extreme possibility of suffering, special mental protective devices are brought into operation. It seems to me unprofitable to pursue this aspect of the problem any further" [!!] (my exclamation marks). (Freud, 1930a, pp. 66, 89)

The dynamic unconscious: repressed or dissociated?

In *The Psychopathology of Everyday Life* (Freud, 1901b), Freud cites the evidence for unconscious processes in the universal phenomenon of forgetting names, words, and phrases as well as their substitution by other dynamically charged replacements. The slip of the tongue has been elevated to premier importance and is now known as the "Freudian slip". In addition, slips of the pen and clumsiness illustrate the endless ways in which conscious thinking is interrupted by internal pressures. It has become so accepted that these "errors" are unconscious in origin and assumed that repression is the underlying defence mechanism that there are remarkably few articles in the literature devoted primarily to parapraxes (Kelman, 1975a; Mintz, 1975; Szalai, 1934). Guidebooks on analytic technique generally add very little (Fenichel, 1945; Glover, 1955; Greenson, 1967; Nunberg, 1955), although Anna Freud noted that trying to interpret a parapraxis might often be unsuccessful and even derail the patient (A. Freud, 1936). So, it is paradoxical that such a ubiquitous facet of unconscious mental life may be one of the most convincing evidences of its existence and yet inaccessible. The usual answer would be that, of course, it might be inaccessible because of the "depth" of the repression.

Early in treatment, an analysand who has a parapraxis might be so oblivious to it that, even if it were brought to his attention, he might not have heard himself, have no memory of it, no curiosity about it, and even think that the analyst heard him incorrectly. This negation (Freud, 1925j) may be so strong that he might employ all measures to avoid exploring it. Over time, however, if the patient becomes able to believe the analyst, realises he has made an error, eventually hears himself without assistance, and then ultimately analyses its own meaning, it is a measure of progress. However, where there is great resistance and little progress, there could be a defensive operation beyond repression and more akin to a mini-trance, since the patient speaks, albeit briefly, without observing ego and is unaware of his vocalisation or gesturing. Freud himself observed how it resembles "somnambulistic certainty" (Freud, 1901b, p. 142), an allusion to his forgotten observation about lapsing into spontaneous self-hypnotic trances (Freud, 1891d).

Evidence of the relationship between parapraxes and dissociative phenomena may be seen clinically. For example, a suicidal patient, after years of treatment resulting in "integration" and self-continuity, became accident prone and started making many parapraxes (I. Brenner, 2001). Apparently, her profoundly self-destructive behaviour, which was perpetrated in amnestic, fugue-like states, became "tamed" but periodically broke through in the form of the "psychopathology of everyday life" (Freud, 1901b), where she would trip or bump into things and become bruised. A clinically useful definition of dissociation that incorporates earlier observations of hypnoid states, repression, and the role of trauma is as follows:

> . . . a defensive altered state of consciousness due to autohypnosis, augmenting repression or splitting. It develops as a primitive, adaptive response of the ego to the overstimulation and pain of external trauma, which, depending on its degree of integration, may result in a broad range of disturbances of alertness, awareness, memory, and identity. Dissociation apparently may change in its function and be employed later on as a defense against the perceived internal danger of intolerable affects and instinctual strivings. Thus, it may be a transient neurotic defense or become characterological, and may even be the predominant defense. The content of associations in dissociation is as important as the defensive purpose it serves and may be accessible through hypnosis, but very resistant to psychoanalysis unless the analyst is aware of its presence. (I. Brenner, 1994, pp. 840–841)

So, there may be a continuum between dissociation and the parapraxes because a parapraxis is typically of very short duration, whereas fugue-like states are longer, and, if time is the main distinguishing factor, perhaps they have more in common than we generally have considered. It might be helpful, therefore, to review what is known about the capacity to banish and keep things out of awareness through defensive altered states of consciousness, which precede the onset of the repression barrier in the young child.

A pathodevelopmental line

The sleepiness of the neonate and the demarcation between wakeful alertness and the sleeping state are the natural origin of dissociation, according to Winnicott (1945), whereas motivated forgetting is usually not observed until about age three. Dissociation may be the precursor of repression that perhaps is never completely replaced by repression. Disorganised attachment patterns (Main & Solomon, 1990) and their correlation with later behavioural and dissociative problems (Main, 1993; Ogawa, Srolfe, Weinfield, Carlson, & Egeland, 1997) are significant because the signs of such a pattern include freezing or confused activity, wandering, fear, and rapid fluctuations of affect. As a two-person model of conflict, symptom, and defence, such an attachment might underlie the "unthought known" (Bollas, 1987), that is, implicit enactive behaviour preceding symbolisation and explicit memory (Lyons-Ruth, 1999; D.N. Stern et al., 1998). Therefore, such an "internalized dialogue as defense", as well as the gaze aversion of the over-stimulated infant who "looks the other way", may be precursors.

It is crucial for the mother to provide her infant with an ongoing, intimate experience in order to develop a continuous sense of self (Bach, 2001). "Knowing and not knowing" (Laub & Auerhahn, 1993) probably begins with a disturbed, dissociogenic mother's need not to know about herself which hinders her ability to know her infant, who then cannot fully know who he is. From a relational perspective, dissociation is a ubiquitous, interpersonal defence against the unthinkable that was not properly recognised by the primary care-taker (Bromberg, 1994). Growing up in a climate of denial and abuse facilitates a dissociative state of mind, that is,

> conflicted approach–avoidance attempts at dialogue of the disorganized child, as well as the inability of the abusive mother to help the child integrate the contradictory aspects of her experience through a collaborative dialogue. (Lyons-Ruth, 2003, p. 901)

Even in less traumatic settings, the mother's need not to know that her infant is in distress seems to be a central dynamic factor.

Working with adults, clinicians familiar with severe dissociative pathology regularly observe that such patients often have excessive and extensive amnesia for not only their early childhood years, but also for events in latency and adolescence, often leaving them with disturbing gaps in memory of continuous self-experience. These "holes" in the memory might be embarrassing and be minimised or covered over by confabulation or reports of alcohol or drug abuse that only exacerbate the problem. Once in treatment, it may be revealed that an unusually dense "repression barrier" is present which, paradoxically, may be easily breached through hypnosis (I. Brenner, 2001, 2004).

A very disturbed early mother–child relationship seems to set the stage for continued problems requiring extraordinary measures for the child to psychically survive. Avoidant attachment disturbances may also be seen, where the child dissociates her needs and appears indifferent and oblivious to the mother's comings and goings.

Discontinuity of the self

If dissociation is linked to the persistence of an infantile state of mind where the mother failed to ascribe meaning (Whitmer, 2001), then acquiring self-knowledge is compromised due to the disturbance in representing one's own experience. As a result, there is little internal continuity or self-constancy, and one remains dependent upon others for definition. Therefore, the disturbances seen in DID, according to Stern's model (D. N. Stern, 1985), would infer a disruption in the development of the core self, especially in the areas of self-cohesion, self-continuity, and self-agency. Sensory input may be accurately perceived consciously, but its meaning would require the input of another because the experience is unsymbolised (Ogden, 1986), unformulated (D. B. Stern, 1997), and unrepresented (Fonagy & Target, 1996). As a result, one would be inclined to subordinate his or her own senses and defer to another's reality in order to stay unaware and protected from knowing very painful somatic and psychological states, a so-called "repression by proxy" (Whitmer, 2001, p. 16).

The "illusion of an autonomous psyche" (Whitmer, 2001, p. 817), is extreme in DID, where seemingly separate selves might deny or not know the existence of others and might literally fight to the death over exclusive control of the body (I. Brenner, 2001, 2004). Not only would there be disturbances in the core self, but also in the intersubjective self and, quite dramatically, in the narrative self (D. N. Stern, 1985), where these selves might have different biographies.

Therefore, DID, in addition to being a "lower-level dissociative character", is also a disorder of the self characterised by overall lack of self-constancy obscured by a cadre of seemingly separate selves with their own cohesion. The vulnerability to sadomasochistic exploitation is often seen in the scared child selves who are essentially very complex, intrapsychic structures that function as compromise formations (C. Brenner, 1982). Such patients employ a pseudo-externalised displacement, in which their instinctual strivings may be disowned, banished from consciousness, and attributed to someone else: not an outside person but, rather, an "inside" self (I. Brenner, 2001). Working with this defence as it emerges in the transference is a crucial part of the treatment, as it involves altered states, amnesia, traumatic memories, and the pathognomic development of dissociated selves. Having achieved a degree of secondary autonomy, they might be willed on by the patient in an effort to take psychological flight or might emerge spontaneously as a result of anxiety in the here and now. When this "switching" from one self to another in response to anxiety occurs in the transference, it enables the analyst to begin to work with this seemingly bizarre symptom/defence constellation.

Maintaining this separateness, as in splitting, may reduce anxiety by "protecting" the "good self" or "good object" at the expense of continuity of identity. In addition, the known problems in symbolic thinking (Bass, 1997; Bollas, 1989; Grubrich-Simitis, 1984; Levine, 1990; Ogden, 1986) might be encapsulated by some selves in DID, allowing others to develop extraordinary creativity and high-level abstract thought. These personifications are defensively shielded by a barrier reinforced by autohypnotic amnesia and analgesia. This type of sequestering might permit normative development to occur in other regions of the psyche (Wholey, 1926) and could even stave off frank psychosis (Kramer, 1993). This barrier appears to function as a very powerful repression barrier and is less amenable to usual therapeutic interventions. It is, therefore, essential to develop a therapeutic alliance with the patient in all these states of mind and empathise with his/her psychic reality of being inhabited by other selves.

Phenomenology of DID

Dissociative identity disorder continues to be perhaps the most misunderstood and vilified condition in the history of psychology, and observations from over sixty years ago still apply: that is, there are two types of believers, naïve people and those with actual contact with such patients (Taylor & Martin, 1944).

The *Diagnostic and Statistical Manual of Mental Disorders, Fifth Edition* (*DSM-5*) describes the diagnostic criteria for DID as the following:

(a) Disruption of identity characterized by two or more distinct personality states, which may be described in some cultures as possession. The disruption in identity involves marked disconti- nuity in sense of self and sense of agency, accompanied by related alterations in affect, behavior, consciousness, memory, percep- tion, cognition, and/or sensory-motor functioning. These signs and symptoms may be observed by others or reported by the individual.

(b) Recurrent gaps in the recall of everyday events, important personal information, and/or traumatic events that are inconsis- tent with ordinary forgetting.

(c) The symptoms cause clinically significant distress or impairment in social, occupational, or other important areas of functioning.

(d) The disturbance is not a normal part of a broadly accepted cul- tural or religious practice. (Note: In children, the symptoms are not better explained by imaginary playmates or other fantasy play.)

(e) The symptoms are not attributable to the direct physiological effects of a substance (e.g., blackouts or chaotic behavior during alcohol intoxication) or another medical condition (e.g., complex partial seizures). (American Psychoanalytic Association, 2013, p. 155)

In contrast to *DSM-5*, which categorises this entity as an "Axis I" major psychiatric illness, the *Psychodynamic Diagnostic Manual* (Ameri- can Psychoanalytic Association, 2006) considers it a "dissociative personality" and thereby promotes the idea of a spectrum of severity of character pathology. This viewpoint is congruent with, but slightly different from, my own clinical understanding of DID, which is equated with the "lower-level dissociative character" (I. Brenner, 1994) and will be discussed later.

Despite the clinical value of such a characterological formulation, it is not the prevailing psychiatric attitude and, paradoxically, might add to the confusion that has accompanied this condition since it was first recognised.

Reflecting this confusion, it has been known as split personality, Gmelin's syndrome, exchanged personality, multiplex personality, double existences, double conscience, dual consciousness, dual personality, double personality, plural personality, dissociated personality, alternating personality, multiple personality, multiple personality disorder, and now dissociative identity disorder (Ellenberger, 1970; Greaves, 1993). The current nomenclature conveys the belief that it is not a problem of too many selves, but not enough of one, and that dissociation is involved. Another source of confusion comes from the introduction of Bleuler's term "schizophrenia", which means "split mind", and replaced "dementia praecox". Since then, the number of published case reports of multiple personality has significantly declined, suggesting that much diagnostic confusion might have ensued between these entities (Rosenbaum, 1980). Because there may be depersonalisation, derealisation, emotional withdrawal, bizarre conversion symptoms, "hysterical" auditory hallucinations, and even so-called Schneiderian first-rank symptoms of schizophrenia (Kluft, 1987a) in DID, at times it might be difficult to differentiate between these conditions. In addition, it could take many years of treatment before DID is definitively recognised (Coons, Bowman, & Milstein, 1988). Furthermore, there may be significant secondary gain in disowning one's behaviour and attributing it to a separate personality, especially when forensic issues are present (Orne, Dinges, & Orne, 1984).

The question of iatrogenic influences through hypnosis or other interventions creating multiple personality (James, 1890; McDougall, 1926) is often considered despite the fact that, to my knowledge, there has not been one documented case of manufactured DID in the literature. However, it has been alleged that it could be created by the military for special missions (Estabrooks, 1945). It is, therefore, not surprising that many still question the validity of DID. So, it is rather ironic that Anna O, whose "talking cure" began the psychoanalytic movement (Freud, 1895d), was actually a case of multiple personality (Jones, 1953) and that her ghost has haunted us ever since.

Further metapsychological reflections

It is now recognised that severe, early sustained trauma, including physical and sexual abuse (Kluft, 1984; Putnam, 1989; Ross, 1989), is highly correlated with DID. Therefore, Janet's (1889) theory of dissociation, which posited a split or disintegration of the psyche in traumatised people with a constitutional susceptibility, has gained renewed interest. The development of autonomous components that could be disowned and treated by hypnosis was the basis of this spatial model to which Jung also subscribed, as he described "personified autonomous complexes" (Jung, 1902).

In the psychoanalytic mainstream much later, Fliess (1953a) described hypnotic "evasion" and Dickes (1965) emphasised the defensive function of the hypnoid state, while Shengold (1989) described the autohypnotic defence in which hypnotic facilitation and hypnotic vigilance may occur. Even Anna Freud (1954) observed that a patient could ward off sexual anxiety by a trance-like sleep, but. as Glover (1943) pointed out, the term "dissociation" has a "chequered history" in psychoanalysis and, until recently, few writers have dared to reintroduce this term.

Interestingly, just as a split in the psyche has been invoked in many types of psychopathology, so, too, have many theories been put forth to explain DID. Freud (1923b) thought that different repressed identifications could take over consciousness at different times. Fairbairn (1952) considered "multiple personality" as simply another model of the mind, where layering and fusion of internal objects varied in complexity in each person. Glover (1943) described early, unintegrated ego nuclei as precursors to dissociation, while Federn (1952) hypothesised the reactivation of various different repressed ego states. Watkins and Watkins (1979, 1997) elaborated upon Federn and described a continuum of dividedness from adaptive and normative to maladaptive and pathological, ending with DID. Abse, an expert on hysteria (1974, 1983), maintained that both splitting of the ego and altered states of consciousness were necessary to explain the dissociation essential to DID. This structure sacrificed repression and a clear, continuous consciousness and, due to the amnestic, dissociated "personalities", reflected identity diffusion as well (Akhtar, 1992).

Berman (1981) also emphasised splitting, citing seriously disturbed mother–daughter relationships followed by the loss of a compensatory, overly intense, eroticised oedipal relationship with the father. Here, separate "personalities" were precipitates—"part object representations which evolve into split self representations" (Berman, 1981, p. 298). A developmental arrest (Lasky, 1978), and psychotic features may also be seen in such a fragmented self, as per Kernberg's (1973) continuum of dissociative psychopathology. In this model, psychosis with poor differentiation of self and object is at one end while hysterical dissociation, mutual amnesia of two personalities, and repression are thought to be at the other.

DID has also been considered a subtype of borderline personality (Buck, 1983; Clary, Burstin, & Carpenter, 1984), a variant of a narcissistic character (Greaves, 1980; Gruenwald, 1977), and a type of transitional object (Marmer, 1980). Kluft (1984) viewed DID as a post trauma disorder of childhood incorporating dissociation proneness and the level of development at the time of trauma. Arlow (1992) postulated

> alternating conscious representations of highly organized fantasy systems, each of which coalesces into a particular idiosyncratic entity . . . [which] are not compatible with each other and . . . can dramatize internal conflicts. (p. 1975)

Most relevant here is his conclusion that "altered ego states . . . may be incorporated, in part, into the *character structure* of the individual" (Arlow, 1992, p. 75). However, the nature of dissociation and its developmental significance were not well integrated into any of these theories. Therefore, the consideration that a pathodevelopmental line may exist from the earliest sleep–wakefulness cycle to dissociation as the central defence in DID allows for assimilation of more recent findings from child analysis into my clinical experience with adults (I. Brenner, 1994, 2001, 2004).

In both outpatient and inpatient settings, I have had the rare opportunity to treat, interview, consult, supervise, and review the cases of several hundred patients with a suspected diagnosis of DID. This condition seems to generate more controversy and schisms in the staff than any other disorder, except that this split, as noted earlier, is unique in that the patient's credibility and the diagnosis are often the issue. Incest survivors often do not believe themselves (Kramer, 1985), or fear that they will not be believed by others (Sachs, 1967), and these patterns are enacted in hospitals.

Many refractory patients with borderline-like pathology, eating disorders, and some in very complex, long analyses might, in fact, suffer from unrecognised dissociative problems (Kluft, 1987b). Some cases of transsexualism (Schwartz, 1988), bestiality (Shengold, 1967), paedophilia, drug addiction, prostitution, and striptease dancing may also be linked to dissociative pathology (Socarides, 1992). If these findings are to be taken seriously, then it would be useful to synthesise the wealth of knowledge accrued by psychoanalysis, but it has been unclear how it best fits in.

The dissociative character

The model that I have found most useful is that of a continuum of dissociative character pathology in which dissociation, rather than splitting or repression, is the central defensive operation (I. Brenner, 1994). In this dissociative character continuum, the most severe end, or lower-level dissociative character, would correspond to DID. The intermediate-level dissociative character would have less cohesive self-organisations, the so-called attenuated cases of multiple personality (Ellenberger, 1970), or DD-NOS (dissociative disorder not otherwise specified). The upper-level dissociative character would have an over-reliance on defensive altered states, but would have more overall self-constancy.

A case report

A memoir written by an internationally renowned expert in Asian studies describes the tortured inner life of a very credible, high-profile individual. Robert Oxnam, PhD, details how he became depressed, developed a serious eating disorder, and drank very heavily to suppress his early memories of sexual abuse. During a therapy session, he blanked out and one of his young alter personalities emerged to introduce himself to the psychiatrist. The patient had amnesia for this time and was shocked to discover that not only was the time over but that an unknown part of himself had been talking while he was in an amnestic state.

Dr Oxnam had a "system" of eleven different selves with different ages, different traits, different intellectual capabilities, different genders, and different responsibilities. Bob's inner selves resided in a psychological castle with a library that contained the "Baby Book", that is, the story of his childhood. In this highly symbolised, dream-like way, his memories of severe early trauma, including anal rape and near death by suffocation, were kept separate and inaccessible until therapy: "And the 'Baby Book' was totally etched in my mind, waiting for me to open it. And as soon as I thought of its possible contents, my smile faded with a shudder . . ." (Oxnam, 2005, p. 38).

Dr Oxnam's selves were so geared toward mastery of knowledge and success that, unlike less gifted individuals with this type of mental organisation, "they" achieved great prominence. Remarkably, he describes his horror at being mercilessly plagued by his voices while hosting a multi-million-dollar fund-raiser in which former President George H. Bush was the keynote speaker.

> Suddenly, just as President Bush arrived, I felt inner vibrations, like a ringing cell phone. I knew there was an incoming Bobby message. 'The president's not happy. He's sad.' Of course he's happy. He's smil-ing. Please not now! 'Just look at his face. He's not happy. He's making a hurt smile. Who hurt him?' OK, I see. But we can't talk now. I mean it. We'll talk later. Goodbye! (Oxnam, 2005, p. 117)

As a cautionary note about the potential lethality of this malady (I. Brenner, 2006a, 2009a), Dr Oxnam reports that after the death of his mother, he took a very serious overdose.

Dissociated selves

The personifications, or alter personalities, the hallmark of DID, appear to be multiply determined compromise formations that encap-sulate disowned traumatic memories, affects, anxiety, drives, and fantasies. The creation of these selves may be attributed to the disso-ciative, or "It's not me!", self, who, like the "man behind the curtain" in the *Wizard of Oz*, wanted to be ignored while he created the illusion of an omnipotent, frightening self.[2] As mentioned earlier, the illusion of oneness, or self-constancy, may result in each self being ignorant of the presence of others.

With an appreciation of dissociation, the reconstruction of a very traumatic childhood might become possible through the development of a therapeutic alliance with the patient in the various states of mind and analysis of the "mosaic transference". Five "organising influences" have thus far been discovered that are exploited by the "It's not me!" self in order to create these seemingly separate identities, kept apart by an amnestic, autohypnotic barrier (I. Brenner, 2001, 2004). Just as Oxnam was not aware of his other selves until his decompensation in adulthood when a child self emerged in therapy, his therapist became an auxiliary memory until he could acquire "co-consciousness" and expand his observing ego.

One organising influence is perverse sexuality, aggressively infused sexuality with part objects and body parts. The individual seems to traverse multiple sexual developmental pathways in different states of consciousness. A triad of personifications—a transsexual self, a homosexual self, and a sadomasochistic heterosexual self—is frequently seen. For example, a married man would become utterly overwhelmed with urges to drink other men's urine in an amnestic, altered state of consciousness. He would lure young men to a private apartment and carefully feed them calculated amounts of beer to dilute their urine just enough so he could swallow it while performing fellatio and while he ejaculated. In another state of mind, he was a flamboyant, transsexual, gourmet cook who prided himself on his special recipes and secret sauces.

Of equal importance is ego in the dream state, especially the "functional phenomenon" (Silberer, 1909), where alterations in consciousness may become symbolised in hypnogogic and dissociative states. The patient might anthropomorphise a traumatically induced dissociated state and symbolise it in the form of a young child or an angry teenager, which could be expressed in both recurrent dreams and in subsequent traumatically induced altered states. For example, Oxnam's hermetically sealed castle in his mind might have been a transformation of the refrigerator he was locked into that nearly suffocated him to death. The terror and fluctuating state of consciousness he experienced at the time might have been represented and crystallised into this imagery.

A third influence is the role of intergenerational transmission in which the perpetrator's own trauma history might become occultly incorporated into the "biography" of a personification, usually one based on identification with the aggressor. Originally described in children of Holocaust survivors (Bergmann & Jucovy, 1982) and subsequently in disturbances of attachment with traumatised mothers, this phenomenon may be obscured by other symptoms. For example, a woman with the perverse triad mentioned above had a destructive male self who wanted to "take over" the body and attempted a crude mastectomy, resulting in massive blood loss. Not only was a dissociated transsexual conflict uncovered, but also the transmission of her father's own trauma, as this male self insisted he was a military man who was sodomised as a young boy (I. Brenner, 2001).

The divisive effects of aggression, originally described by Freud (1920g), accompanied by identification with the aggressor and the unusual manifestations of near-death experiences (Gabbard & Twemlow, 1984), such as autoscopic and even psi phenomena, might also factor into the creation of these selves (I. Brenner, 2001, 2004). In one such case, it appeared that a patient who sustained a near-death experience in childhood by poisoning had encapsulated that experience in the form of a "dead child" self who had uncanny powers of perception and, perhaps, extrasensory perception (I. Brenner, 2001).

While dissociation itself is a compromise formation, the defensive aspects of it enable the analytic clinician to work with it. While it typically may encompass qualities of both repression and splitting, thus perpetuating confusion over its categorisation, it is a distinct means of dynamically keeping mental contents separate. In her comparison of repression and dissociation, Howell points out that while both are motivated and defensive, the latter may occur spontaneously during acute trauma or hypnosis (Howell, 2005). Indeed, peritraumatic dissociation is highly correlated with the development of post traumatic stress disorder (PTSD) and is recognised in *DSM-5* (American Psychiatric Association, 2013). In addition, repression typically refers to actively forgotten declarative memories, whereas the latter often refers to unformulated experiences (D. B. Stern, 1997). However, clinical experience makes me question this clear-cut distinction. As one patient succinctly described it, "I can't think about what I remember." Her other selves protected her from quite disturbingly clear memories of severe early sexual abuse.

With regard to splitting (Kernberg, 1975), the intrapsychic world is divided into aggressively and libidinally self- and object representations: that is, "bad" and "good". In dissociation, however, such a division is not as clear-cut and amnesia is typically present. And, in an attempt to link the two from a relational perspective,

... what we call 'splitting' involves a re-enactment of posttraumatic dominant–submissive relational patterns ... a particular organization of alternating dissociated helpless/victim and abusive/rageful self-states ... [which] may have developmental underpinnings in attachment style and biological states. (Howell, 2005, p. 163)

Despite the clinical blurring in extreme situations, such as with fluctuating amnestic states of consciousness seen in DID, the underlying mechanism of dissociation seems most clear. Analysing not only the timing of such a dissociative switch but also the content of what is being said in that state of mind is significant. These clinical findings, along with the reconstruction of childhood trauma with adults, correlate with data derived from child observation and developmental research.

Dissociation of trauma in adulthood

Case report

The traumatically induced breakdown of the reasonably well-formed adult psyche may result in dissociated states but is not likely to manifest itself as DID proper, since the self will have already developed in childhood and adolescence. As a result, what may be seen can resemble the lower-level dissociative character without the profound disturbance of self- and object constancy. Auschwitz survivor, Yehiel De-Nur, the acclaimed Israeli author better known by his tattoo number, Ka-Tzetnik 135633, described this phenomenon after testifying in the Eichmann trial in 1961 when the judge asked him why he hid behind his *nom de plume*. De-Nur writes,

A routine question, ostensibly, but the moment it flashed into my brain all hell broke loose. Not only did they want me to melt the two identities into one, but they wanted a public confession, an open declaration that this was so. Escaping to no-man's land was my only solution—becoming a vegetable in a hospital ward. (Ka-Tzetnik 135633, 1989, p. 70)

He further elaborates on the dissociation of his personality in Auschwitz and his subsequent attempts at integration, marvelling at finally being able to write in the first person:

All I've ever written is in essence a personal journal, a testimonial on paper of . . . I, I, I, till half through a piece, I suddenly had to transform *I* to *he*. I felt the split, the ordeal, the alienation of it . . . I knew unless I hid behind the third person, I wouldn't have been able to write at all. And lo and behold, here I am in the thick of the manuscript and totally unaware of how naturally I am allowing—from the first line onward—the connection with *I*. How did I miss this until now? . . . Without the shadow of a doubt I can at last acknowledge my identities, co-existing in my body. (Ka-Tzetnik 135633, 1989, p. 71)

During his treatment with LSD years later, De-Nur revived an intolerable memory of being caught peering through a window of an SS barracks where they were raping Jewish women and the traumatic division of his psyche:

I behold *Feld hure* [field whore] branded between my sister's breasts. And I see myself instantly splitting in two.

I see how I leave my body, separating into two selves: I stand and stare at my body, in a dead faint on the ground. . . . I couldn't hear the camp commander's order, then. I was unconscious.

Depersonalised and peering down at himself, he continues,

Now that I have left my body, I am also able to see the way Siegfried is dragging me by the feet back to the block: I am my own cortege; I am behind my own bumping head . . . I stare at myself, dragged by the feet back to the block and see the key to my nightmare . . . This time I don't fall into a faint, because I've split myself in two. Just as then and now are actually a single unit of time multiplied by two, the *I* of Then and the *I* of Now are a single identity divided by two. I look at my unconscious self, and I look at the self staring at my self; I look and see the key to the split . . . the secret of the split, deciphered . . . My mother. I see her naked and marching in line, one among Them, her face turned to the gas chambers. "Mama! Mama! Mama!" (Ka-Tzetnik 135633, 1989, pp. 99–100)

His dissociative experience of "knowing and not knowing", "being here and not here", and being "me and not me" is quite clear. However, his assigning a name to his "traumatized self" (Volkan, 1996) appears deliberate and conscious in contrast to a more structured personification that is relatively more autonomous, unknown, and separated by its own amnestic barrier. Furthermore, we have no evidence of defensive efforts to camouflage a lack of self-constancy or a need to create the illusion of self-cohesion. Instead, De-Nur clings to the Ka-Tzetnik persona consciously and uses him as a device that enables his creative expression. As such, his symptoms might be more consistent with DD-NOS (American Psychiatric Association, 2013).

Conclusion

Under severely traumatic conditions in childhood, one's mind might not be able to reconcile the contradictions necessary for psychic and, possibly, physical survival. For example, in order to maintain an attachment to a murderous, sexually violating mother, there might be a coalescing of self- and object representations into seemingly separate selves maintained in hypnoid states. Analytic work with this lower-level dissociative character (I. Brenner, 1994), that is, DID (American Psychiatric Association, 2013), reveals the presence of organising influences that seem to contribute to the creation of these personifications. These influences include perverse sexuality, the autosymbolic phenomena seen in dreams, hypnoid, and hypnogogic states (Silberer, 1909), near-death experiences, the overall mentally divisive effects of aggression, and intergenerational transmission of trauma (I. Brenner, 2001). This unique and idiosyncratic assemblage has survival value and, despite major disturbances in relationships, may result in areas of very high ego functioning in creativity, language, and mathematics (Oxnam, 2005).

Whereas it is a generally accepted principle that the unpleasurable or "bad" self- and object representations are externalised and the "good" self- and object representations remain internalised (Freud 1915e), the analyst may see a pseudo-externalised displacement to the inside as an additional aspect. The amnestic, autohypnotic barrier adds to the unique qualities that make them more encapsulated and distinctive than the contradictory selves separated by disavowal and the vertical split described by Kohut (1971). As a result, these structures are quite resistant to a classical analytic approach alone.

CHAPTER FOUR

Seeing and not seeing

"He did not want to see, and did not see . . . He did not want to understand, and did not understand . . . He did not allow himself to think about it, and he did not think about it; but all the same, though he never admitted it to himself, and had no proofs, nor even suspicious evidence, in the bottom of his heart he knew beyond all doubt that he was a deceived husband, and he was profoundly miserable about it"

(Tolstoy, 1917[1877], p. 267)

Introduction

As advancements in psychoanalytic technique have enabled more difficult patients to benefit from this modality, a group of patients generally thought to be outside the realm of treatment have provided new opportunities to re-examine basic concepts. For example, it is my contention that the conscious aspects of self-observation have been over-valued and that unconscious aspects of self-perception have, over time, been minimised or subsumed under other conceptualisations. The influence of unconscious forces on self-perception may be fruitfully studied in those patients who employ defensive altered states of consciousness because of the preponderance of periodic irruptions of dissociated, unconscious aspects of the self. I begin with an observation made when I was an undergraduate psychology student.

The first time I witnessed someone having a "bad trip" on a drug, the young woman's repeated utterance made such an indelible impression upon me that, over forty years later, her simple but haunting words continue to disturb and fascinate me. She was standing a bit ahead of me in line with her friends at a film theatre near the university campus. A popular new film had just arrived and a huge crowd had showed up early to wait for tickets. After a while, this young woman suddenly blurted out: "I'm here and I'm not here—and I'm here and I'm not here—and I'm here and I'm not here—and I'm here and I'm not here—and I'm here . . ."

The townspeople took note of her confusion, registering their feelings of concern and disdain by their silent expressions. Her friends tried to quiet her down but to no avail. She only became more insistent and persistent in her disorientated wonderment. Her voice became more hollow and eerie-sounding as she repeated her mantra while her entourage embarrassedly escorted her away. Clearly, she was in no condition to watch the film, as she had apparently experienced an abrupt change in her mental state that altered her perception of her self and her surroundings.

While I have long forgotten what film was actually playing that evening, seeing this young woman decompensate has remained quite memorable, and many times I have asked myself why my seeing this woman's disturbance of perception made such an impression upon me. At the time, as I said, I was an undergraduate student, fortified with only my introductory courses and a semester of abnormal psychology, but had instantly become fascinated by the subject. So, on one level, here was a real, live demonstration of a mental aberration I could ponder. I knew this young woman slightly and was struck by her shyness and almost secretiveness. Despite being superficially friendly, she exuded a type of aloofness that, back then, could have easily been mistaken for snobbery or conceit. Most importantly, I had heard through the proverbial campus grapevine that on the evening in question she had smoked marijuana for the first time prior to going to the theatre. None of her friends had had any adverse reaction, so the likelihood of it being contaminated with a toxic hallucinogen was quite low. In perhaps one of my first psychodynamic formulations as a psychology undergraduate, I crudely speculated to myself that perhaps there was some underlying vulnerability in her psyche that made her especially sensitive to losing contact with her ability to know where she was. Moreover, I wondered where it was that she "went to" when she exclaimed that she was "not here", as she gave the impression that she had somehow left her body, which had remained in line. In other words, she might have experienced a sense of her body as being quite different from her usual feelings about her overall self.

This disturbance in her perception, I came to realise many years later, had a certain quality to it that one might indeed attribute to depersonalisation, or derealisation (Arlow, 1966; Guralnik & Simeon, 2010), which is now subsumed under the larger category of her having had a "dissociative" experience. An extreme of the dissociative continuum would be those cases of DID, or multiple personality. In my work with those who live with such phenomena, which has also been described as a lower-level dissociative character (I. Brenner, 1994, 2001, 2004, 2009a), a person can feel that I am "here and not here", it is "me and not me", and I "know and do not know" a painful truth, quite often of a traumatic nature. Freud, in likening one's becoming aware of one's own mental processes ". . . to the perception of the external world by means of the sense-organs" (Freud, 1915e, pp. 170–171), thus provides an avenue for comprehending what might have happened to this temporarily deranged young woman. She might have experienced alternating awareness of her unconscious mental processes and, thus, taken leave of her usual senses. Freud states:

> Just as Kant warned us not to overlook the fact that our perceptions are subjectively conditioned and must not be regarded as identical with what is perceived though unknowable, so psycho-analysis warns us not to equate perceptions by means of consciousness with the unconscious mental processes which are their object. Like the physical, the psychical is not necessarily in reality what it appears to us to be. We shall be glad to learn, however, that the correction of internal perception will turn out not to offer such great difficulties as the correction of external perception – that internal objects are less unknowable than the external world. (Freud, 1915e, p. 171)

As Freud lays out his understanding of the unconscious and reminds us that the nature of mentation follows different principles associated with primary process thinking, he attempts to diminish the significance of those ever problematic cases of multiple personality in the following way:

> ... analysis shows that the different latent mental processes inferred by us enjoy a high degree of mutual independence, as though they had no connection with one another, and knew nothing of one another. We must be prepared, if so, to assume the existence in us not only of a second consciousness, but of a third, fourth, perhaps of an unlimited number of states of consciousness, all unknown to us and to one another. In the third place – and this is the most weighty argument of all – we have to take into account the fact that analytic investigation reveals some of these latent processes as having characteristics and peculiarities which seem alien to us, or even incredible, and which run directly counter to the attributes of consciousness with which we are familiar. Thus we have grounds for modifying our inference about ourselves and saying that what is proved is not the existence of a second consciousness in us, but the existence of psychical acts which lack consciousness. We shall also be right in rejecting the term "subconsciousness" as incorrect and misleading. The well-known cases of *"double conscience"* (splitting of consciousness) prove nothing against our view. We may most aptly describe them as cases of a splitting of the mental activities into two groups, and say that the same consciousness turns to one or the other of these groups alternately. (Freud, 1915e, pp. 169–170)

The question of these ". . . different latent mental processes [which] enjoy a high degree of mutual independence, as though they had no connection with one another, and knew nothing of one another" (Freud, 1915e, p. 169) has continued to vex theoreticians and clinicians ever since. This especially is the case when there are more than "two groups", which is often the case in this population. In an effort to reconcile classical theory with findings in self-psychology and relational theory, Slap and Slap-Shelton elaborate on the notion of schemas and describe pathogenic, sequestered schemas as residues of early childhood traumata that colour perception and function on the level of the dynamic unconscious and then reappear. In their view, their reappearance accounts for the repetition compulsion. Extending their thinking to dreams, they consider such night-time mental processes as "the product of the interaction of the sequestered schemas with a current day event or situation" (Slap & Slap-Shelton, 1991, p. 79). They go on to say that

> The sequestered schema is understood as an organization of the mind, having at its core traumatic impressions and situations of the past which have been separated from the generally interconnected mass of ideas and which function at a primitive cognitive level in which assimilation prevails over accommodation. (Slap & Slap-Shelton, 1991, p. 79)

Thus, they account for disturbances in perception in terms of "anachronistic templates" (Slap & Slap-Shelton, 1991, p. 80) that colour the input.

In the following vignette, a patient with one of these ". . . well-known cases . . ." (Freud, 1915e, p. 170), with several splits in her "mental activities", could not accept her psychical reality of sequestered schemata and dissociated selves, which resulted in a serious surgical mishap.

Case report

Cindy had contemplated getting laser eye surgery to permanently correct her near-sightedness. She was especially low on funds at the time, so her sense of urgency to undergo such a procedure was notable and brought to her attention. Despite her conscious intention to see better than ever and no longer need her eyeglasses, deeper forces were simultaneously at play that were determined to obscure her delving into her incestuous relationships with key male relatives. Having been in analysis for several years at this point and having observed profound changes in her demeanour, identity, and memory, as well as episodic self-destructive behaviour, there was much clinical evidence to support her having a severe dissociative disorder (I. Brenner, 2001).

As I listened to her rationalisation about the forthcoming surgery, I was reminded of the fact that in another of her states of mind, named Candy, she wore a different pair of glasses that had a different prescription. In this state of mind, a rather carefree, capricious, seemingly separate, and hypersexual self would exude a very different air about herself and berate Cindy for her old-maid-like behaviour. She had her own relationships as well as a wardrobe that was kept separately that Cindy had no recollection of buying. Moreover, Candy could know

Cindy's mind but not *vice versa*—like a one-way mirror. Candy also had knowledge of the inner population. Cindy was loath to acknowledge her amnesia about such times when this other self had ascendancy, but the clues about her secret life that were left behind became a source of analytic enquiry. In yet another state of mind, her vision was reportedly perfectly fine and she wore no glasses. At such times, she cross-dressed and hid her long hair under a baseball cap. This transgender self was prone to paranoid violence. In addition to the already complex and devastating situation the patient was contending with in the state of mind where she dressed as a man, the patient was also quite menacing in the transference. This "male" self tried to acquire a penis and absolutely hated being trapped in a female body. It occurred to me that her wish to permanently change the structure of her eyes might have also been an upward displacement of a wish to change her genitals. However, enacting this symbolic solution would adversely affect her capacity to see clearly.

I had observed this phenomenon of fluctuating visual acuity in other patients, but I could not find any reports in the literature. I surmised, therefore, that the changes in acuity were not of a hysterical nature but were, rather, more of a psychophysiological fluctuation of her extraocular muscles of accommodation.[3] At this point in her therapy, she was confronting yet another level of very painful truths about the traumatic nature of her background and severe abuse that were not well tolerated in her usual state of mind. Suicidal impulses re-emerged. Clearly, there were things that she wanted to see and did not want to see about her past that greatly affected how she saw herself. A personification of her superego was vicious and punishing. In a desperate moment, she sought an external, concrete solution to her internal problem. However, this interpretation had no effect on the patient, as she continued headlong into her medical misadventure. Not surprisingly, after the procedure, her vision was blurred for well over a year. Her ophthalmologist was alarmed and puzzled. While she became depressed, despairing, and withdrew, her new preoccupation with this visual fog seemed to diminish her suicidality.

Discussion

It could be argued that the heart of the psychoanalytic enterprise is the exploration of unconscious influences upon perception. We see what our minds enable us or need us to see and do not realise it unless we understand what is going on out of our awareness. With regard to seeing oneself, Jacobson described it this way:

> By a realistic image of the self we mean, first of all, one that correctly mirrors the state and the characteristics, the potentialities and abilities, the assets and the limits of our bodily and mental self: on the one hand, of our appearance, our anatomy, and our physiology; on the other hand, of our ego, our conscious and pre-conscious feelings and thoughts, wishes, impulses, and attitudes, of our physical and mental functions and behaviour.

> At present it may suffice to point to the enormous and rather disruptive influences which the processes of infantile denial and repression exert upon the formation of our images of the self and the object world . . . the cutting out of a considerable sector of unpleasurable memories by infantile repression eliminates a large amount of unacceptable aspects of both the self and the outside world. The defects caused by the work of repression may be filled in by screen elements, by distortions or embellishments produced by the elaborate maneuvers of the ego's defense system. (Jacobson, 1964, pp. 21–22)

Cindy was unable to tolerate her psychical reality of having multiple, dissociated selves. She needed to maintain an illusion of cohesion that was apparently quite limited and subject to dynamic influences. In her flight from seeing the state of her self-organisation, she severely damaged her capacity to see the external world. This extreme example of reciprocity between inner and outer perception, once better understood, helped explain seemingly bizarre and quasi-psychotic symptomatology. In less complex, more mundane cases, such a principle is axiomatic.

From transient distortions of basic sensory experiences to analysis of the transference, the basic question is how all of our unique dynamics affect "what we see". While this viewpoint is hardly new or original, the fact that it is so well known is perhaps why there seems to be diminishing interest in the topic among analysts. An emphasis on perception was primary in Freud's early work as the Pcs./Cs. was a central tenet of topographic theory (Freud, 1900a). In the original model, perception was seen as accurate and non-conflictual, as has been pointed out (Slap & Slap-Shelton, 1991). As Freud's thinking evolved and the primary process of mental functioning was recognised as manifesting itself in derivatives (Freud, 1915e), the distinction became less clear. With the introduction of the structural theory (Freud, 1923b), where perception was relegated to an ego function—albeit a very important ego function—there seemed to be less concern over the conscious–unconscious differentiation. Then, with the study of unconscious fantasy (Arlow, 1969) with its central organising influence upon ego functioning, although it undoubtedly included perception, the emphasis was more on mental creation and instinctual influences. The Kleinian object-relations perspective, which focused on the crucial importance of splitting and projective identification (Klein, 1946; Bion, 1959), also enlarged our understanding of how unconscious factors might affect what we perceive. But here, too, the emphasis on the defensive operations seemed to receive more attention.

In my experience with adults who have sustained severe early trauma, there might be a preponderance of defensive structures organised around altered states of consciousness and amnesia which may resemble "very deep" repression and a division of the psyche, which Breuer and Freud described as splitting of consciousness (Freud, 1895d). In this type of mental organisation, those who dissociate and who suffer from major disturbances of self-constancy could have alternating, seemingly separate, self-organisations that appear to take over the conscious and utilise secondary process mentation, not unlike what was described in the legendary case of Anna O. They also manifest a ". . . cutting out of a considerable sector of unpleasurable memories . . . and elaborate maneuvers of the ego's defense system" (Jacobson, 1964, p. 21). Freud retreated from such cases in the end, convincing subsequent generations of analysts that this condition was either easily explained, unimportant, or so mysterious that analysts had nothing to offer (I. Brenner, 2009a). In the following vignette, I describe the clinical challenge of addressing a patient's rather sudden and dramatic change of self-perception that was dynamically significant and that raises some technical questions for contemporary analysts.

Case report

Minh, a tall, thin, strikingly beautiful, but aloof Asian-American woman was in her fifth year of a five-time-a-week analysis. As she lay on the couch in the middle of an hour, she was sobbing over the forthcoming anniversary of the untimely death of her uncle, a problematic and extremely ambivalent relationship that came to an abrupt end just as he was beginning to recognise how important his niece was to him. He was trying to make amends. Since her father was absent much of the time due to military obligations, her maternal uncle served as a father surrogate. Struggling with her bitterness and grief over having lost him again—this time permanently—she then turned on her side and tucked her head under her arm. Her crying stopped and she became perfectly still and completely quiet. In my own affective resonance and my attunement to her states of mind, I felt a sudden rupture of our connection at this moment. I then waited quietly for what might ensue, be it an extended silence or more outpouring of emotion. Shortly thereafter, she started speaking in a different tone of voice, but one with which I was familiar. It had a playful, sing-songy quality and she addressed me informally as Doc. In her usual states of mind, she never addressed me by any name, careful to avoid being too formal or informal, a longstanding theme that had come up not infrequently. This cautiousness appeared to be a derivative of her effort to achieve optimal distance (Mahler, Pine, & Bergman, 1975) and reflected her attempt to rework in the transference a healthier, pre-oedipal maternal relationship. It had been profoundly disturbed throughout her childhood, and separations were often characterised by rageful protests punctuated by prolonged ruptures of our rapport of the type described above. Periods of chaos and altered states of consciousness were suggestive of adult manifestations of a disorganised, disorientated attachment.

So, upon hearing how I was being addressed, it immediately signalled and confirmed my intuition that another self, one seemingly separate from her "regular" self, had emerged and taken over the executive functioning of her ego. She spoke differently, often with more colourful, raw, and direct phrases consistent with a precocious adolescent who was rather street smart and wise beyond her years. In sharp contrast, Minh exhibited extreme politeness, correctness, and great sensitivity so as not to offend others and often appeared timid and easily frightened. This other self, Linh, was extremely devaluing of Minh, calling her an idiot for being so emotional, naïve, and trusting of others who quite often took advantage of her good nature and her fear of antagonising others. In addition, she was extremely jealous of Minh, who spent so much time "out" and who seemed to have become stronger as a result of analysis, thus making it more difficult for her to "push through" and take over.

However, there were still times when Minh would be so overwhelmed with intolerable affects, such as grief and deep sadness, as well as instinctual anxiety over libidinal and aggressive currents, that she would take leave either by literally exiting the office or taking leave of her body and dissociating. At such times, Linh would be most likely to take over, following prodromal symptoms of debilitating headaches, flushes, and nausea. The patient had consulted several neurologists in the past for these mysterious symptoms that could literally cripple her and render her unable to function for periods of time. Diagnosed with ocular migraines, the patient was incredulous to discover that, over time, these also heralded a change in her self-states.

Other selves less regularly involved in the therapeutic process but, none the less, having an enormous influence on the process included an intellectual, rageful self with a lesbian predilection who would scream and yell about how she hated and mistrusted me. She would leave furious telephone messages for me, calling me by my first name, and pronouncing it in a slow, mocking, and derisive way. Together with Linh, this dyad appeared to have the power to internally persecute and punish Minh, causing her to lock herself of her house in bad weather and out of her car in dangerous neighbourhoods. From a vantage point outside the patient, such "bungled actions" would be entirely consistent with the "psychopathology of everyday life" (Freud, 1901b). As though this were a personification of a punitive superego, as with Cindy, such times were clearly associated with unconscious motivation and attributed to repressed wishes for punishment due to unrecognised guilt. Minh, whose longstanding awareness of these selves had been a very private and contentious issue laden with deep shame and embarrassment, had more or less "known and not known" about them for years, but could not allow herself to articulate the problem to herself, let alone to an outsider, such as her analyst. Like elusive floaters in the eye that quickly disappear into peripheral visual fields when trying to focus upon them, Minh likened these selves to this phenomenon. They were just out of reach of consciousness, and she could not see herself as sharing her body with other selves. However, she would dream about having a birthday party with four empty chairs and fully understand the symbolism.

Significantly, Linh had access to the patient's inner population and spoke freely about the problem, offering insight and detailed historical information about the uncle's perverse, incestuous violations of her young body that often foreshadowed Minh's progress in treatment. At first, Minh could only acknowledge a very aberrant relationship with her uncle that she could not put into words. Instead, all she could really say for the first several years was succinctly expressed as "I can't think about what I remember!"

As noted, Linh could not only remember such things, but she could think about them and talk about them. She protected Minh and had taken over when the pain had become too much to bear as a child. However, she refused, or was unable to acknowledge, that she shared the same physical fate with Minh and essentially wanted my help to eliminate her.

Over time, the rivalry between Minh and Linh became quite palpable and real for the patient in both states of mind. Extremely jealous of all my patients, especially the female patients, her possessiveness was apparently represented and played out both internally and externally. So, when I heard the patient call me "Doc", it confirmed that a significant defensive shift had taken place, probably due to affect intolerance associated with grief, as it was now Linh's turn to be out. At such times, the clinician is presented with a technical dilemma that has enormous implications for the analysis and has been debated in virtually every session of our discussion group on dissociative disorders at the American Psychoanalytic Association meetings. Does one acknowledge the dissociated self and engage with the patient at that level? Does such an approach "play into", reinforce, and perhaps reify a quasi-delusional belief about other people inhabiting someone's mind? Or would that stance be empathic and respectful of the patient's psychical reality? Does such a direction introduce iatrogenic complications into the treatment? Or should the analyst simply listen to the patient's utterances like any other associative material and treat the patient as he or she would any other analytic patient (Gottlieb, 1997)? After all, if the patient has the requisite ego strength for analysis, would she eventually simply give up such a defensive stance for more adaptive, healthy defences? Are we dealing with a fantasy of multiplicity, or are the structural changes of such a deep nature that additional work in addressing these selves is warranted? Is this a disturbed self-perception or a perception of disturbed selves?

Discussion

Psychiatrists in training are generally taught not to confirm or play into the schizophrenic's delusions for a number of reasons, not the least of which is the concern about further weakening the patient's grasp on reality. Instead, the clinician is instructed to tactfully listen and not aggressively confront the psychotic thinking, as further decompensation and violent or suicidal repercussions might ensue. Such a shibboleth has often been applied to the situation in those with "multiple personality", as, even today, those with little experience (Taylor & Martin, 1944) with the condition might conflate schizophrenia and DID. Since Bleuler's term "schizophrenia" is derived from root words meaning "split mind", and since Freud made short shrift of it, DID continues to have an identity problem of its own (I. Brenner, 1999) and is, ironically, often seen as outside the realm of psychoanalysis.

So, given these historical circumstances and the particular dynamics of the patient in question, the technical challenge over how to listen and respond to the patient's dissociated and unconscious perception of herself was critical. Failure to acknowledge that a change had occurred would have insulted and enraged the patient, whereas undue attention and favouritism might have had negative repercussions as well. Linh had revelled in her capacity to slip in and out of sessions with "their" former psychotherapist who, despite his good intentions and considerable overall clinical experience, was apparently clueless about these shifts and made little headway after almost a decade of treatment.

In my view, the idea that if the analyst does not acknowledge or recognise such shifts they will eventually cease and not be problematic is tantamount to behavioural therapy masquerading as psychoanalysis. One would be wittingly or unwittingly employing the treatment strategy of trying to "extinguish" an unwanted behaviour by ignoring it rather than analysing it. In addition, since many such patients have a significant history of early sexual trauma (I. Brenner, 1994, 2001, 2004; Kluft, 1986) and were threatened with serious consequences if they told anyone and/or were brainwashed (Shengold, 1989) into thinking nobody would ever believe them, they had become quite adept at reading others and sensing when to essentially shut up, hide, and become like a chameleon. From a Winnicottian perspective, their pseudo-compliant false selves would prevail (Winnicott, 1955).

The issues of observing ego, self-awareness, self-perception, and perception of the self are critical here, as quite often there may be considerable cohesion within a given self or a "narcissistic investment in separateness" (Kluft, 1986). At the same time, by definition, such patients are sorely lacking in self-constancy. This seeming contradiction appears to ward off deep annihilation anxiety through this illusion, whereas, ironically, the presence of other selves might, at times, provide company or companionship for the patient and defend against separation anxiety. Not unlike imaginary playmates in this regard, such selves serve multiple functions in the psyche. Such a complex psychical arrangement serving multiple functions (Wälder, 1936) must be dealt with carefully, as the extent of internalised aggression could precipitate a suicidal regression. In the following case, the clinician did not appreciate such a nuanced approach and a near-fatal catastrophe occurred.

Case report

A colleague was providing inpatient coverage for a severely traumatised patient many years ago while I was on vacation. During this time, the patient complained to him about how she had become more aware, or "co-conscious", of another self trying to take over her mind. She feared that such a takeover would consign her to getting lost somewhere in her mind forever, which was associated with profound abandonment anxiety. Seriously underestimating the extent of her conflict, he made the bold pronouncement that he would try to get rid of this particular self who was harassing her. Mistakenly believing that such a psychological exorcism was indeed possible by this imposing, authoritarian presence, the intervention reactivated a malevolent, paternal, internalised object. The patient panicked and retreated into her bedroom where, in a dissociated state, she found a razor blade that she had smuggled in and, while in the bathroom, severed her radial artery. As conflicted as she was over staying alive, she had intended to exit the bathroom, turn right, and bleed to death on her bed, but instead, turned left and promptly fell on the floor in the hallway. An alert member of the nursing staff rushed to her side and applied direct pressure to stop the spurting of arterial blood. Emergency vascular surgery saved her life.

Following my return and careful exploration of this new disaster, it appeared that the patient's sense of abandonment in the transference left her feeling unprotected and vulnerable to the covering doctor's intrusive directive. Just as her mother retreated into her nightly alcoholic stupors and enabled her father's vicious sexual attacks to occur with impunity, so, too, her protective analyst disappeared and left her at the mercy of the substitute doctor.

Reviving fear and old memories of her father's repeated violent sexual intrusions into her unprotected young body, this schema became enacted by an internal perpetrator in the form of a dissociated self who, out of fear of being caught, brought to justice, and subsequently eliminated, had reverted to suicide. Here, the patient's unconscious, disorientated self-perception was of being a hunted sexual criminal who, backed into a corner with no escape, gave into a desperate, life-threatening impulse. The question of perception of the self becomes rather complicated when there is an organisation of multiple dissociated selves who may, alternately at times, or at times conjointly, become, as it were, conscious or take over consciousness.

Perception of the bodily self

As Freud reminded us, first and foremost, the ego is a "bodily ego" (Freud, 1923b) and, therefore, the somatic basis of the self is generally accepted to be sensory–motor in origin. The infant's growing awareness of bodily position and muscular co-ordination, as well as sensory and perceptual input, are organised into schemas (Schilder, 1950; Piaget & Inhelder, 1969). Multiple schemata and perceptions of bodily image are then created which, under normative conditions, blend more or less seamlessly into a cohesive sense of self (Kohut, 1971). A nodal point of development, erroneously thought by Lacan to occur at eight months in his "mirror stage" (Lacan, 1953), is the recognition of one's self in a mirror. This stage is in contrast to Kohut's "mirror stage" (Kohut, 1971), where the infant basks in the gleam of the mother's eye. Although infants may react to their image at such an early age, more recent research concludes that this capacity is more likely to be achieved between the ages of fifteen to eighteen months (Asendorpf, Warkentin, & Baudonnière, 1996).

Coinciding with other crucial milestones at this time, such as anality and rapprochement, along with their affective and cognitive accompaniments, this acquisition appears to have a very important organising quality to it. While studies have concluded that other species, such as chimpanzees (de Veer et al., 2003), Asian elephants (Plotnik, de Waal, & Reiss, 2006), and bottlenose dolphins (Marten & Psarakos, 1995) may also acquire the capacity to recognise themselves in a mirror, the obvious language barrier between humans and these animals precludes a deeper understanding of the full implications of this achievement in these species.

Our fascination with our reflection quite probably predates the myth of Narcissus, as even Palaeolithic cave art from almost 30,000 years ago has revealed reflections of actual human hands in the form of colourful, stencil-like representations carefully applied to the wall. Much more recently, it has been incorporated into many genres of literature. For example, this theme is found in fairy tales such as Snow White, where the wicked, vain queen reportedly asks, "Looking-glass, looking-glass on the wall, Who in this land is the fairest of all?" (The Brothers Grimm, 1812). It is also seen in preternatural stories, such as the story of Dracula, the vampire, who did not have any reflection in the mirror. In the sequel to *Alice in Wonderland*, entitled *Through the Looking-Glass, And What Alice Found There* (Carroll, 1871), Alice found a bizarre and wondrous world on the other side of the looking glass. Stepping through the mirror on her fireplace mantel, she encountered a land of opposites, reversals, and time travel. A clinical correlate to this fictionally fanciful account is seen in the following case.

Case report

During a particularly anxiety-laden session with Christine in which she became very aware of my presence in the room, I made a statement to her that in some ways I was like a mirror, listening and reflecting things that she was saying. Much to my surprise, shortly thereafter, there was a change in her affect, in her syntax, in her tone of voice, and in her body language, and a very young self emerged, giggly, saying, "You're a mirror?" I was aware of this change in her self-state, and listened on as to what was forthcoming. What emerged was a series of recollections in this child's voice and, later on, in the patient's usual voice, of experiences when she was a young girl. Following painful, sexualised torture at her mother's hands, she would retreat into the bathroom and see her tear-streaked face in the mirror. Looking at her reflection in the mirror she saw a girl there whom she did not perceive as herself. In her depersonalised state, she then experienced herself going into the mirror, looking for help and solace from the girl whom she believed lived in the mirror. A period of amnesia would result then, which was relieved during the session. As we attempted to reconstruct what had happened to her when she was young, it appeared that another self, called the "Mirror Girl", or the "Girl in the Mirror" would emerge dissociatively, take over, and absorb the pain. The patient was very confused, and it took a number of weeks for her to find words and make sense of this aspect of her experience. Her relationship to her reflection in the mirror and her attempts at flight into the world inside the mirror to get help from her dissociated reflection seemed to be an autohypnotic effort on her part to escape an intolerable affectively and physically painful situation.

Closing comments

In *Don Quixote de la Mancha* (de Cervantes, 1605), the master and his servant encounter the Knight of the Mirrors, a neighbour who uses mirrors to obscure his own identity in the hope of tricking the Don into giving up his quest and returning home. Ultimately, Don Quixote was to be cured of his madness by being forced to see himself realistically in the mirror so he would give up his delusional self-perception, which emerged from his unconscious. The mirror as a symbol of realistic perception is also seen in Shakespeare's philosophy of the theatre. It was expressed through Hamlet when Hamlet said that "... [the] end, both at the first and now, was and is, to hold ... the mirror up to nature ..." (Shakespeare, 1978a, p. 227) and reflect life as it is. The great Italian playwright, Pirandello, a contemporary of Freud, whose deep understanding of human nature informed his writing, also considered the mirror to be essential to his work:

> When a man lives, he lives and does not see himself. Well, put a mirror before him and make him see himself in the act of living, under the sway of his passions: either he remains astonished and dumbfounded at his own appearance, or else he turns away his eyes so as not to see himself, or else in disgust he spits at his image, or again clinches his

fist to break it; and if he had been weeping, he can weep no more; if he had been laughing, he can laugh no more, and so on. In a word, there arises a crisis, and that crisis is my theater. (Pirandello, in Bassanese, 1997, p. 54)

A monologue by the character, Laudisi, in *Right You Are! (If You Think So)* offers a theatrical illustration of the emergence of disowned aspects of the self:

LAUDISI: [left alone, walks up and down the study a number of times, nodding his head and occasionally smiling. Finally he draws up in front of the big mirror that is hanging over the mantelpiece. He sees himself in the glass, stops, and addresses his image.] So there you are! [He bows to himself and salutes, touching his forehead with his fingers]. I say, old man, who is the lunatic, you or I? [He levels a finger menacingly at his image in the glass; and, of course, the image in turn levels a finger at him. As he smiles, his image smiles.] Of course, I understand! I say it's you, and you say it's me. You—you are the lunatic! No? It's me? Very well! It's me! Have it your way. Between you and me, we get along very well, don't we! But the trouble is, others don't think of you just as I do; and that being the case, old man, what a fix you're in! As for me, I say that here, right in front of you, I can see myself with my eyes and touch myself with my fingers. But what are you for other people? What are you in their eyes? An image, my dear sir, just an image in the glass! "What fools these mortals be!" as old Shakespeare said. They're all carrying just such a phantom around inside themselves, and here they are racking their brains about the phantoms in other people; and they think all that is quite another thing! (Pirandello, 1921, p. 193)

In closing, while such concepts as observing ego focus our attention on the conscious perceptions of the self, unconscious, dissociated influences must be considered in order to "really" see ourselves in the mirror.

PART III
SOCIETAL REALM

CHAPTER FIVE

Intergenerational transmission

"I wish and I ask that our rulers who have Jewish subjects . . . act like a good physician who, when gangrene has set proceeds without mercy to cut, saw, and burn flesh, veins, bone, and marrow. Such a procedure must also be followed in this instance. Burn down their synagogues, forbid all that I enumerated earlier, force them to work, and deal harshly with them, as Moses did in the wilderness, slaying three thousand lest the whole people perish"

(Martin Luther, 1543)

"To take the place of emigration, and with the prior approval of the Führer, the evacuation of the Jews to the East . . . should be of great importance in view of the coming *Endlösung* [final/definitive solution] of the Jewish question"

(Reinhard Heydrich, Speech at the Wansee Conference, Berlin, Germany, January 20, 1942, p. 304)

Introduction

Results of a twenty-year study of children of Holocaust survivors have concluded that they are no more psychologically disturbed than a matched control group—except in "extreme situations" (Van IJzendoorn, Fridman, Bakermans-Kranenburg, & Sagi-Schwartz, 2013). Such findings might come as a relief to those who have felt stigmatised by being labelled with a diagnosis that does not exist. It might also come as a relief to certain agencies and governments that might have been asked to provide expensive services or restitution payments to offspring of survivors of genocidal persecution. However, such a conclusion might also inadvertently obscure the findings of more than forty years of psychoanalytic experience with this group. In this chapter, I wish to review these findings, drawing upon the unique form of research that can only be derived from an in-depth study of the unconscious mind.

Case report: extreme trauma

I once knew a man who believed that if he never talked about his experience during the Holocaust, he would have protected his children. They would have been spared the horror, pain, sorrow, grief, and rage that he did his best to keep inside. They should never know about his suffering, for what he had seen and endured surely should have killed him, but somehow he survived. So, when they as children asked about the little blue numbers on his arm, he would laugh and tell them it was his old girlfriend's phone number. They did not quite believe it, but somehow sensed that they better not ask any further, as his forced jocularity tried to belie an abyss of such depth that everyone might be swallowed up by it. His eyes would dart away while his mouth would smile, signalling his anxiety at the end of the conversation. He survived beatings, starvation, degradation, humiliation, dehumanisation, cruel punishment, and the constant threat of being murdered on the capricious whim of any guard at any moment, as well as witnessing the torture and murder of friends, family, and esteemed religious leaders. At a very low point in his life, shortly before the evacuation of Auschwitz in January 1945, he risked his life to help two boyhood friends escape. Unbeknown to him, they witnessed his group of survivors on their death march through that most brutal winter while they were in their temporary hiding place in a nearby village. The man miraculously hung on and was sent to a munitions plant associated with Buchenwald for several more months until the Allies liberated the facility in April 1945. All told, he spent more than five-and-a-half years as a human slave in the most notorious death camps known to exist in the Nazi regime, from shortly after the invasion of Poland in September 1939 to the end of the war. Reduced to a ninety-pound skeleton, he required months of careful feeding at a field hospital before he could go back to his hometown to look for any surviving relatives. He then made his way to the USA, where he got a job, married an American woman, and started a family, hoping to put his "nightmare years" (Shirer, 1984) behind him. But, as Kitty Hart, an Auschwitz survivor, starkly declared upon her return to Auschwitz years later, "I knew I ought never to have come back, because it has proved I've never been away" (Hart, 1981).

This man made it a priority to protect his children from knowing about such horror, and did his best not to think about it. However, it pervaded every aspect of his daily life. For example, his wife cooked excessively and he ate everything on his plate, including the marrow of chicken bones. While voraciously consuming his food, he projected his memories of starvation on to his children, saying, "You don't need to eat your food so fast. Don't worry. Nobody will take it away from you." He also refused to wear heavy clothing in the wintertime, seemingly oblivious or immune to the elements. This habit was seemingly disconnected in his mind from a disturbing memory of his first experience of life in the camp.

He and his father, along with many others, were taken from their hometown at gunpoint early in the morning and sent by armed guard on a specially commandeered commuter train, the S-Bahn, to Sachsenhausen. It was a hot, mid-September day, and the newly inducted prisoners were required to wear heavy winter uniforms designed and manufactured by the Hugo Boss company, whose deep Nazi connections only recently became well known. The doomed prisoners were then locked into an overcrowded barracks for several days with no provisions.

Needless to say, many died. After this crude but effective selection process, those who survived were assigned to various "jobs" and, most importantly, a quarry and brick factory. The building products were intended to supply materials to house the superior race that was to conquer Europe and start the Thousand-Year Reich. The work was backbreaking, dangerous, and relentless. As an eighteen-year-old adolescent with endurance and strength, whose dreams of college and a medical career were replaced by the daily reality of roll call, shootings, and endless hours of slavery, his youth, instinct for survival, and luck ultimately prevailed. One day merged into the next as he saw his father deteriorate during their periodic encounters. Caught trying to give the ailing man his own meagre portion of bread, the man was beaten mercilessly by his SS overlord and locked in an underground cell for twenty-four hours where the quarters were so narrow that he could only stand up. Intended to "teach him a lesson", this man was left with lifelong claustrophobia, such that should he be required to take an elevator, he would become very quiet and distant in an effort to keep his profound anxiety at bay. He was also very reluctant to visit relatives or friends in hospitals or nursing homes, which, no doubt, brought back memories of deteriorating prison inmates waiting to be sent to the gas chamber. The daughter of another death camp survivor succinctly described the problem in her poem, "Things My Father Won't Do" (Kirchheimer, 2007):

Things My Father Won't Do

wear striped clothing
go to the doctor
tell me his dreams
live in a house surrounded by a fence

(Kirchheimer, 2007, p. 4)

Children and grandchildren of survivors

Growing up with a massively traumatised parent can leave its mark directly and indirectly, but, while it has become a cliché that yesterday's abused children become today's child abusers (Blum, 1987; Steele, 1970), even today, much less is known about the subtle and indirect transmission that occurs even when parents try to protect their offspring. The daily absorption of the adult's traumatic past, taken in by the developing psyche of the child as a function of mothering and/or fathering, might be overlooked (Bergmann & Jucovy, 1982;

Jucovy, 1986; Kestenberg, 1972, 1982a,b, Klein, 1973). The poet Paul Celan wrote how the trauma of the Holocaust was transmitted through ashes in the mother's milk (Celan, 1948). While this aspect of intergenerational transmission may be considered strain trauma (Kris, 1956), or cumulative trauma (Khan, 1963), there are several reasons why it might not even be recognised as a contribution. It is likely to be overlooked if overt, gross abuse, deprivation, or shock trauma (Furst, 1967) overshadows it, or if the parent's trauma history is not clear. In addition, countertransference issues might induce the analyst to unconsciously collude with the patient's silence to avoid painful affects, such as grief, anxiety, shame, and guilt, that might accompany the parent's past (Danieli, 1980; Moses, 1978). Then, if we consider the theoretical problems related to differentiating a repressed memory of trauma from an unconscious fantasy (Person & Klar, 1994) in just one person, we see that this dilemma is only confounded by the challenge of evaluating its impact across generations.

Nevertheless, it has been possible to examine transmission in cases where the history of parental trauma is not in doubt, when it was time-limited prior to the child's birth, and where the child himself was not directly affected. Sadly, there has been no shortage of documented human tragedy and the Holocaust, most notably, has provided most of the data on transmission, but it has also been studied in other realms, such as in the children of Nazis, Second World War POWs, the Armenian genocide, Cambodia, ethnic cleansing in Yugoslavia, Japanese-American internment, the children of hibakusha, African-American slavery, and the plight of indigenous peoples such as Australian aborigines and Native Americans (Danieli, 1998).

The genocidal destruction of two-thirds of the European Jewish population during the Second World War has been termed the Holocaust. The term has been trivialised, commercialised, politicised, exploited for secondary gain, denied, and also applied to other recent mass atrocities, such as those in Cambodia, Rwanda, and Bosnia. It is not possible to assess the extent of an individual's suffering based on the magnitude of the catastrophe or the number dead in any given event. Also, as a result of many variables, including premorbid factors, the extent of traumatisation may be different, not only among Holocaust survivors, but also among survivors of other genocidal persecution. None the less, the Holocaust is by far the most widely studied, and, almost seventy years after the liberation of the concentration camps, the number of survivors is dwindling quickly, with fewer than 200,000 in Israel, according to recent reports (Haaretz, 2012). They have produced a second, a third, and even a young fourth generation. The lessons to be learnt about politics, religion, and human nature are endless. Our understanding of the long-term effects of massive psychic trauma (Grubrich-Simitis, 1981; Krystal, 1968; Ornstein, 1986) on both adults and on the developing child (Kestenberg & Brenner, 1996) has also greatly increased.

The passage of time has allowed us to examine multigenerational transmission. In a recent documentary by Rivka Bekerman-Greenberg, *I Am Carrying The Holocaust In My Pocket* (2011), herself a member of the second generation, she clearly shows the deep emotional connections that four women have with their survivor grandparents. Transmission in the third generation seems to occur in two ways: one, through the second-generation parents and, two, through direct survivor grandparents themselves. When they die, the mourning process revives all of their losses, which adds to the burden of the third generation. However, with the passing of time and the metabolism that occurs, much of the irrational shame of the survivors has been transmuted into a sense of pride in their grandchildren. Evidence of their preoccupation may be seen in their sublimations, career choices, and problems. In such cases that I have seen, one patient became immersed in the study of an obscure, persecuted minority in the Middle Ages, another took up the cause of cruelty to animals, whereas another kept running away, travelling abroad, and becoming involved in toxic relationships that she magically hoped would cure her. She grew up listening to her grandparents mythologising their time in the camps and romanticising their meeting in South America after liberation. However, her parents essentially avoided the Holocaust, thus creating a secret bond that skipped a generation, at least consciously. I am quite convinced, however, from the detailed study of approximately thirty analyses that have been presented since I have been involved in the Holocaust Discussion Group of the American Psychoanalytic Association, that unconscious effects might be quite significant.

The phenomenon of living in two worlds simultaneously, born of trauma and not of psychosis, was described by Kestenberg as a "time tunnel" (Kestenberg, 1982a). She observed that in Holocaust survivors, there appeared to be a profound communication of their traumatic experience to their children, resulting in a transposition of the past, whereby they might feel that they, too, were living a Holocaust reality. Consequently, the developing ego in the second generation was confronted not only with the usual tasks of adaptation, but also with the integration of their parents' traumatic reliving of the Holocaust. As a result, there could be an intensification of developmental dangers and a characteristic preoccupation with survival, loss, persecution, and Jewish identity. The resulting feeling of almost "being there" can have a surreal, uncanny, or dissociative quality to it, and has raised important metapsychological questions about the specificity of Holocaust trauma and the transmission of trauma in general.

At a most basic level, it might be that certain conditions merely accentuate and fixate the tendency in young children to assume they have always been part of their parents' earlier lives. For them to ask a question such as, "Where was I before I was born?" is not only a function of the separation–individuation process (Mahler, Pine, & Bergman, 1975), but also a cognitive milestone, for it requires a comprehension that there was a time in the world before their existence. As with other universal, anxiety-laden issues, this theme is depicted in popular literature and films and it is often in the form of time travel. Interestingly, the hero is frequently a child who goes back in time and is caught up in the dilemma of changing the past in order to avenge a crime, correct an injustice, or prevent a tragedy.

The underlying oedipal component to this reparative fantasy was humorously depicted a number of years ago in the very popular film *Back to the Future* (1985). Here we see a young man who is very ashamed of his parents and seems to want to disown any relationship to them. He then travels back in time and lives out his prehistory with the help of a wild-eyed but affable scientist (who is not an analyst!). He becomes entangled in a love triangle with his parents when they were of high-school age, but they do not know he is to become their son. He resists his future mother's amorous advances and helps his pathetic, defenceless, pushover of a father stand up to the class bully who humiliates him on a daily basis. In so doing, his future father gains strength, pride, respect, and, most importantly, the love of the boy's future mother. The son, the hero, avenges his father's past victimisations and rehabilitates him. He helps the father become the kind of man that he can look up to. In order to do so, he must renounce his own oedipal desires. In return, he creates a strong and successful father with whom he can develop a healthy male identification. And, as is the case in transpositions, there was an ambiguity between the past and the present. This ambiguity can progress to confusion and disorientation when there is blurring among dream, fantasy, memory, and reality that accompany severe early trauma (I. Brenner, 1995a). Unconscious reparative fantasies of rescuing a family member from the Nazis may be seen in children of survivors.

The "selection"

A related organising fantasy frequently seen in children of survivors is one of "selection" (I. Brenner, 1988). Woven into this Holocaust scenario, both oedipal and pre-oedipal conflicts may be played out with sickeningly real imagery from the parents' past. Here, too, this motif has emerged in popular literature with *Sophie's Choice*, by William Styron (1979). Ilany Kogan (Kogan, 1995a,b), in the analytic literature, described such a woman with a "selection" fantasy whose mother was a survivor. She could neither escape the symbiotic engulfment of this perpetually grieving mother, nor tolerate the anxiety and guilt of an oedipal victory. Consequently, she found refuge in a perverse solution characterised by sadomasochism and a phallic woman fantasy (Bak, 1968) in which she became a female Doctor Mengele in an SS uniform wielding a deadly phallic baton. In her fantasy, she made the "selections" on the entry ramp to Auschwitz, deciding who would live or die by a casual wave of her powerful stick. People were used or discarded at will. Within her inner life, she could then maintain total control over her object world, being the omnipotent Nazi "angel of death" (Abraham, 1986). Another poem of Kirchheimer's, "A Daughter's Dream", describes it this way:

> I was standing in a line,
> sent to the left, but I was still
> alive. I should have been
> sent to the right, and

I tried to change the dream,
tried to stand in another line
but was sent to the left again and
given a number written
on a piece of paper,
23344,
and it was wrong.

And I went back again, and
I was standing in a line,
sent to the right, and
I got a number, this time
on my arm, and I finally felt better.

(Kirchheimer, 2007, p. 88)

The Holocaust "culture"

The Holocaust "culture" (Kestenberg & Gampel, 1983) may completely saturate the mental life of children of survivors, *as though* they are transported back to a time when reality was worse than fantasy. Almost eerily, some would unconsciously recreate elements of the past when they reached the age their parents were during their ordeals. Such an internalisation of the parent's past seems to extend beyond the symbolic or metaphorical world, suggesting a very deep, pre-verbal communication between parent and child (Herzog, 1982). Volkan (1981), in his work on pathological grief, describes a depositing of the parent's traumatised self-representation into the child. Faimberg (1988) has conceptualised a type of identification with a "telescoping of generations". She postulates an intergenerational narcissistic problem in which the parent appropriates the capacity for experiencing pleasure from the child and is internalised as a dominating and intruding object. It is similar to Bollas's notion of extractive introjection (Bollas, 1987). In this structure, a condensation of three generations may occur in which elements of a secret history not belonging to the patient are incorporated. These identifications are unconscious, timeless, and may be uncovered in the transference. In such cases, a pervasive anhedonia with a feeling of inner deadness is reported. As the child becomes the "container" (Kogan, 1995a) for the parents to deposit their losses, fears, rages, and hopes, the role of projective identification is considered to be a central mechanism here. Anna Freud (1936) had long since concluded that "identification with the aggressor" was often seen in trauma, recognising that projection of guilt was at the core of it. Consequently, the projection of what was later to be coined as "survivor guilt" (Niederland, 1961) would be an essential part of the intolerable burden transmitted to the second generation. Blum (1986, 1987), however, reminds us that identification with the rescuer and identification with the victim are other important outcomes in the resolution of trauma.

Although first recognised in children of survivors, intergenerational transmission of massive psychic trauma is not unique to the Holocaust (Apprey, 1993; I. Brenner, 2001), and its effects may be diluted in succeeding generations. This cultural transmission may be by way of the superego (Freud, 1940a) and through the incorporation of shared images of such tragedies that become woven into a large group's fantasy life (Volkan, Ast, & Greer, 2002). Such a legacy most likely contributes to the oral traditions and distinctiveness of a given family, an ethnic group, or a whole society. Such images have even been exploited in the fashion world. For example, the Hugo Boss company, which made uniforms for everyone from prisoners to the Nazi elite SS during the war, was recently criticised for billboards of emaciated models with shaved heads and tattoos on their arms. Even more recently, the trendy clothing company, Urban Outfitters, introduced an "Auschwitz chic" T-shirt in bright yellow, complete with the image of the Star of David that was required to be sewn on to clothing in order to identify Jews in the ghettos of Europe. Holocaust video games and Nazi costumes worn by musicians or high-profile people at parties also make the news, as these images still have enormous shock value many decades later.

The "second generation"

The knowledge of the importance of "transmission" became widespread in the late 1970s and 1980s as the commonality of their experience spawned the Second Generation movement, including specialised group therapy (Fogelman & Savran, 1979), a proliferation of local organisations throughout North America, and autobiographical books, such as Helen Epstein's now classic *Children of the Holocaust*

(1979). She struck a very responsive chord as she wrote of the "iron box" (Epstein, 1979, p. 9) full of the most dangerous unspoken secrets of her parents' Holocaust past. Her book became the handbook for many thousands, and marked the coming of age for this surprisingly resilient and creative population whose prognosis was somewhat guarded in earlier psychiatric reports (Krystal, 1968). In the books, *Maus I* and *Maus II* (Spiegelman, 1986, 1991), a controversial but very effective use of the medium of the comic book depicted Spiegelman's experience growing up as a child of survivors. His family's story of genocidal persecution was illustrated. Nazis were drawn as malevolent cats while Jews were sketched as vulnerable mice. Here, the Nazi propaganda of the Jew as dangerous vermin was ironically and subtly incorporated into Spiegelman's imagery.

In 1974, the New York-based Group for the Psychoanalytic Study of the Effects of the Holocaust on the Second Generation (GPSEHSG) was formed, as it was recognised that analysts frequently overlooked, minimised, or defensively avoided the importance of the parents' survival experience. Under the leadership of Judith Kestenberg, Martin Bergmann, and Milton Jucovy, it met monthly to study the issue of transmission of trauma. Analysts presented case material to the group that, over the years, probably had more collective knowledge of the subject than anywhere else in the world. They sought to tease out so-called private pathology from Holocaust-related pathology and study the interaction of both as they emerged in the analytic process. In addition, they offered an annual discussion group at the winter meeting of the American Psychoanalytic Association in New York and published the ground-breaking text, *Generations of the Holocaust* (Bergmann & Jucovy, 1982).

After attending this discussion group in 1980, I joined the monthly study group in 1981. Eventually, I had the good fortune of being offered the chairmanship of the annual discussion group when the senior leadership retired in 1990. Dori Laub was appointed co-chair, and we have collaborated in this endeavour ever since. In addition, my participation in Kestenberg's international study of child survivors produced a number of papers and presentations, culminating in our book, *The Last Witness: The Child Survivor of the Holocaust* (Kestenberg & Brenner, 1996). In this volume, we, among many other things, examined the issue of transmission of trauma from the survivor's perspective.

Dissociative aspects of transmission

Transmission takes on a more pathogenic quality when it is associated with symptomatic disturbances of memory, awareness, consciousness, and identity. While most of the reported cases pertaining to the Holocaust emphasise transposition associated with defensive operations based on repression or splitting, one report does describe dissociative symptoms. Even though the aetiology of dissociation itself remains somewhat of a debate, many authorities share the view put forth by Van der Kolk and Kadish (1987) that, barring organicity, it is caused by psychic trauma. In this vignette (Gampel, 1982), a seven-year-old girl presented with amnesia, disorientation, learning difficulties, and "absences". Her father was the sole survivor of his family who, as a young boy, endured the Warsaw Ghetto and a concentration camp. He never spoke of his past, but his daughter was privately preoccupied with the fantasy of an electrified fence in a ghetto that could deliver a deadly charge to the children who were placed against it. Her parents were appalled and mystified to learn of the girl's knowledge of such things, a subject that had consumed her so intensely that it apparently made her ill. Her dissociative symptoms, which were thought to be almost psychotic in nature, reportedly resolved after several family meetings in which the father's Holocaust experience was openly discussed in front of the child. While it is unclear what, if any, other traumatogenic influences might have existed in this secretive family, it does appear that she identified with her father as a child victim. A similar phenomenon was described after 9/11, where a three-year-old child literally drew her father's nightmares of how he imagined his co-workers were killed after he survived the World Trade Center attacks. He had not gone to work that day and was wracked with survivor guilt, but could not talk about it (Coates, Schechter, & First, 2003).

Psychic trauma and its myriad repercussions appear to have effects on both time and potential space. From the frequently reported sense of a slowing of time in the acute state to the disorientation to time in the sub-acute and chronic traumatic states, the overwhelmed and helpless ego undergoes a regression associated with neurophysiological changes, cerebral blood flow, and stress regulating hormones (Yehuda, 1999). Kitty Hart, a survivor of Auschwitz who was deported there from her ghetto at the age of fifteen, described it this way:

Keeping track of time was impossible. One hour of the morning was memorable: four o'clock, when the whistles screeched and there was shouting and bullying and you turned out for roll-call. But you soon lost track of the days and months. The seasons ran into one another ... There was no way of working things out from the vegetation—there was not a blade of grass, only vast tracts of mud. (Hart, 1981, p. 96)

As though the psychic apparatus becomes frozen in time, one may experience a reliving of trauma in dreams, flashbacks, and fantasies, and in unconscious behaviour. Recognised by Freud over eighty years ago as contradictory to the pleasure principle, this compulsion to repeat (Freud, 1920g) and its vicissitudes might occupy a central role in one's mental functioning. So, when the offspring of such massively traumatised individuals manifest the stigmata of the scars of their parents, a number of explanatory mechanisms may be invoked, from strain trauma (Kris, 1956), or cumulative trauma (Khan, 1963) to inter-generational transmission of trauma (I. Brenner, 2002b; Kestenberg, 1980, 1982a,b; Kogan, 1995a,b). In her poem, "How To Spot One of Us", the child of survivors describes it this way:

> We're the ones who didn't know our relatives
> spoke with accents, the ones whose parents
> got nervous if we didn't come home
> on time, were afraid to let us go
> places by ourselves, who
> told the neighborhood kids the numbers
>
> on their forearms were their phone numbers,
> who won't visit Germany, who wake up
> night after night from dreams, who never talk
> about the past, or never stop
> talking about the past, and we're the ones
>
> who dream about big families, who
> wish words could just be words, wish "camp"
> or "selection" didn't make us flinch,
> and sometimes we're the ones
> who do everything we can
> so you don't know who we are.
>
> (Kirchheimer, 2007, p. 69)

Attachment

It was recognised during the bombing raids on London during the Second World War that securely attached children who stayed with their mothers suffered much less than those who were separated and sent to the countryside. Even though the dangers there were less in actuality, being removed from a loving, attentive mother caused much more distress for these youngsters (Freud & Burlingham, 1943). More recently, as Bowlby's ideas have been more widely accepted and expanded upon, it has been observed that disturbances in attachment to the mother, such as those characterised by a disorganised/disorientated pattern of reacting, may occur in children whose mothers have been seriously traumatised but have not abused them directly (Hesse & Main, 1999). A young child's psychosexual fantasy world might then become suffused with images of unseen horrors, repetitive survival scenarios of unspoken brushes with death, and transmitted unresolved grief over unknown relatives. It might be that such transmitted trauma accentuates a basic assumption in very young children that they were always part of their parents' lives.

Fuelled by instinctual pressures and the inevitable frustrations over never truly being able to possess one's parents, the desire to be part of their all-consuming world of trauma might heighten such children's anxiety over primal scene issues and add another dimension to it. Citing her position as somewhere between McDougall's (1992) and Laplanche's (1976), Davies (2001) postulates that the parent's own unintegrated sexuality is transmitted to the child unconsciously in our Western society child-rearing practices, which results in an area of dissociated, unarticulated, early somatic experiences of sexual arousal. It might be that in some cases of intergenerational transmission of massive psychic trauma, this inchoate sensory experience also contains the parental traumatic affects, which contributes to the feeling of living in the parent's past. Such confusion may then be associated with this population's reportedly increased lifetime risk to develop PTSD (Solomon, Kotler, & Mikulincer, 1988; Yehuda, 1999). Children of survivors seeing combat in the Israeli army have been more vulnerable (Solomon, Kotler, & Mikulincer, 1988), and analytic reports from Israel (Kogan, 1995a,b), as well as our Holocaust discussion group's findings in the aftermath of 9/11, suggest a powerful merging of Holocaust pathology with here-and-now trauma.

It might be that in their metaphorical time travel, as the theory of relativity would predict, a shortening of space–time occurs and is associated with a constriction or collapse of the "potential space" in the psyche of the second generation. Indeed, such a collapse of time (Volkan, Ast, & Greer, 2002) has been postulated in which the capacity for symbolisation is either unable to develop or to be maintained. Problems in abstract and metaphorical thinking in severely traumatised people, and even in some of their offspring, have long been described (Grubrich-Simitis, 1984; Herzog, 1982). In one of the manifestations of this disturbance, the reality of a given experience or situation might be so overwhelming that it confirms in the child's mind that one's worst fears and wishes could indeed come true. This was the Holocaust nightmare in which reality was worse than fantasy. As a defensive solution, the child might then hyper-cathect elements of this reality as a defence against fantasy and, in so doing, might become unduly preoccupied with certain details, structure, or functioning of the external world. As a result, "The dialectical resonance of realistic and fantastic meanings is foreclosed, leaving the patient incapable of imagination" (Ogden, 1986, p. 221). Yet, unconscious preoccupation with Holocaust-related themes is quite prevalent.

Reis (1995), in his efforts to translate cognitive–behavioural trauma theory into analytic language, has thought of the so-called trigger reaction in terms of a delayed quality of traumatic memory, reliving of trauma, and the inherent disturbances in the subjective sense of time. He cites Bion (1962a) and Ogden's (1994) emphasis on the analytic task of symbolic transformation of the patient's unarticulated experience which, according to Winnicott, cannot ". . .get into the past tense unless the ego can first gather it into its own present time experience and into omnipotent control now. . ." (Winnicott, 1974, p. 105). The non-verbal realm has been described by a variety of overlapping terms, such as primal repression (Freud, 1915d), beta-elements (Bion, 1962a), the unrememberable and the unforgettable (Frank, 1969), the unthought known (Bollas, 1987), multisensory bridges (I. Brenner 1988), unformulated experience (D. B. Stern, 1997), presymbolic representations (Beebe, Lachmann, & Jaffe, 1997), and zero process (Fernando, 2009). Kitty Hart, upon her return to Auschwitz more than thirty years later, described her life-long challenge to put her ordeal in the past this way:

You see grass. But I don't see any grass. I see mud, just a sea of mud
... Open my eyes and see grass. Close my eyes and see mud ... The
watch-towers still look down. There must still be guns in there, trained
on you. I belong here. I knew I ought never to have come back,
because it proved I've never been away. The past I see is more real
than the tidy pretence they have put in its place. (Hart, 1981, p. 162)

If psychic trauma damages the ego's synthetic functioning and
prevents an experience from ever becoming "in the past", one would
be thrust into a state of timelessness (Bromberg, 1991) and a perpetual
living of the trauma. Therefore, it could not become a memory to be
repressed because it never stopped happening intrapsychically in the
first place. So, instead of a benign event becoming traumatic after a
future experience augmented by development, the opposite would be
true. A traumatic event could only hope to become detoxified after it
becomes part of one's past as a result of some experience in the future.
For those survivors of genocidal persecution during the Holocaust,
that developmental experience was having children. Becoming a
parent held the most promise of any healing whatsoever.

Starting a new generation of Jewish children proclaimed ultimate
victory over Hitler's decrees to destroy all of their kind. It would give
them a sense of purpose or meaning to their senseless suffering and
immeasurable grief to name their offspring for their murdered parents
and siblings. Wardi (1992) described these children as "memorial
candles". But it also put a huge burden on many of the second generation to alleviate their parents' daily torment and to justify their own
improbable existence (Kestenberg & Brenner, 1996). The developing
child's psyche might have become appropriated by the parents, serving as a repository for their intolerable mental contents as well as
becoming an auxiliary ego to assist in their negotiating a strange, new,
post-liberation world in a strange, new country. In addition, for many
who returned to their original homelands, the familiarity of the past
was overshadowed by the hostility of the local townspeople over their
return as well as a further collapse of time.

A unique aspect of treatment

In the analysis of children of Holocaust survivors, Kestenberg was
emphatic about the need to thoroughly reconstruct the parents' lives,

a feature of analysis not typically thought to be essential. In so doing, the "child", to paraphrase Hoffman (1983), then became the interpreter of the parent's experience in order to differentiate from them and free themselves from the time tunnel that transported them back to the camps. In Bion's way of thinking, the developing child would become the container of the parents' unmetabolised beta-elements, a reversal of the expected pattern (Bion, 1956; Kogan, 1995a,b). It is the transmission of these traumatically induced dissociative states that have been described as an empty circle (Laub, 1998) or psychic hole (Kogan, 2002), whereby something unknowable enters the developing child's mind. It has also been referred to as an "affect propeller" (Kaplan, 2006), in which affects invade the present rather than explicit memories, linking the generations through unmetabolised emotion (Kaplan, 2006). A unique phase of treatment, the "joint acceptance of the Holocaust reality", has also been described (Grubrich-Simitis, 1984) as a profoundly affect-laden time for analyst and analysand, in which grief and authenticity replace denial and dissociation of what the parents could not symbolise as a result of their trauma. The pathogenic nature of the parents' silence has been seen in family therapy research (Slipp, 1984). It was also very well portrayed in the documentary film, *Breaking the Silence*, written by Eva Fogelman (Fogelman, 1984). Indeed, an austere, classical, psychoanalytic approach to treatment might, in fact, re-enact the parents' silence and be quite detrimental (Bergmann & Jucovy, 1982).

Inanimate objects

The use of inanimate objects incorporated by children that belong to their survivor parents could provide clues as to what is dissociated and conveyed unconsciously. Such transpositional objects might resemble, or function as, linking objects and generational objects for the parent(s), but could then be used by the child for any possible developmental or pathological purpose. They might be used as transitional objects or fetishes, or for a more neurotic, oedipally based purpose such as a pair of boots being incorporated into a young boy's masculine self (I. Brenner, 2009a). Another boy knew that his father still had a tiny Bible that he had hidden in his camp uniform. It was his most treasured possession then and now, and no one was allowed to touch it in its special place. It seemed to have magical powers. In another case, a woman grew up with a photo of her dead half-sister, who was murdered in the ghetto well before she was born; this idealised child was never spoken of. The extent to which such objects are present and how they might be utilised in others requires more research and listening for such items in the clinical material. However, it appears that such items might promote unusual areas of weakness in the fabric of the developing child's mental space–time continuum. If stretched to a point of rupture, such tears could result in a psychic wormhole suddenly catapulting him/her back in time to the parent's Holocaust mentality.

An obscured manifestation of intergenerational transmission

An obscured manifestation of transmission may be uncovered at the most severe end of the dissociative character spectrum in DID as a contribution to the creation of a self, based on an abuser such as a "persecutory father alter". Abusive or incestuous scenarios would be enacted between the various alters in the form of self-injurious behaviour to an outside observer. It used to astound me how even the most profoundly traumatised patients would often have an alter who felt so tenderly and sympathetically about their parents' own miserable, early lives. Quite often, this alter is especially removed from the others and hated by the others for betraying them and giving in (I. Brenner, 2001).

The seemingly delusional preoccupations and quasi-psychotic symptoms of even the most severe type of dissociative pathology may become comprehensible through an appreciation of the many vicissitudes of trauma. For example, the transmitted trauma may be a factor in the confusion between the past and present seen in more regressed patients. It appears that such individuals might have been severely traumatised in childhood by parents who had been traumatised themselves. Parental trauma, childhood trauma, and developmental processes apparently condensed into complex autohypnotic, defensive altered states of consciousness. Depending on the level of integration of self- and object representations at the time of trauma, the internalisation of the traumatising parent could be experienced as a separate, dissociated, inner persecutor. Under those circumstances, the transmitted trauma of the parent seemed to become incorporated into the life history of the personification, instead of a more diffuse, global sense of living in two worlds simultaneously. Recognition of this possible contribution to the development of dissociative pathology might be helpful in translating seemingly bizarre symptoms into potentially treatable complications of trauma. Thus, the idea that transmission goes beyond identification is given more credence in such cases. However, we might be more likely to see a more typical case such as the one below.

Case report: a second-generation victim

Several years ago, while spending a few days in the Midwest after giving a talk on the Holocaust, arrangements were made for me to see a woman in consultation. She knew someone who knew someone who knew one of the members of the group who sponsored the talk. A child of two Holocaust survivors, this woman was a member of a small but active Jewish community with a specialised group for the second generation in which she had actively participated. This woman had some familiarity with my work and involvement in this area, so she eagerly hoped that I could help her. The problem that she presented with, and the immersion in her situation that I experienced, illustrate many of the issues, challenges, complexities, and controversies that the clinician encounters with this population.

Here is what she told me.

She had been working for many years in an industry that, although regulated, was lax in the implementation of its policies, which not infrequently endangered its workers. Although she was a highly valued and skilled employee with an excellent record who was in line for a major promotion, a new regime took over and she was overlooked. Moreover, a climate of lawlessness took over, with thefts on the job and harassment of females. Her new boss seemed to turn a blind eye and even rebuked her for her requests for help. As conditions deteriorated, one day she was injured by a prank that became vicious during which she was pinned down by a man and trapped between two large pieces of equipment. As she screamed in pain, helpless, terrified, and humiliated, a group of onlookers did nothing to help and laughed in sadistic delight at the sexualised spectacle.

When she finally wrenched herself free, she developed shooting pain down her back and her legs and limped away feeling quite literally broken. Her supervisor was unavailable and she felt desperately alone.

Unable to go to work the next day, she called in sick and saw the company doctor. He was unsympathetic and determined that she was still able to work despite her back pain and her terror. He then told her that, given the nature of the industry in which she had chosen to work, she should expect such things might happen to her—they were basically occupational hazards. Outraged and despairing, she began to question herself. While she was on sick leave, she returned to work one day in order to help another downtrodden co-worker fill out some paperwork related to a grievance. While she knew that she was not permitted on the premises while on sick leave, in her mind, her mission to help her friend transcended the company policy. Naturally, she was spotted by her boss, with whom she was already on bad terms, and was severely reprimanded and ordered off the premises immediately. Yelled at in his harsh voice in front of others, she once again experienced deep humiliation, fear, and degradation.

Reverberation of his screaming at her started to haunt her and she became quite unsettled. "I felt like a Jew in Nazi-occupied Europe," she confided to another friend at work, a woman who, significantly, was also Jewish. Her preoccupation with her mother's life during the war began to consume her. She wondered how her mother would have felt were she subjected to the same mistreatment at work after all she had been through. Would not such a response have been natural for her? As she became more consumed by what she imagined her mother would have done, her friend did something to her that seemed quite inexplicable and that was the final insult. The friend told their boss what she had said and he became incensed that he was accused of being a Nazi. He then officially reprimanded her for her slanderous comment and made it part of her permanent personnel file. At this point, she felt utterly overwhelmed, misunderstood, and defeated. She could not return to work, filed a claim against her employer for PTSD, and was scheduled for psychiatric evaluation to determine the status of her condition. Fearing that her background as a child of Holocaust survivors would not be taken into consideration as an important predisposing factor to her vulnerability to traumatisation, she hoped that my expertise could help her case in some way.

At this point, I did not know any specifics of her parents' background other than that they suffered terribly and that her father was quite strict in that he was always trying to teach her a lesson in survival. She inferred that her mother was a very difficult person as well and was pleased that they had been able to make peace with each other before the old woman died a number of years before. The patient also took a certain pride in her mother's use of an ambiguous Yiddish term of endearment for a mischievous, impish child. Now, it appeared that this imp had grown up and was now in an awful situation. She had, perhaps, gone too far.

From a phenomenological and diagnostic standpoint, the clinician might have been struck by her pressured and loud presentation, wondering if some hypomanic energy were fuelling her psyche. In addition, one might have also been struck by a perhaps histrionic quality to her presentation and a sense of narcissistic entitlement, as well as more than a tinge of masochism and victimisation. A previous psychiatric history of treatment for depression with medication might then satisfy the clinician's need for diagnosis, such as an Axis I mood disorder and Axis II characterological problems. The extent to which the recent insult in question actually fulfilled criteria for PTSD might then be arguable because of her pre-existing "condition". However, she kept reliving the assault, was terrified to return, and felt betrayed and totally isolated.

Her immediate transference reaction to me was twofold: one, of an idealised rescuer, and two, being a part of her world—a "landsman" as it were. As such, her sense of our being part of the same fold seemed to reflect a twinship-type of narcissistic transference as described by Kohut (Kohut, 1971). Indeed, she correctly sensed that I understood the "Holocaust culture" (Kestenberg & Gampel, 1983) of her childhood.

I sensed her exquisite vulnerability thinly masked by her bravado and could immediately see how easily misunderstood she could be by others. Moreover, she had asserted that she had dealt extensively with Holocaust issues in her psychotherapy and felt that she understood everything she needed to know about the effects of the Holocaust on her. She strongly identified with the second generation and thoroughly psychoanalysed herself—or so she believed. As a result, she would have me believe that she understood the Holocaust contribution to her psyche and it was under control.

As mentioned earlier, the extent of the effects of the Holocaust on the second generation continue to spark controversy and confusion. It is especially delicate regarding the issue of financial compensation, the so-called restitution, or *Wiedergutmachung*, given by the German government. To my knowledge, there has never been a successful claim for damages transmitted from survivor parents to the child. That does not mean, however, that psychological scars and perhaps biochemical markers are not present. Indeed, the work of Rachel Yehuda shows elevated cortisol levels in children of survivors (Yehuda, 1999), and, as mentioned earlier, studies of Israeli soldiers have suggested an increased risk of PTSD in those whose parents were Holocaust survivors (Solomon, Kotler, & Mikulincer, 1988). The Dutch government has provided for psychotherapy, and charitable organisations have done so as well, but children of deceased survivors who had received restitution could not inherit their parents' cheques. Only the widows were eligible.

Since the early reports of children of Holocaust survivors described them as being profoundly damaged, their prognosis of a life of disability, to paraphrase Mark Twain, has been greatly exaggerated. Yet, the early experience of psychoanalysts treating such patients suggested that the analytic dyad avoided the topic completely and that the patients did not do nearly as well in treatment as they might have (Kestenberg, 1982a). However, a more classical position suggests that these patients are no different from anyone else, their analyses should be no different from anyone else's, and psychosexual issues prevail no matter what. In a now rather inglorious, oft-quoted opinion, Charles Brenner once said, "I do not think it is possible to separate the effects of being a replacement child—Holocaust or no Holocaust—from the effects of other individual and ubiquitous influences in childhood conflict" (C. Brenner, 2003a, p. 773). If, however, we take a step back and just listen to the story that the patient has told, it does not take a great imagination to hear the themes of injustice, persecution, betrayal, indifference, tremendous fear, helplessness, rescue, and a sense of needing to prove that she was indeed injured.

I hypothesised that this woman grew up so saturated with her parents' Holocaust trauma that, even with her insight, she did not realise how much she was living in two time zones.

I was especially struck by her plea for justice and compensation, as she even suggested that her case might set a precedent for children of survivors. Indeed, her need to return to her workplace, now forbidden and off limits, to rescue a comrade seemed to have an over-determined nature to it.

As with so many members of the second generation, nodal points in their parents' lives often correlated, almost uncannily, with events in their own lives. In the course of analysis, their unconscious fantasies of living through a Holocaust and being over-identified with a survivor parent could then come to light and be examined. In this way, as Martin Bergmann described it, the private psychopathology could become teased out from the Holocaust psychopathology, as the latter often intensified the developmental dangers of the former (Bergmann & Jucovy, 1982). So, as I listened to the patient's history, I took note of such landmark events. For example, when she was sixteen, her parents separated after years of bitterness, rage, and verbal abuse. Following allegiances along oedipal lines, she went to live with her father while her older brother sided with the mother and lived with her while he went to college. He married at a very young age, left the mother all alone, and had little to do with his younger sister, who felt isolated and trapped living with the father. The patient lived with the father throughout college and felt guilt-ridden and torn over leaving him all alone as well. Ironically, the only way that she was freed was through a serious car accident at the age of twenty-three that left her quite injured and disabled, requiring many months to recover. At that time, needing assistance, she went to live with her brother and his wife for an extended period of time. Interestingly, she reported not being at fault for the accident, as another motorist slammed into her, but was unable to prove her victimisation and receive any compensation because the witnesses lied. She felt doubly victimised, and I listened carefully to this story.

The patient eventually met her husband-to-be but could not marry him until her father was dying, as she felt guilt over not taking him in at his greatest hour of need. Her husband was verbally abusive also. Their first child was born when she was thirty-five years old. She reconciled with her estranged mother when she was dying and, not wanting to repeat the scenario of the dying father, brought the old woman to live with her. Broken dreams, loss, guilt, and mourning pervaded her life, and she grew up on the "bad" side of her mother's splitting while the brother was the idealised "good" child.

Once I elicited the patient's history and made my speculations about transmission, I then sought the parents' Holocaust history. Her father had a very difficult childhood and as a teenager fled to Russia, where he was captured and spent the war years in a series of labour camps. While not in any death camps *per se*, the living conditions were extremely harsh with high morbidity and mortality and he was beaten numerous times. He was the sole survivor of his family and went to a displaced persons camp after liberation, where he met his wife-to-be. Prone to irritability, rage, and verbal abuse, he was perceived by the patient to be the kind one despite his own harsh form of discipline and brutal insistence on punctuality.

The patient's mother, also from Eastern Europe, lived with her family until the age of sixteen, at which time conditions deteriorated and she went to live with other family members. She was caught by the Nazis, probably betrayed by local neighbours, and soon was deported to Auschwitz. Somehow, she befriended an older woman who took a liking to her and got her reassigned to the *Effektenkommando*. These were the women who took the clothing and emptied the suitcases of the newly processed prisoners who were immediately sent to the gas chambers and the crematoria. This assignment offered privileges to the women in this work assignment in that they were given larger rations and had access to clothing that they were occasionally able to smuggle out and give to other people. They lived in relative comfort. However, the proximity to the gas chambers and the crematoria had them living and breathing in the shadow of death all the time. The patient recalled asking her mother if she knew what was going on. Mother saw the smoke in the chimneys and knew that people were being killed, but she was psychologically numb. All she could say was that the stench was unbearable and that it never left her nostrils.

The location of the storage rooms was nicknamed *Kanada*, as the rooms were overflowing with clothing, shoes, and other personal effects, like a wealthy foreign land. These belongings were distributed among the guards and their families and were also sent to the Reich for needy families of soldiers sent to the front. The mother was liberated at the end of the war, barely alive. She was twenty-three years old. She and a cousin were the only survivors of their large family. As mentioned earlier, she met her husband-to-be at the displaced persons camp where they recovered. They made arrangements to come to the

USA in the early 1950s, where they had their first child. Interestingly, the father did not receive any restitution payments and the mother, though quite eligible for restitution because of her documented slave labour, did not receive any payments until very near the end of her life, at which point she received an inappropriately low monthly payment. When asked about this, the patient shrugged her shoulders and said she did not understand why she did not get her compensation either. She felt a strong need for vindication. When the mother was thirty-five, she gave birth to the patient. When the patient mentioned this to me, she made this connection for the first time. However, when I asked her if she thought it was significant, she emphatically denied it.

The patient complained of having organisational problems and had great difficulty with throwing out things in her home. As a result, it was piled high with clothing, papers, personal effects, and items that she could not get rid of. Essentially, it looked like a storage room and she considered herself a hoarder. Here, too, she could not see any deeper significance to this remarkable congruence, which we have seen might take years of analysis for one to fully appreciate.

The "coincidences" that emerged were that both the patient and her mother had to leave home under dire circumstances at age sixteen. Both were subsequently trapped in an untenable situation, and both were liberated but disabled at age twenty-three. Then they both married abusive men and had a child at the age of thirty-five. Both were victimised, cheated out of compensation, and lived in the storage room at Auschwitz—one in an unspeakable reality, the other unconsciously in a self-created hoarder's paradise. Unfortunately, this woman could not enter analysis, which, in my view, would have been the only way for her to have a chance to become psychologically liberated from a transmitted repetition compulsion and a dissociated living through a Holocaust.

Conclusion

It is a life-long endeavour for members of the second generation on both sides of the barbed wire to integrate the past and the present. There can be identity conflicts and intensification of the developmental dangers of childhood—for example, abandonment, fears of punishment through bodily injury and retaliation, or aberrations of the superego, as one has to grow up in two psychic realities where the Holocaust past was worse than fantasy. In a world of victims, perpetrators, rescuers, and helpless bystanders, simple decisions could have life-and-death implications that might saturate all aspects of the person's inner life. Secrecy, silence, and denial of the painful realities of that time are likely to perpetuate the transmission of pathological trends such as unresolved grief, irrational guilt, and the avoidance of responsibility. Through analytic therapy and other life-affirming activities that promote a reconciliation with unmetabolised introjects from the Holocaust, one may then achieve growth, healing, creativity, and the opportunity to pass on a new legacy to future generations. This is the legacy of wisdom, understanding, and humanity.

CHAPTER SIX

Playing and survival

> "A hundred children—a hundred individuals who are people—not people to be, not people of the future, not people of tomorrow, but people now . . . right now . . . today"
>
> (Korczak, 1967, p. 254)

Of the roughly six million unanswerable questions that may be asked about the Holocaust, one of the most perplexing pertains to the nature of "play". While it is indeed amply documented through diaries and journals, as well as survivor testimonies, photographs, artwork, and poetry, it is not yet possible to have a full understanding of the meaning, purpose, and capacity to play under the conditions of sadistic, dehumanising, genocidal persecution. A young girl in the Warsaw ghetto simply put it this way:

> When I am in play, I forget my hunger. I forget that outside are such evil Germans even existing. Early in the morning I rush to the child care center and I wish that the day would never end, because when it is getting dark, we all have to return home. In my room it is so full with dark shadows and black fear. (Eisen, 1988, p. 101)

In an eyewitness report to his superiors in London, Jan Karski, a representative of the Polish government in exile who secretly entered the Warsaw ghetto to document the conditions, noted,

> Everywhere there was hunger, misery, the atrocious stench of decomposing bodies, the pitiful moans of dying children. We passed a miserable replica of a park—a low square of comparatively clear ground in which a half-dozen nearly leafless trees and a patch of grass had somehow managed to survive. It was fearfully crowded. Mothers huddled close together on benches nursing withered infants. Children, every bone in their skeletons showing through their taut skins, played in heaps and swarms. "They play before they die," I heard my companion on the left say, his voice breaking with emotion. Without thinking, the words escaping even before the thought had crystallized—I said: "But these children are not playing. They only make-believe it is play." (Eisen, 1988, p. 107)

Karski's enigmatic words warrant deeper consideration of what it is these children were doing. In my own work with Judith Kestenberg interviewing child survivors (Kestenberg & Brenner, 1996), it became abundantly clear that they felt robbed of their childhoods and many felt that they either never learnt or had lost their capacity to play. When they became parents, many complained that they could not play with their own children. Indeed, Auerhahn and Laub (1987) corroborate this finding through their analytic work with three Holocaust survivors and conclude that the extent to which one can rediscover her lost playfulness is an indicator of her potential to heal.

Anna Freud and Sophie Dann (1951) describe an "experiment" determined by "fate" in which six orphans from Terezín, aged three to three-and-a-half, were treated in a group living situation at "Bulldogs Bank" in 1945. These children, whose parents were murdered by the Nazis, entered the camp under the age of twelve months and were cared for as best as possible in the Ward for Motherless Children. They had no toys, access only to a bare yard, and the only food they had was a pasty, starchy porridge. When they arrived in England, they did not know how to play and were ignorant about the natural world, with the exception of dogs, which reminded them of Nazi guard dogs and terrified them. At first they destroyed their toys and much of the furniture and were aggressive or indifferent towards the adults. However, the group loyalty and libidinal ties to each other were very strong.

Over time, they chose soft toys as transitional objects, which they took to bed and used for masturbating. Although they learnt quickly and became more socialised, the very strong ties to one another in lieu of object ties to parents were most noteworthy. To extrapolate from these findings, the older ghetto and camp children of latency age who were on their own quite probably developed very strong bonds with each other also in order to survive, adding another important dimension to the significance of the nature of their "play" (Freud & Dann, 1951).

The games that ghetto children played reflected what they saw and lived with, such as "Aktion" (a sudden raid upon the prisoners ending in murder or deportation), "Breaking Into Hiding Places", "Gravedigging", "Massacre in Ponary" (a re-enactment of the massacre of Vilna Jewry who were decimated by the Germans in the woods of Ponary, Lithuania) or "Returning the Clothing of the Dead" (Eisen, 1988). Latency-aged children were regularly seen in the streets playing with corpses, tickling them to see if they would move, checking to see if they were breathing, and incorporating them into their play. Even if one of them were to drop dead in their midst, they would continue with their play. In a sense, there was a grotesque transformation of their play into a "play", which could be thought of as improvisational street theatre performed by dying children. In contrast, a child survivor, Henri Parens, who escaped from the detention camp, Rivesaltes, in the foothills of the Pyrenees in the south of France, described more typical play, that of "Three Musketeers" with his fellow young inmates. At the age of twelve, on the cusp of adolescence and not having been exposed to death, this optimistic boy and his friends were

> . . . pretending we were the heroes encountering and, of course always, winning over the evil Cardinal Richlieu and his henchman. That this was early in the winter of 1940–1941, before the worst to happen reached us directly, that it was early in the Holocaust denouement probably was the factor that allowed us to still play . . . (Parens, 2004, p. 49)

Now reflecting upon his young life with the wisdom of a senior psychoanalyst, Henri Parens observed,

> We could fight evil, even if only in play, that medium which children use naturally to cope with fear, with anxiety and stress. We played it,

we played it, and we played it. It must have worked fairly effectively for us, otherwise, we would have soon abandoned the game. (Parens, 2004, p. 49)

Parens escaped from the camp, never to see his protective and loving mother again, and noted that even upon his transatlantic voyage to freedom and safety in America, he still had not known about the horrors of Auschwitz. It appears that this form of play was not yet saturated with the inevitability of death as with the ghetto children. Furthermore, at his age, the emergence of sexuality was in the air. (On his voyage, he later described his first sexual experience with an older girl who submitted to three boys in succession.) Indeed, Parens tells us that "The other way we tried to go on living was by dancing" (Parens, 2004, p. 49). Musically inclined at a young age, he sang and, thus, provided the music for their precious moments. Music was important to prisoners of all ages.

Nightly concerts

There is a secret tunnel under a Nazi concentration camp where something very unexpected took place. This tunnel connects the "infirmary" with the morgue. It allowed the SS doctors to murder their ill or injured "patients" and unobtrusively have them transported to the pathology lab where their bodies could be desecrated in the name of "science". Fraudulent death certificates were crafted here to mask their crimes. Then their remains would be incinerated in the crematoria at the far end of the campus. Their ashes were then dumped in the river which separated the facility from a beautiful park where the locals loved to picnic with their families on Sunday afternoons after church. This disposal system allowed for the quiet, systematic removal of unwanted or useless prisoners who lost their value as human slaves without arousing mass panic and a possible uprising of the other inmates.

The main product of this closed and secret society, just a short train ride from the centre of Hitler's universe in Berlin, was the manufacturing of bricks and building materials for the new world that was being eagerly constructed by the architects and builders of the Third Reich. Strategically located near a quarry, which provided the raw materials, and the river, which enabled efficient transport of the finished products by boat, the Sachsenhausen camp in Oranienburg, Germany, was a vital part of the war effort. In this way, those enemies of the Reich who were deemed "life unworthy of life" (Binding & Hoche, 1920; Glass, 1997) and were taken there could redeem themselves by working to death or providing entertainment for the overlords whose sadism is now legendary.[4] I might add here that during my first visit to this camp before its overhaul in preparation for tourism, I was also shown the remains of a huge bakery that was also a source of German pride. In addition, I saw the rusting remains of the crematoria, which were eerily sinking into the ground like a lopsided and doomed sailing vessel. So it was here at Sachsenhausen that they baked bricks, bread, and bodies.

But it was a story related to the tunnel that I learnt from my guide that day that is especially relevant to this chapter. On this particularly grey, rainy day there was a biting wind that ripped through the open expanse, or *appellplatz*, where prisoners in their thinly clad uniforms were forced together to stand at attention for as long and as often as commanded, or face dire consequences. It was so cold, wet, and bleak that day that it felt impossible not to shiver and long to seek shelter somewhere inside. But here at Sachsenhausen there was no respite. It was even worse inside. In the morgue, the white tile, the stainless steel, and the concrete were as cold as ice. It left little to the imagination as gruesome life-sized photos of dissected inmates hung on the walls. I was then asked if I wanted to see the tunnel in question and rather numbly agreed. We descended a ramp into the dank darkness that was illuminated by bare light bulbs overhead. In this quiet echo chamber under the chamber of horrors, I learnt that a bizarre occurrence would occur regularly there at night. As the report went, a group of musically talented prisoners would secretly gather with their smuggled instruments and quietly but defiantly play their repertoire, risking their lives for those moments of sanity, solidarity, and mournful expression of their souls. Unbeknown to them, however, the guards were quite aware of these secret concerts but, curiously, did not forbid or punish them for it. On the contrary, they, too, secretly entered the tunnel, but from the far end, and unbeknown to the inmates surreptitiously listened to the nightly concerts. So, for those brief, transcendent moments, there was no perpetrator and no victim hopelessly locked into their respective roles of predator and prey.

There were just two groups of people joined together in the very human activity of making and listening to the sounds of music, under most bizarre conditions.

Such a story, as unbelievable as it seems, has been portrayed on a one-to-one basis in the highly acclaimed film, *The Pianist*, in which the actor, Adrian Brody, plays a concert pianist and persecuted Jew in wartime Warsaw, who softens the heart of his would-be SS executioner who discovers him hiding in an abandoned house, barely clinging to life as he is starving to death in the freezing cold winter. The German master commands the wretched Jew to play the decaying piano that is left behind in the house. The hidden Jew is so weak and frozen with both terror and the cold that his fingers barely move at first. Given the capricious abuse of power that so often characterised the Nazi, it is unclear to the viewer whether the SS man will shoot Brody on the spot for lying about being a concert pianist, but then he marshals a superhuman effort to be able to play. Suddenly, in the midst of the bombed-out rubble of the city in the bleak winter night, this utterly horrendous and crazed, caged animal of a man produces exalted music. The officer is quietly but clearly moved by this unexpected musical performance and, more unexpectedly, hides the Jew from the other soldiers, provides him with some food, and even gives him his overcoat. We know the old adage "Music soothes the savage breast" and the Biblical story of how young David calmed the irascible King Saul with his music. Under these conditions, the capacity of the weaker, oppressed other to soothe the perpetrator, at least temporarily, is illustrated in the context of genocidal persecution.

A musical fad in the ghetto

An entry in *The Chronicle of the Łódź Ghetto, 1941–1944*, dated August 25, 1943, written by one of its chroniclers, Oskar Rosenfeld, describes a musical "fad" that swept through the ghetto. It might have started when a child took two small pieces of wood between his fingers and created a pleasing clicking sound:

> For several days now the streets and courtyards of the ghetto have been filled with a noise like a clatter of wooden shoes . . . The observer soon discovers that this "clattering" is produced by boys who have

invented a pastime, an entertainment. More precisely, the children of the ghetto have invented a new toy.

All the various amusing toys and noisemakers . . . are things our youngsters must, of course, do without . . . And so, on their own, they invent toys to replace all the things that delight children everywhere and are unavailable here.

The ghetto toy in the summer of 1943: Two small slabs of wood—hard wood if possible! One slab is held between the forefinger and the middle finger, the other between the middle finger and the ring finger. The little finger presses against the other fingers, squeezing them so hard that the slabs are rigidly fixed in position and can thus be struck against one other by means of a skilful motion . . . Naturally, the artistic talents of the toy carver and performer can be refined to a very high level.

. . .

The streets of the Litzmannstadt ghetto [the Germans renamed Łódź to Litzmannstadt and Aryanised it] are filled with clicking, drumming, banging . . . Barefoot boys scurry past you, performing their music right under your nose, with great earnestness, as though their lives depended on it. Here the musical instinct of Eastern European Jews is cultivated to the full. An area that has given the world so many musicians, chiefly violinists—just think of Hubermann, Heifetz, Elman, Milstein, Menuhin—now presents a new line of artists. (Dobroszycki, 1984, pp. 373–374)

Here we see the desperate inventiveness of these doomed children who communicate to one another and to all the grown-ups in the ghetto that they are still alive. Like the cacophony of a swarm of crickets, they make their music and their fervent defiance known to all.

An entry about a month before, on Saturday, July 24, 1943, provides another view of these massively traumatised and starving children's ingenuity under most devastating conditions. This report describes their creation of playing cards from cigarette boxes:

The so-called Belgian cigarettes have been a disappointment to smokers in the ghetto, even to those who have smoked poor-quality tobacco all their lives. The countless packs with their gaudy colors and equally gaudy names could not alter the devastating judgment that has been passed on the quality of the cigarettes. However, a smoker's passion overrides any reservations. The cigarettes go up in smoke, the cardboard box remains. Since every object in the ghetto, no matter how worthless, acquires some value, even these boxes have come to be cherished. The smoker does not throw them out. He saves them, and makes sure that they do not go to waste. Children's eyes beg for those boxes, children's hands reach out for them.

Outside the ghetto, children receive beautiful and appropriate playthings as presents . . . Our children collect empty cigarette boxes. They remove the colorful tops and stack them in a pile, until they have a whole deck of cards. Playing cards.

And they play. They count the cards and deal them out. They arrange them by color and name. Green, orange, yellow, brown, even black. They play games that they invent by themselves, they devise systems, they let their imaginations take over. (Dobroszycki, 1984, pp. 360–361)

The importance of toys and other inanimate objects is quite well known (Akhtar, 2003b; Volkan, 1981, Winnicott, 1953) and under these conditions they became even more highly prized (I. Brenner, 2009a; Kestenberg & Brenner, 1996). About a year later, the Łódź Ghetto was finally liquidated and the wretched survivors were sent to their final destinations, the extermination camps of Chelmno and Auschwitz. There, the remnants of a once vibrant Jewish community were reduced to ash and smoke.

The Family Camp

Described as ". . . one of the most diabolical inventions of the Nazi mind" (Eisen, 1988, p. 47), the Family Camp, B-IIb, was created in 1943 when approximately 5,006 Czech Jews were forced to the Auschwitz/ Birkenau extermination camp from Theresienstadt. Theresienstadt, located in north-western Czechoslovakia in the walled fortress town also known in Czech as Terezín, was the so-called "model Jewish settlement" known for its cultural and arts programmes for adults and children. Literally advertised as a refuge that would protect them and help them prepare for their move to Palestine, terrified, well-to-do Czech Jews paid tens of thousands of marks to gain entry. We now know that the "final solution" to the Jewish question was not migration but genocide, and this model camp was designed to hide the inconceivable truth. Even the International Red Cross, which visited the camp in 1944, was either fooled by this cynical ruse or too intimidated to accurately report its findings. The ancient walled city, which never housed more than 8,000 people, became the desperate, crammed quarters of about 60,000 prisoners at a time who, after a "deportation to the east", made room for the next transport. Of the 15,000 children sent to Auschwitz from Theresienstadt, only one hundred survived and none of these was under the age of fourteen.

Although the Auschwitz prisoners found a way of extending and preserving their human dignity for as long as possible, it, too, had its horrors and was eventually to be totally liquidated. In order to avoid panic and possible trouble from the prisoners who had been ousted from the relative luxury of Theresienstadt to the depths of hell in Auschwitz, Adolf Eichmann continued the elaborate deception to the end, commissioning the painting of a giant mural of Snow White and the Seven Dwarfs in the children's barracks at Hut 31. A German-Jewish star athlete by the name of Fredy Hirsch, who developed a youth programme at Theresienstadt, was among the deportees. He was then to become the "Head of the Children's Day Block" and oversaw the building of a playground and creation of a daily schedule of activities for the children who numbered about five hundred. He was even able to procure better food for them, such as milk and eggs. Seeing the children playing openly and freely had puzzled, surprised, and confused the inmates. As one Auschwitz survivor who escaped, named Rudolph Vrba, said, "I saw them set aside a barrack for the children, a nursery, no less, in the shadow of the crematorium. I saw a blonde, athletic man of about thirty [Fredy Hirsch] organizing games, then lessons" (Eisen, 1988). Tragically, however, when the Family Camp was liquidated and all the prisoners were gassed and cremated, Fredy Hirsch committed suicide by poisoning himself. He was forewarned by the underground resistance about what was to happen and could not believe it, given the favourable treatment they had received. He was asked to lead an uprising in the Family Camp that had no chance of succeeding and he could not bear to see the children murdered in either manner. Perhaps like Janus Korczak, who could not live without his charges and accompanied the children of his remarkable orphanage in the Warsaw ghetto on their train ride to certain death, Hirsch, too, saw no purpose without his children. Hirsch's children were led to the gas chambers and as they were taking off their clothes, they spontaneously started singing the Czech and the Israeli national anthems. The cold facts of the Family Camp are documented in the *Auschwitz Chronicle* this way:

> September 8, 1943: 5,006 Jews are transferred from Theresienstadt . . . 2,293 men and boys, given Nos. 146694–148986, and 2,713 women and girls, given Nos. 58471–61183. (Czech, 1990, p. 483)

> February 29, 1944: . . . SS Lieutenant Colonel Adolf Eichmann, views the Theresienstadt Family Camp . . . Camp B-IIb in Birkenau. Dr. Leo Janowitz, [of] the Theresienstadt ghetto, and Fredy Hirsch, a teacher and children's attendant in Camp B-IIb, report to him. . . . (Czech, 1990, p. 591)

> March 7, 1944: With the end of the six-month stay of the first group of Jews from the Theresienstadt Family Camp B-IIb . . . it is decided to liquidate them. To prevent unrest, it should appear that the camp inmates were being transferred to labor camps . . . Consequently, all prisoners who are healthy and are able to work are transferred to the Quarantine Camp B-IIa in Birkenau. . . . First the men are brought over and put up in other blocks; later the women are also brought over and put in other blocks. They are allowed to take their entire belongings with them . . . from Theresienstadt. . . . (Czech, 1990, p. 593)

> March 8, 1944: . . . The prisoner Fredy Hirsch . . . commits suicide, because he cannot protect the women and children from destruction, and does not want to be a passive witness.

> . . .

> Around 8:00 P.M., Camp B-IIa is put under curfew. A large number of SS men . . . arrive in the camp. Capos and Block Commanders . . . are called for support. Half an SS company with dogs surrounds the camp. Around 10:00 P.M., 12 trucks covered with tarps drive up. The Jews are ordered to leave the heavy luggage in the barracks and are promised that it will be brought to the train. To maintain order and quiet, 40 people at a time are left on the truck loading platform and the trucks leaving Camp B-IIa do not turn left, i.e., the direct route to the crematoriums, but right, so it looks as though they are driving to the train station. This operation lasts several hours. First the men are driven to Crematorium III, then the women to Crematorium II. After waiting several hours for their departure, the Jews in one of the blocks become anxious and around 2:00 A.M. begin to sing a Czech folk song. In the next block singing also begins. Startled, the SS men begin to fire

warning shots. The Jews are forbidden to sing, under the threat that the transport will be stopped. The disrobing rooms in the crematoriums have been prepared in such a manner that the waiting prisoners hope, to the end, that they are leaving for a labor camp. Only the order to disrobe makes it clear that they are in the crematorium. The women . . . already in the gas chamber . . . sing the "Internationale," the "Hatikva," at that time the Jewish national hymn, and the Czech national anthem, and a partisans' song. . . . 3,791 . . .—men, women, and children—are killed in Crematoriums II and III. (Czech, 1990, p. 595)

While the sight of seeing children play was an inspiration and a source of rejuvenation for the beleaguered and doomed population of adults, there soon developed great concerns in the ghettos about the creation of such playgrounds, as they would have made round-ups by the SS quite effortless. The children would be localised and "concentrated" in such an area, making them much more easily captured, like being baited in a trap. Still, it was incomprehensible to most that their Nazi captors were sending them to extermination camps, to be killed *en masse* like annoying or useless insects. Indeed, even those in Auschwitz, like Hirsch, found it inconceivable until the last minute. The utterly cynical and merciless exploitation of displaced, dehumanised, and demoralised civilians could not be hidden from the older children, however, who saw the degradation and murder of their elders. Their reliance on their own ego strength and their own judgement, even when it countermanded their parents' values, may have made the difference between life and death for some (Kestenberg & Brenner, 1996). Their capacity to adapt more creatively and flexibly to the conditions than the grown-ups has been thought to have been mediated through their surreal form of "play".

More reflections

Dr Adina Blady Szwajger, who worked in the children's hospital in the Warsaw ghetto, poignantly described how, prior to the destruction of the ghetto, the sick and dying children were seeing the world "with the eyes of adults". These "ageless creatures" (Szwajger, 1990, p. 31) from four to twelve years of age, who were precociously aware of their impending deaths, had profoundly serious eyes that expressed "all the sorrow of two thousand years of Diaspora" (Szwajger, 1990, p. 31). Yet, some of these children had retained a capacity for play. For example, she described one boy who screamed in constant pain due to contractions in his extremities until a staff member placed a pencil between his nearly useless fingers. At such times he would calm down and draw pictures from his memory and imagination. Toddlers played in a makeshift playground there pretending to be grown-ups lighting the Shabbat candles on Friday night and cooking soup with "real potatoes".

Toddlers and latency-age children in the Warsaw ghetto would imitate in their play what they witnessed, such as funerals and raids by their Nazi captors. And, as noted earlier, if a child dropped dead during their play, they would continue in their fantasy world, seemingly unaffected by the latest fatality in their midst (Eisen, 1988). Their attempts at mastery were noted at the death camps also, where ". . . children played Blockaeltester (block elder), roll call, caps off, and even gas chambers. They played what they needed to understand, and what they did understand was the horror of an adult world gone mad" (Kestenberg & Brenner, 1996, p. 135). The depiction of this play in the cinema was poignantly portrayed in the film *Life Is Beautiful*, where a father, played by Roberto Benigni, tried to help his son survive by telling him that it was all a game and that if he could earn enough points, tanks would come into the camp and rescue him.

Among the older children, writing diaries and poetry was quite prevalent in hiding and in the camps. Ann Frank's diary is by far the most well known one. Development continued and sexual interest was evident but often not spoken of (Kestenberg & Brenner, 1996; Nir, 1989). Themes of despair and hope were omnipresent themes in the poetry, and reading them aloud was reported to have boosted the spirits of all who listened (Sender, 1986). Most notably:

> The children of Terezin left a remarkable legacy in their poetry and art . . . [with the help of their] teachers who defied camp rules to offer the children art therapy in the guise of art lessons, to teach literature, and to organize poetry contests, recitations, and cultural programs in the girls' and boys' dormitories. One such teacher was Friedl Dicker-Brandeis . . . of the Bauhaus in Weimar, Germany . . . [who] brought what art materials she could to the camp . . . [and] saw that the children . . . needed a form of artistic expression as a way to moderate the chaos of their lives. (Volavková, 1993, p. viii)

Of those who survived, many child survivors further developed their creative abilities in the realms of painting and sculpture as well as writing. Here are some representative poems written by children in Theresienstadt.

The Little Mouse

A mousie sat upon a shelf,
Catching fleas in his coat of fur.
But he couldn't catch her—what chagrin!
She'd hidden 'way inside his skin.
He turned and wriggled, knew no rest,
That flea was such a nasty pest!

His daddy came
And searched his coat
He caught the flea and off he ran
To cook her in the frying pan.
The little mouse cried, "Come and see!
For lunch we've got a nice, fat flea!"
(Koleba, 1944, in Volavková, 1978, pp. 40–41)

The Jewish prisoners' identification with being treated like vermin and their own identification with the aggressor in their treatment of insects is humourously described in this poem. Themes of hunger, hiding, being caught, and being burned alive are encapsulated here.

A ten-year-old girl, Gabrielle Silten, who was also in Theresienstadt, described her relationship with rats this way:

In the spaces between the beams [in the attics] lived rats with their families. We would walk on the beams to get to the spaces where the rat families lived (or sometimes just to walk on the beams) and then poke at them and watch them jump. Surprisingly, they never harmed us or attacked us at all. (Friedman, 1982, p. 61)

This young girl and her friends played the game of "aktion" with the rats who, like the Jews, never fought back. This identification with the Nazi aggressor persisted in an ageing child survivor who would periodically perform "selections" on the yellowing, dying leaves of my plants, insisting with great urgency they be removed from the healthy leaves (I. Brenner, 2004).

Homesick

I've lived in the ghetto here for more than a year,
In Terezin, in the black town now,
And when I remember my old home so dear,
I can love it more than I did, somehow.

Ah, home, home.
Why did they tear me away?
Here the weak die easy as a feather
And when they die, they die forever.
                    (Anonymous, 1943, in Volavková, 1978, p. 46)

This child seems to have grasped one of the essential factors of death—that is, the permanent and irreversible nature of object loss.

The Butterfly

The last, the very last,
So richly, brightly, dazzlingly yellow.
Perhaps if the sun's tears would sing
    against a white stone . . .

Such, such a yellow
Is carried lightly 'way up high.
It went away I'm sure because it wished to
    kiss the world goodbye.

For seven weeks I've lived in here,
Penned up inside this ghetto.
But I have found what I love here.
The dandelions call to me
And the white chestnut branches in the court.

Only I never saw another butterfly.
That butterfly was the last one.
Butterflies don't live in here,
    in the ghetto.
                    (Pavel Friedman, 1942, in Volavková, 1978, p. 39)

Wanting to fly to freedom but being trapped, the struggle for survival is painfully represented through his appreciation of the simple beauty of nature. This boy died in Auschwitz.

Discussion

In this brief sampling of creativity and play during the Holocaust, I have focused mostly on the plight of children which, until fairly recently, was a largely untold story (Dwork, 1991; Glassner & Krell, 2006; Kestenberg & Brenner, 1996; Marks, 1993; Moskowitz, 1983). The approximately 1.5 million children who perished were killed in every way imaginable: they were stabbed, starved, suffocated, and shot. They were abandoned in knapsacks on the way to slave labour camps, sent into hiding where some were sexually abused, drugged, drowned, smashed against walls, run over, frozen, or died of infectious diseases. And, of course, they were gassed and cremated. Their cries could signal the presence of Jews in hiding under floorboards or behind false walls. Their discovery by raiding SS troops would lead to the certain death of all who were caught. Moreover, any healthy grown-ups with a child on the selection ramp at the death camp would immediately be sent to the left, directly to the gas chambers. Children, therefore, became a liability of lethal proportions. So, the young offspring who, under "expectable" conditions (Hartmann, 1939) would represent the hope and future of any group, became deadly baggage for their parents and an utterly useless commodity for the Third Reich. Indeed, their extermination was especially important to those whose mission it was to cleanse Europe and the world of the Jewish menace—that is, to make it "Judenrein". In this climate of death, dying, and impending death, or living in the constant terror of being caught and sent to death, the children tried to adapt in ways that were characteristic of their ages, stages of development, and state of health.

With what we currently know about the child's developmental acquisition of the awareness and meaning of death in others and for himself, it is clear that within a certain range there is considerable individual variation based on experience and psychodynamic factors (I. Brenner, 2010). Furthermore, precocious exposure to death well before the child's maturational capacity to comprehend it may be traumatic in and of itself and may be thought of as the inverse of a fixation (Kestenberg & Brenner, 1988). As such, the function of play under these most dire conditions of the ghetto might, in part, help the child learn more quickly about what awaits him in very short order.

Akhtar, in his definition of "play" (Akhtar, 2009), which syn-
thesises the contributions of Balint (1959), Erikson (1950), Freud
(1920g), Wälder (1933), Winnicott (1942, 1953, 1971), and others, states,

> Play enriches life, and enjoyment of playing is a hallmark of the grow-
> ing child's mental health. Playing was the result of acting from the
> centre, so to speak, and fearlessly being imaginative and innovative
> . . . a spirit which would not torment itself with questions of reality
> and unreality; instead, it will peacefully accept the paradox that some
> activities are neither real or unreal. (Akhtar, 2009, p. 211)

This definition might better apply to the type of play that Parens
described where, for example, he and his friends might spontaneously
go into character and become the "Three Musketeers" if they encountered one another on the way to the latrine. However, I would contend
that it does not apply to the previously mentioned ghetto games, such
as "Aktion" and "Returning the Clothing of the Dead". Here, the
complex activity seems to go beyond the binary distinction between
reality and fantasy, beyond being a life-enriching activity indicative
of mental health and to be, as Freud stated, "beyond the pleasure
principle" (Freud, 1920g).

From this perspective, it might be seen as a child's ego's best effort
at managing an overwhelming upsurge of pressure from *Thanatos*, the
death instinct. The repetitive enactments of real life activities, which
were far more macabre than fantasy, incorporated the well-known
defence of identification with the aggressor, reflected an attempt at
turning passive into active, and also seemed to have an additional
level of significance. What exactly did Karski mean when he blurted
out, "But these children are not playing. They only make-believe it is
play" (Eisen, 1988, p. 107. And what did the writer in *The Chronicle of
the Łódź Ghetto* mean when he described the boys playing their musical toys ". . . as though their lives depended on it" (Dobroszycki, 1984,
p. 374)? Could it be that indeed the children were more aware of the
inevitability of their deaths than their parents? They

> . . . did not simply copy the atrocity surrounding them; rather, they
> imposed on reality their own construction and interpretations. In fact,
> all surviving evidence indicates that the children had a clear grasp of
> reality and were aware of their fate. Play of the Holocaust, however,

reflected this reality in a "bent" form, fitting the players' existing level of cognitive functioning. (Eisen, 1988, p. 114)

If this were the case, how might we understand how they could have acquired an appreciation of reality at a much earlier age than might have been expected? Perhaps a deeper consideration of the nature of this "improvisational theatre" and its relationship to reality might offer a clue. And, perhaps, there might even be a clue derived from the ambiguity (Adler, 1989) of the analytic situation.

A number of years ago, an analysand who was trying to make sense of the complex nature of the analytic relationship commented in passing that it had the quality of a Pirandello play. This woman, a gifted academic with wide-ranging interests and knowledge, said that it felt like "a play within a play within a play". In her metaphor, she was alluding to this ambiguity from which analysis is such a powerful modality. The reality of the "frame" of the analytic situation is one level. The fundamental rule, the "signposts" of neutrality, anonymity, and abstinence which are most aberrant in human relationships and contribute to the creation of the asymmetry, make it another level. Under these conditions, the transference may be cultivated in a way that enables the projection of the analysand's internal world to become visible, comprehensible, and interpretable. In the process, the analysand's reality testing becomes strengthened. But then, of course, there is another level to contend with, and that is the unconscious communication between the two, which exerts an additional influence in the transference–countertransference matrix, manifesting itself in the enactments throughout analysis. Through interpretation, containment, and co-creation, it then becomes possible for deeper meaning, understanding, and strengthening of one's sense of inner and outer reality to occur.

For Luigi Pirandello, the Pulitzer prize-winning playwright and novelist who was deeply affected by the horrors of the First World War in his native Italy, much of his work dealt with the multiple layers of consciousness, reality, relativity, and self-deception in a chaotic world governed by "arcane" forces. A contemporary of Freud and a playwright like Shakespeare, for whom "All the world's a stage . . ." (Shakespeare, 1598), Pirandello saw all experience as theatrical. The quest to understand the mysteries of the world through one's consciousness and self-awareness are major themes in his work. The essence of the creative process, as he saw it, consisted of *spontaneita* (spontaneity), *sincerita* (the most honest effort to represent things as authentically as possible), and *smania di vivera* (the "mania to live"), which psychoanalysis might reductionistically think of as the manic defence (Akhtar, 2001; Winnicott, 1935). Pirandello recognised the twentieth-century preoccupation with consciousness and was quite aware of unconscious forces that he saw as multi-dimensional. He wrote extensively about death, as it most profoundly represented those dark, arcane forces at work, which are always waiting to become manifest and induce people to become totally authentic and truthful about themselves.

As Pirandello thought of theatre as "a form of life itself" and a true and proper "active life", he most probably would have seen the ghetto games as a necessary part of existence which, driven by the children's "mania for life", was a true creative process characterised by their *spontaneita* and *sincerita*. They were a cohesive group of sick, starving, and dying children, deciding on who would get to play the coveted rule of Nazi commandant in charge of the raids and rounding up of Jews. That decision process, in and of itself, was yet another drama within the drama. They were loitering on street corners littered with detritus and filth and, to add to the authenticity of their performance, would not infrequently find a dead body nearby to incorporate into their scenarios. Perhaps it might have been a corpse of someone who was known to them, or perhaps one of their relatives—yet another drama within the drama and another level of reality for them to contend with. Then, the doomed child would handle the dead body in the context of the play, trying to determine if there was any life left in it and learn more about death; another drama ensues within the larger game, and on and on. And then, how would it be decided when the performance would be over for the day? Would a real life "aktion" actually occur?

The strength of the group would empower each child, and by verbalising, symbolising, and representing the unrepresentable through repetitive enactments, they could learn what lay in wait for them. They could become more prepared to survive another day and perhaps outlive the masters of death whose own fate would eventually be out of their hands, too, as a result of the advancing Allied Forces. From this rather complex process, perhaps the children met their deaths with a wisdom and understanding that far exceeded what any child should ever have to know.

Concluding remarks

It has been said that play

> . . . became an instinctual form for understanding the absurd and for accommodating the irrational . . . The children suffered, cried, laid down their broken bodies and died: sometimes they played. They played for the few moments they were given with the vehemence and desperation that only the doomed can have. (Eisen, 1988, p. 122)

In addition to this observation, it seems, from the descriptions and kinds of play of children in hiding, in ghettos, and in death camps, that it was complex and multiply determined, owing to their life-and-death circumstances, their health, and their stages of development. Perhaps the saturation of their "play" with death is analogous to Volkan's description of the malignant regression in cultural rituals in societies under totalitarian and terrorist rule (Volkan, 2006), where aggression infuses and contaminates what were once light-hearted traditions. Here, in the children's play of the ghetto, their "making believe" they were just playing had the quality of improvisational street theatre of desperate and dying children who were trying to comprehend what was happening around them. The ideas put forth by Pirandello about levels of reality in the creative process might help deepen our understanding of this phenomenon.

CHAPTER SEVEN

Geopolitical identity disorder

"The tragedy is that there is a clash here between two truths; but the justice of our cause is greater"

(Jabotinsky, 1926, p. 303)

"The Arab is culturally backward, but his instinctive patriotism is just as pure and noble as our own; it cannot be bought, it can only be curbed by . . . *force majeur*"

(Jabotinsky, 1922, p. 53)

Introduction

The seemingly insolvable situation in the Middle East, referred to as the "Palestinian–Israeli Conflict", has been conceptualised in a number of ways, including political, ethnic, religious, psychological, etc. (I. Brenner, 2004, 2007; Lesch & Lustick, 2005; Morris, 1999; Volkan, 2004). From a geographic point of view (Derrida, 1998), it could be seen simply as a fight between different groups over the same piece of land. Competing claims over ownership of land have occurred since time immemorial, from the most exclusive suburban neighbourhoods in America to many of the "hot spots" in the world today.

In his work on the psychological understanding of political and societal processes, Volkan (1997, 2004) emphasises the importance of large groups—ethnic, religious, ideological, or national—and the threats to their identity. He posits that under stress a regression may occur in these groups to fixation points in their history, such as the reactivation of a "chosen trauma". An example of this phenomenon would be what was experienced in the USA after September 11th (I. Brenner, 2006b). The helplessness, shame, and humiliation experienced by Americans revived nationalistic feelings similar to the reaction to Pearl Harbor sixty years before, which resulted in an immediate need to wage war, destroy the enemy, and restore a sense of integrity to the country. Another symptom of large-group regression would be the activation of border psychology, whereby the dynamics of creating and managing borders become infused with enormous symbolic as well as "real" significance, as though there is a shared psychological skin. First described by Falk (1974), the rituals pertaining to maintaining the integrity of the boundaries might have life-and-death significance for the respective large groups.

Variations of border disputes and/or rights to holy places occur in a number of war-torn areas, such as Kashmir, where the Indians and the Pakistanis are at a perpetual standoff. Here, too, as in the Middle East, there is a legacy of British colonialism that complicated life in this idyllic haven of natural beauty where people of two great religions once lived in peace. In this case, however, it is the Hindus and the Muslims, not the Jews, the Muslims, and the Christians.

In that part of the Middle East of concern to us here, the Jews' original claim to Israel started with the purchase of a parcel of land. Interestingly, this transaction was actually described in an ancient document. An old man, who was originally from out of town, bought a large cave in which to bury his dying wife. He insisted on paying full price for it, despite it being offered to him for free. He did not even try to get a deal, lest there be any cause to challenge his ownership. That is because, over the years since he had moved there, he had become familiar with the local laws of the land, which stated that unless purchased outright, any land given to a non-Hittite reverted back after the man's death. So, perhaps not without reason, this cave in Hebron where an old woman named Sarah is buried—the oldest site in Jewish history—is currently one of the most hotly contested areas between the Palestinians and the Israelis today. After all, according to this legendary writing, both Isaac, the legitimate son and heir, as well as Ishmael, patriarch of the Muslims, together eventually buried their father, Abraham, there too. Since that time, over the millennia, much has been said about the fate of the rivalry between these two brothers (Roith, 2006).

Brief review of the land

Following the Roman conquest and destruction of Jerusalem about 2,000 years later, Jewish domination of this land ended. The Jews' mournful longing to return as a people to their promised land has been incorporated into ritual and holiday commemorations, most notably in the concluding line of the Passover Seder: "*L'shanah haba'ah b'Yerushalayim!*" or "Next year in Jerusalem!" Even Freud, the supposed atheist (I. Brenner, 2003–2004), alluded to this perennial lament in a letter to Wilhelm Fliess on 16 April 1900, where he sarcastically writes, "If I closed with 'Next Easter in Rome,' I would feel like a pious Jew" (Masson, 1985, p. 409). In fact, however, there has been continuous but limited habitation by Jews since then, but the ascendancy of Christianity, the phenomenal spread of the teachings of the Prophet Mohammed, the Crusades, the Ottoman Empire, and then the British influence greatly changed the demographics and political landscape there.

Setting the stage for problems in the twentieth century, separate arrangements and promises from the British to both Arabs and Jews over the disposition of land further complicated the matters. The McMahon–Hussein Agreement of 1915 promised much of the land to the Arabs in return for their helping the British oust the Turks. The secret Sykes–Picot Agreement in 1916 between Britain and France drew up boundaries in the Middle East in the post Second World War period. In 1917, the Balfour Declaration supported ". . . the establishment in Palestine of a national home for the Jewish people . . ." These conflicting and overlapping treaties greatly added to the confusion over the sense of ownership and national identity associated with the land.

Following the United Nations' resolution in 1947 to partition the land to allow for a Jewish state, the historical events of 1948 were subsequently remembered quite differently by each side. One view is that the War of Independence was fought and won by Israel, whereas the Palestinians experienced these events as the *Nakbah*, or catastrophe. Since then, Israel's survival of its periodic wars with its neighbours, its alliance with the USA, its lightning victory in the 1967 war that expanded its borders (the narrowest part of pre-1967 Israel—nine miles across its midsection—is shorter than the distance from one end of the city of Philadelphia to the other) made it an occupier country, and the development of its ambiguous "nuclear option" in Dimona has ultimately made this country a reality that has to be reckoned with. This last achievement has been thought to be so monumental that

> Almost certainly, when historians look back with the added perspective of another two decades, they will conclude that Israel's nuclear capability was the decisive element in persuading the Arab world that the Jewish presence in the narrow strip of land at the eastern end of the Mediterranean sea was a permanent reality. (Karpin, 2006, p. 337)

Despite the existential anxiety that might reverberate from the legacy of genocidal persecution of its founders and their progeny, the identity and existence of Israel are geopolitical facts. Its recognition by others of its right to exist and *vice versa*, however, remains an intransigent and, according to Sadat's famous statement to the Knesset, an essentially psychological problem (Volkan, 2004). While Sadat was specifically referring to the Sinai, his profound declaration may apply here as well.

If it is so that the problem is largely psychological, then there might be some value in applying a psychological model. There are large-group models, small-group models, and individual models, the latter often used as a basis for the former. We all know, however, that extrapolating from an individual patient in the clinical situation to complex events in the outside world of large-group behaviour is fraught with difficulties. With this caveat in mind, I will draw a parallel.

In the case of disputed land, such as in Israel–Palestine, at least two narratives and two identities exist for the same body of land. Each group of inhabitants claims ownership and at times would prefer to deny or eliminate the presence or legitimacy of the others. Such a problem, in my view, lends itself to the analogy of a severely traumatised patient with a fragmented, dissociated mind as seen in DID, formerly known as multiple personality disorder. In this condition, which is highly correlated with severe early trauma, there is excessive internalised aggression that interferes with the development of a unified identity, and the different selves that are created appear to have the power to take over executive functioning of the mind and control of the body. Amnestic states may initially prevent the recognition of the presence of the "others", but dissociated suicidality is often experienced as a deadly fight among the different selves over the body (I. Brenner, 2004).

The application of the model of such a psyche has previously been applied to the fragmented society of Israel following the assassination of Itzhak Rabin in 1995 (I. Brenner, 1996). To make such a comparison to Israel might seem rather arcane, but the idea came to me because I had just presented a paper on exactly that subject (I. Brenner, 1995b) on the day that Rabin was tragically murdered, and I was struck by some ironic similarities.

Learning that the assassin was an Israeli Jew who believed it was his religious duty to kill the Prime Minister to save the country from a ruinous peace with the Arabs was shocking, but it momentarily relieved me. It was somehow "better" that the destructive force had come from within and not from foreign extremists. I had the same feeling when hearing that the Oklahoma City bombing was also committed by a "domestic" terrorist. I soon realised that this peculiar feeling was due to the fact that since there was no "enemy" to blame, there could be no retaliation that could escalate into a war. At least for now, the threat was from within.

At the same time, the destructive schism in Israeli society was clearly exposed to the world, shattering any naïve illusion that such a crime could ever happen there. The once-unifying vision of an emerging nation, building and gaining strength as it evolved from a haven for the persecuted remnants of the Diaspora, seemed like ancient history. Indeed, there was even talk of restricting Jewish immigration. Furthermore, now we all knew that a Jew could kill another Jew— even a head of state—a deed which some thought was impossible. Any claim to moral superiority deriving from being the "Chosen People" who received the Ten Commandments from God was also called into question.

While Rabin's assassination destroyed an image of modern Israel, a parallel was found with a different trauma in Israel's history: the destruction of the Second Temple 2,000 years ago (Keinon, 1995a). Bitter infighting between political factions over how to handle the Roman occupation of Jerusalem led to a weakening loss of unity, tremendous internal mistrust, religious extremism, and alliances between Jewish factions and outsiders against other Jews. Eventually, Jerusalem and the Jewish state were decimated in the first century AD (Flavius Josephus, 1900). And now, on the eve of the 3,000-year anniversary of Jerusalem, Israel was issuing commemorative coins and having gala celebrations but, simultaneously, seemed on the verge of massive self-destruction, once again edging closer to total oblivion.

It was as though history was repeating itself. In the last 2,000 years, the Jewish people have suffered exile, enslavement, exploitation, expulsion, witch hunts, massacres, pogroms, ghettos, and even the "final solution".[5] But, to have finally returned to their homeland and lose it once again—would that be the ultimate calamity?

The repeating of painful or traumatic experience is well known to psychoanalysts as the "repetition compulsion". Freud tried to explain why, for example, people would become plagued by recurrent nightmares of traumas or return to the scene of the crime only to re-experience emotional pain. This phenomenon seemed contradictory to his classic "pleasure principle", which explained motivation on the basis of seeking gratification, good feelings, and libido. He concluded that ". . . the aim of life is death. . ." (Freud, 1920g, p. 28) and theorised that, in opposition to the life instinct, a so-called "death instinct" oper-ated silently and unobtrusively ". . . to return to the quiescence of the inorganic world" (p. 62). While the notion of a true "death instinct" is highly controversial and has all but been replaced by more contem-porary theories of aggression, the compulsion to repeat is readily observable in the human psyche. Especially noticeable in traumatised individuals who seem to have an uncanny ability to become re-victimised, this repetition does not always seem to be in the service of mastery or adaptation and, indeed, might result in one progressively coming closer to death. The extent, however, to which one may apply this theory to the collective psyche of a people over two millennia is certainly subject to debate.

Unlike the plight of Israel during the Roman occupation, today Israel is the occupier. Nevertheless, this reversal also lends itself to another facile psychoanalytic interpretation—"identification with the aggressor"—that is, turning a passive trauma into an active attempt at mastery. But this expression may, unfortunately, provoke invidious comparisons: instead of citing the 2,000-year-old trauma, one needs only to look back a half-century to the trauma of the Holocaust, where some have drawn deeply emotional comparisons of Arab detention camps to concentration camps, of Israeli interrogation techniques to Gestapo tactics, and of Rabin himself to a Nazi. A notorious poster showing the Prime Minister in an SS uniform, which was displayed at a right-wing rally shortly before his death (Gordon, 1995), seems to epitomise this perception.

With Rabin's assassination, Israel suddenly lost its leader, its warrior turned peacemaker, as Yigal Amir's bullets struck home. Ironically, they tore through a folded paper bearing a song of peace, which Rabin had just jubilantly sung in front of 10,000 people. Whether the assassin acted alone or not (Oren, 1995), it is clear that he literally answered the prayers and wishes of the powerful religious right wing (Hirschberg, 1995). While many mourned, others had reason to rejoice. In a moment, the state of Israel was, at the very least, re-traumatised and, at the worst, decapitated, like a person who was trying to inflict a mortal wound upon himself. What was going on? In attempting to find my own answers, I was able to draw some parallels from my clinical experience.

A case of "multiple personality"

A severely traumatised patient, Tracey, was bent on self-destruction. I had hypothesised (I. Brenner, 1994) that her repetitive suicidal behaviour was not in the service of mastery and was best understood—at least metaphorically—by invoking the death instinct theory. Ironically, she had an alter personality who claimed to be a religious leader and wanted to destroy the patient for betraying certain secrets and for trusting "outsiders", that is, other human beings. This personification was violently opposed to the direction she was taking in her life and felt as though "he" would lose his power over her if she persisted. "He" did not believe or care that "they" shared the same body, but, instead, insisted that divine powers would enable "him" to survive and take over exclusive control. In other words, the "reverend", the religious fanatic self-state, maintained a quasi-delusional belief that "his" fate was unrelated to that of the "others", and not subject to the laws of nature or medical fact. As a result, he methodically planned numerous ways to kill Tracey that, to the outside observer, were tantamount to suicide.

Tracey's system also included other personifications who trusted no one and took a tough, no-nonsense stance against the world. In doing so, the patient's "foreign policy" of social isolationism was a form of protection against being re-victimised were she to fraternise with "the enemy" again. The enemy was linked to her childhood, when she was sent to live with relatives: her uncle, a self-styled fundamentalist, sadistically abused her in the name of the Lord. During that time, she felt exiled, unloved, and mercilessly persecuted. Interestingly, she was fascinated with the Holocaust and felt closely identified with the Jews. The "reverend" alter was a personification of this malevolent uncle, an ill-fated way of mastering her trauma. Her mind was also populated with dissociated, victimised children, apathetic or helpless bystanders, and a care-taker "mother" who meant well but was actually in league with the "reverend". The "mother" alter was a double agent, as it were, who tended to the inner child, but turned a blind eye when the "reverend" wanted to have his way, that is, self-mutilate.

When Tracey was "liberated" as a teenager, she returned home and "never looked back". Amazingly, she did well in school, even though she lived a dissociated, secret life of high-risk sadomasochistic exploits. Her repetition compulsion constantly put her in harm's way through her sexuality and through her high-risk professional work in which she excelled. The "reverend" rejoiced when she finally became HIV-positive. He insisted that it was God's will, a punishment for her sins, and he wanted to hasten her demise as he was eager to "take over".

Essentially, the massive trauma of Tracey's early life intensified her aggression to such a degree that it had to be encapsulated by the various dissociated personifications in order for some healthy development to take place (I. Brenner, 1996). This encapsulation took the form of different alter personalities who embodied omnipotent, religious extremism, a belligerent exterior, a double agent, and several child-like parts frozen in the past, doomed to relive the loss, abandonment, pain, and degradation. Amazingly, when all this could be contained and kept in the dark recesses of Tracey's mind, she was able to pursue a normal life. However, her delicate psychic equilibrium could be easily disturbed by perceived threats of danger or reminders of the past, which activated flashbacks, profound survivor guilt, self-destructive behaviour, and paranoid, aggressive behaviour as she readied herself for attack at any moment.

Israel's dissociated society

As a psychoanalyst, I have wondered if a society of traumatised and re-traumatised people, such as Israel, could become similarly organised to the mind of a traumatised individual in order to function successfully. Not being an expert on the Middle East, it is perhaps easier to make such psycho-historical speculations from afar. For example, Israel, as a tiny nation in a treacherous region, has had to rely on its wits, its strength, and its powerful friends for survival. Like Tracey's inability to look back on her past, the current realities of daily life in Israel make it difficult to "look back" on its past trauma for more than a moment at a time, despite all the memorial ceremonies, holidays, monuments, and museums. Even if there are strong political and historical arguments that the Holocaust did not actually "result" in the creation of the state of Israel, the mere fact of its temporal connection, that is, three years after the liberation of the camps in 1945, is very compelling circumstantial evidence that Israel was indeed born of trauma.

The psychological link between the Holocaust and the founding of Israel (Kestenberg & Brenner, 1996; Segev, 1993) was impressed upon me when I presented a paper at a conference in Israel on the transmission of Holocaust trauma (I. Brenner, 1988). At the time, I heard Yehuda Bauer, the historian, succinctly conclude that "The Jews are a traumatized people" (Bauer, 1988, personal communication). Throughout this conference, I learnt that there was much latent national shame about the stereotypical Holocaust victim who went "like sheep to the slaughter" in Europe. This European heritage was the antithesis of the rugged, independent, and resourceful *Sabra*, the invincible fighter, who became a modern-day Israeli legend during the raid on Entebbe and the Six Day War. As a result, those who dwelled on the Holocaust for any more than the duration of a ceremony could not reconcile the two images. Dramatic evidence of this dichotomy was revealed by Associated Press in November, 1995,[6] where it was reported that almost twenty per cent of Israel's institutionalised mental patients, roughly 900 people, were Holocaust survivors who may have been unnecessarily hospitalised (Associated Press, November 27, 1995). Apparently, the uniqueness of their circumstances was never addressed in treatment, which, through bureaucratic oversight, created an islet of immigrants segregated from society and frozen in their traumatic grief from fifty years ago. Such an enclave seemed analogous to Tracey's child alters, who were frozen in their past traumas as well.

Furthermore, among some Jews there is an ultra-religious belief that the Holocaust was God's punishment for not properly obeying the laws of the Sabbath. Reminiscent of Tracey's "reverend" alter, proponents of such a conviction have little interest in the daily political affairs of the Israeli state, secure in their belief that their fate is independent of their country's. Whereas other ultra-religious extremists require an active stance regarding national policy, these *Haredim* remain aloof and dissociated, as it were, from corporeal concerns. The political "death" of democratic Israel is of little concern, and possibly even wished for.

Particularly relevant to Rabin's assassination, however, are those ultra-religious, right-wing Israelis who do take an active interest in national issues. They are trained in elite military units, but might have a divided loyalty between their commanding officers and their rabbis (Keinon, 1995b). With no Jeffersonian tradition of separation of church and state, religious and secular issues are easily intertwined. Moreover, there are inherent conflicts in the basic pillars of Israeli society— it is intended to be both a democracy *and* a Jewish state. Therefore, returning the West Bank to the Palestinians becomes not only a military–strategic issue but also a profoundly emotional Biblical issue. As a result, there has been confusion between the secondary-process thinking of economic and political realities of the day and the primary-process thinking, as it were, of religion. To complicate things further, the investigation of Rabin's death had suggested a possible government conspiracy, or at least some unconscious sympathy, with the extreme right, leading up to a security lapse during his assassination. Whether a double agent actually existed in the General Security Services (GSS), like Tracey's "mother" alter, there is at least the possibility that agents who were planted to monitor right-wing activities might have actually stimulated anti-government sympathies to a deadly pitch (Collins, 1995; Oren, 1995).

Discussion

If a patient with multiple personality survives a severe suicide attempt, extreme measures may be needed to prevent an immediate recurrence. These options include chemical and physical restraints, twenty-four nursing surveillance, and hypnotherapeutic techniques to put the murderous personifications to sleep. Such interventions are only stop-gap efforts and cannot be used indefinitely. It is crucial for the therapist to develop a treatment alliance with the patient in the different altered states of consciousness, especially the most destructive ones. These most inner parts of the mind that are influenced and held in sway by the "death instinct" are the least accessible but the most necessary with which to make contact. In so doing, it might be possible to neutralise some of the deadly inner aggression, abreact old traumata, grieve past losses, and promote unification of the mind. The patient may then become able to recognise the differences between the past and the present, inner and outer dangers, and fantasy and reality. The ego is strengthened by improved reality testing and control over destructive impulses. The disowning of one's body, which facilitates the near-lethal error in judgement, is, thus, corrected when the patient realises, accepts, and "owns" his or her body and mind. The divisive dissociation is then replaced by a more normative repression that relegates much of the primary-process thinking to the unconscious and allows more secondary-process thinking in the conscious part of the mind. This integration of the mind and body is a long-term task that can only be accomplished if the will to live is strengthened by freeing the patient from the vice-like grip of the "death instinct".

If such a formulation is valid and has any applicability to Israeli society, then, in the case of the Rabin assassination, it would have been expected that things would have been quite precarious for some time. "Death instinct" or not, the compulsion to repeat is very powerful. Immediate "life-saving" measures to prevent a recurrence of murderous violence would understandably have included tightened security, legislative action, confinement of suspects, and even the restriction of certain freedoms. However, just as with the patient, such short-term external limitations will not change anything underneath. The extent to which "the truth" about the assassination was determined ultimately by the Shamgar Commission and the extent to which the public felt that all facts about government intrigue and right-wing extremism were revealed should have been important "insights" for society. Furthermore, the extent to which religious extremists can accept the fact that they, too, belong to the state of Israel and share a common fate would seem to be an essential aspect of the quest for national unity.

Sometimes, a near-death experience can have a profound effect on a suicidal individual, causing him or her to develop an increased appreciation for the value of life (I. Brenner, 1996). Is it possible that such a close call in a nation could have the same effect? If so, then the aggressive underside of religious extremism might be neutralised a bit and destructive, irrational views could be replaced by a more rational, secondary-process thinking. Maybe steps could also be taken to develop a safer division between rabbinical and governmental leadership. Finally, regarding the need for catharsis, mourning (Volkan, 1981), and working through of trauma, the trial of Yigal Amir could have been a catalyst. His trial might have been the most sensational one held in Israel since Adolf Eichmann's testimony thirty-five years prior reopened the wounds of the Holocaust. As history has a way of repeating itself, I even wondered if Rabin's assassin would also have found himself in a glass booth during his trial.

To summarise, I hypothesised that the model of the mind in a severely traumatised individual with dissociated, "multiple personality" may be applied to a society of traumatised people such as the Israelis. Clearly, the situation is enormously complex, multi-faceted, and beyond a single theory. Nevertheless, there appear to be parallels. In an individual, early traumatic loss, overstimulation, and injury might intensify aggression to such an extent that it may become organised into a number of encapsulated, dissociated personifications. For example, a child personality might relive past traumas totally disconnected from the realities of the present. The institutionalised Holocaust survivors mentioned earlier could be analogous to such a mental construct. Other personifications might disown the body and express internalised rage by attacking the body, believing that it belongs to "someone else". In the clinical vignette of Tracey, one of her alter personalities was a violent religious extremist under the influence of a self-destructive, repetition compulsion, allegedly in the name of the Lord. In Israel, the ultra-religious right wing might be the societal representation of this phenomenon. Some feel totally disconnected from the fate of the country, whereas others rationalise that murdering its leader is necessary to save the country. Tracey also had a personification who was a "double agent", and such a suspicion was raised about the GSS in Israel. Based on this model, the assassination of Rabin might be interpreted as a national suicide attempt. Following the principles of psychotherapy, all parts of society would have needed to mourn their losses, work through their multiple traumas, learn from this near-death experience of the nation, and accept that they all share a common fate. If not, they might be doomed to repetitive self-destructive acts leading to annihilation. It was hoped that the trial of Yigal Amir would have been a catalyst to promote a catharsis and a rapprochement between these dissociated facets of the Israeli population.

However, during that time, four suicide bombings resulted in over sixty deaths and hundreds of injuries, bringing the "peace process" to an explosive halt and plunging the Jewish State into its biggest nightmare siege since the Scud missile attacks of the Gulf War in 1991. The Palestinian extremist group, Hamas, took responsibility for these acts, seeking revenge for the death of their notorious alleged bombmaker, Yahya Ayyash, whose assassination was attributed to Israeli agents. According to *The New York Times* (Schmemann, 1996), Yassir Arafat alleged once again that Israeli extremists had provided the explosives to the Islamic militants for the suicide bombings in order to further undermine the peace negotiations, but offered no proof. The grief, rage, fear, and re-traumatisation of the Israelis then transformed the question of whether there ever could be peace with their ancient rival into a declaration of war against Hamas. Then Mayor of Jerusalem, Ehud Olmert, gravely announced, after viewing the charred remains of bus number 18, that Jerusalem was now the battleground.

At that time, the threats to Israeli society from both within and without intensified the timeless struggle for Jewish survival into yet another cycle of hatred and violence. Perhaps it was no coincidence that, in addition to the main shopping area in Tel-Aviv, the two buses targeted for destruction were on Route 18, which is the numeric equivalent of the Hebrew word *chai*, an almost sacred word meaning "life". What better way for terrorists to demonstrate their capacity to seemingly strike at will and demoralise and hold a nation hostage than to destroy both vital and symbolically important parts of its infrastructure while killing as many people as possible? With a very uncertain future, further societal dissociation could have resulted in political paralysis, massive civil unrest, and more destructive aggressions turned inward. Therefore, a step toward unification in the service of self-preservation and an appropriate expression of externalised aggression seemed absolutely necessary in order to re-establish trust in Rabin's successor, Shimon Peres, and to recreate a sense of safety for the population before any further détente could occur.

In that situation, the extremist right-wing militants were seen as analogous to a destructive alter personality, the ultra-orthodox as a pious self, and a recently discovered group of institutionalised, ageing Holocaust survivors whose own trauma history was not acknowledged or recognised by hospital staff was seen as a repository of unmetabolised, unacknowledged trauma frozen in time as another dissociated self.

Fast forward

Almost twenty years later, as of this writing, the Israeli–Palestinian conflict is even more entrenched despite periodic hopeful moments of a political solution. There are two traumatised societies that are regressed, separated by a wall, unable to accept their common fate, and locked in mortal combat over control of the same land. I will present another clinical case report to illustrate this aspect of the geopolitical problem. Consider it a parable and just an approximation.

A clinical parable

Isabel was a patient with DID who was in a lifelong struggle over her identity and the fate of the body. She never felt a complete sense of ownership or control of her body, even though her name was on the birth certificate and she held the original claim. Isolated from siblings and ignored by an alcoholic father, Isabel was a victim of maternal neglect and abuse (I. Brenner, 2004). Growing up in a very disturbed household, Isabel recalled that mother hated sex with the father and would scream and fight as he took her by force on a regular basis. It occurred to Isabel after years of treatment that a *secret treaty* must have been made between the parents, because the father would drink himself into oblivion and disappear on a regular basis whenever the mother desired the patient sexually. In return, the mother would let the father rape her, thus creating a terrifyingly unsafe family environment. Yet, Isabel's mother appeared to the outside world as a responsible citizen and dutiful mother who lived by the Bible. Her overt identity as a good mother belied her secret relationship with her overwhelmed daughter. Isabel, therefore, grew up as an undifferentiated psychological extension and literally a sexual slave whose main function was to provide sexual pleasure for her mother's sadistic, soul-murdering whims. So, in other words, she was *colonised* and exploited by the mother, who only paid lip service to her child's developmental imperatives and need for independence. In fact, the incest persisted into adulthood, well into her married life and even into the early years of treatment. Significantly, treatment could not proceed and there could be no progress until the trauma and the violence stopped.

Murderous rage coexisted with a desperate need for the mother, as object constancy was not acquired and she felt that she could not live without her. Internalisation of this profoundly conflicted relationship was lived out by the constant battling among her inner selves in the form of a chronic murder–suicide fantasy. On more than one occasion, it was almost realised. Ironically, Isabel's only source of peace of mind and feeling protected was knowing that at all times she had the means to do just that. Efforts on my part to "disarm" her, that is, confiscate or in other ways have her get rid of her large cache of pills, razor blades, knives, and so forth terrified and destabilised her. One time she bought a gun and needed involuntary hospitalisation in order to avert a most dangerous situation. After that major confrontation, a near-fatal overdose, and a period of supervised external control, we developed a better understanding of each other. Isabel was absolutely convinced that her mother had tried to kill her more than once when she was young and, as a survivor of filicidal persecution, she vowed "Never again!" She felt that she needed to have her escape route ready at all times if the mental pain became intolerable. Having the means to kill her external and internal persecutors readily available at all times actually calmed her down, so we negotiated peace treaties and cease-fires in the form of safety contracts.

Isabel was so divided and at war with herself that in certain states of mind, she completely believed that a horrible mistake had been made and that a "he" was born into the wrong body—a female body. At those times, "he" insisted upon being called another name (his name, Lester) or he would not respond and go into a rage. Because of a thick amnestic wall when "he" was "out", Isabel initially did not recognise that there was another self laying claim to the body and subsequently denied it until the evidence was overwhelming. Apparently, Isabel had left the body for extended periods of time when the abuse was overwhelming, and Lester was created and took over. In other words, the patient's early trauma was so profound and chronic that she lapsed into altered states for extended periods of time as a last-resort defence. Subsequently, these states became organised and personified and became the mental state known as Lester. Having inhabited the body during these most difficult times, he felt entitled to it, but was not even acknowledged until he became violent and demanding. Feeling utterly vulnerable and humiliated over "his" fate and the loss of control of what he believed was his, "he" was driven at all costs to claim the body. His vision was to alter the geography and boundaries by wanting to flatten the mountains of "his chest", by expanding "his waistline" to become more substantial in size, and by trying to dam up and stop the flow of his own "Red Sea", that is, the bloody waters flowing from the delta that regularly depleted him through some mysterious force controlled by his enemies. Lester was baffled, uncertain, always on guard, and chronically in a rage. If "he" had his way, "he" would kill off Isabel and her minions who threatened him and who, at times, had the power to take over the governance of the mind that made decisions about what should and should not be done with the body. His attacks were sporadic ambushes with knives and razors, causing much bloodshed, like terrorist attacks. Isabel lived in fear of these dreadful surprises and felt the most secure by having a powerful, hidden, secret weapon at all times just in case the pain became so great that she could kill herself and her persecutors once and for all. It was a huge bottle of pills kept in a top-secret location. Attempts to "disarm" her were frequently met with temporary regression and despair, so it eventually seemed more prudent to maintain the safety contract with her and trust her with her doomsday weapon. Significantly, she proved to be rather reliable in this realm.

Regarding the management of the body, there were huge disagreements over where things could be grown and when they could be harvested. When "he" was in control, the forests of his underarms and legs were free to grow as wildly and naturally as possible. On the other hand, when she had domination, the hair could not be more than stubble before the blades removed any evidence of growth. On many occasions, bloodshed resulted from major disputes over who had such growing rights and what the contours of these fields should look like. The bitterest fights occurred over the hair on the head, which was the most visible to the world and conveyed gender identity quite prominently. Attempts to alter the original plan by introducing very powerful chemical agents would have tipped the scales in favour of him, as this biological warfare would darken the hair, promote its growth on the face, and prepare the topography for permanent restructuring at the hands of an amoral technician who would excavate and remove from some areas while fabricating and erecting in another. Once completed, this massive rebuilding process would have obliterated all outward traces of the earliest claims to this highly contentious territory. This massive influx of male hormone from outside sources from all over the world could be a major, irreversible decision of such life-altering proportions that, unless there is total unanimity from all voting members in the mind, that is, the female, male, and child selves, any misgivings or dissent could ultimately erupt into full-scale internal civil war leading to anarchy, despair, and total deterioration. Indeed, when in control, Lester had not demonstrated any consistent ability to take care of the body for any extended period of time. His rage, trauma, and confusion did not allow him as yet to develop the necessary ego strength and psychic infrastructure to maintain this responsibility. If he were truly serious about living and not just destroying, it would take time and much external support. Given the patient's long history of periodic self-destructive behaviour of life-threatening severity, I tried to oversee the internal referendum in order to prevent any voter irregularities or fraud that was likely to occur. Nevertheless, knowing that I, the patient's analyst, did not have the wisdom to make the decision myself as to what the final shape and governance of the body should be, I encouraged a thoughtful period of reflection and open and honest internal debate as well as trying to anticipate what the future would look like.

Then all hell broke loose when Isabel's partner of many years staged a major revolt and threatened war, unable to tolerate the growing likelihood of having to shift from having a sexual relationship with a woman to being intimate with a bearded man. Neighbour and partner who had lived side by side under extremely harsh conditions for a long time were quickly reaching a point of irreconcilable differences. Neither could be likely to survive without the other, an uncannily similar situation to the patient's internal crisis, and the patient became paralysed with indecision and pessimism.

She could not proceed with the sex change, as it would not only destroy her relationship with her partner, but with herself. Yet, the profound realisation of both inner and outer interdependence meant that, in order for my patient to survive, there would have to be serious negotiations requiring major compromises, leaving all parties more than a bit dissatisfied. Not proceeding with it, however, perpetuated impotent rage and perpetual suicidal attacks. Ultimately, however, it needed to be realised that there had to be acceptance of the fact that all parts of the mind were connected, shared a common fate, were there for some reason, and had to be reckoned with.

Back to psychopolitics

If total integration or coalescing into a seamless, unified self were not possible, at the very least there needed to be mutual respect, ongoing internal communication, and accommodation for the different cultures that shared the body—in a sense, a psychological two-state solution with peaceful borders. In addition, any future major decisions required a mandate from all internal parties, from the most outspoken militant males to the weak, little-girl "cry-babies". Consequently, there would be no attempts to deny anyone's right to exist or to enact harsh regulations to suppress their freedom or rights of travel as long as they did not damage the body through bloodshed, hunger strikes, poisoning the water or food, biological warfare, or attempts to secede by amputation of body parts. A cessation of hostilities was essential, so a fragile truce—a psychological *hudna*, as it were—was established under the supervision of an outside observer. This external authority—one who supported the recognition and respect between the selves—was capable, under the most extreme circumstances, of implementing a form of martial law through involuntary hospitalisation in order to disarm the militants, provide emergency aid to the starving, and renegotiate the peace plan. Nevertheless, it was quite clear that the ultimate success of this therapeutic alliance, which was contingent upon something as strong and as weak as one's words, was based upon acceptance and trust out of necessity. Without some basis for trust and goodwill, such an alliance could not develop, even in the quiet times, so that there would be no foundation on which to stand during very difficult times. So, deciding on the final shape of the body might be analogous to negotiating the fate of the territories and the pre-1967 borders. Deciding on the control over the appearance of the head—or *caput* in Latin—might be analogous to the disagreements over the fate of Jerusalem—the capital—and the return of all displaced Palestinians and their descendants, which some Israelis fear might dilute, overwhelm, and possibly destroy the Jewish state, might be analogous to the patient's infusion of large amounts of male hormone to obliterate the traces of the original female body.

In contrast to the usual theories about the endless cycle of revenge and counter-revenge as a major dynamic for the hostilities in this part of the Middle East, the issue of internalised aggression perhaps needs to be considered also. What might appear as aggression in the service of survival and self-preservation could, in fact, be disguised suicidal aggression. While in some situations the suicidality might be quite blatant, especially with Palestinians who strap bombs to their chests in order to kill others, other policies and strategies might ultimately backfire if, indeed, the perceived enemy is part of the same "geopolitical self". With the ongoing confusion over identity, it is tempting to simplify things, which may only obfuscate matters further.

So, under the current conditions of ongoing trauma and violence, such regressed societies revert to black-and-white thinking, resulting in stereotyping the other and virulent xenophobic prejudice. In this situation, all Palestinians then become Muslims and all Muslims become suicide bomber terrorists, whereas all Israelis become Jews and all Jews become the purveyors of evil who conspire to take over the world. Then, through a perverse twisting of historical fact, Israeli Jews become equated with Nazis, so, by default, the Palestinians would have to become the victimised Jews! Furthermore, should Israel feel mortally endangered and exercise its nuclear option, or Sampson option (Hersh, 1991), Israel, like the biblical hero, would then destroy her enemies and quite possibly herself in the process. Israel would then become the ultimate suicide bomber. Perhaps such equations conceal a truth that, underneath it all, they are more the same than they are different and need one another for their mutual survival and welfare. Coming to this realisation is a political challenge that may be facilitated by applying certain psychological principles.

CHAPTER EIGHT

Post-9/11 world

"... a race from the kingdom of the Persians, an accursed race, a race utterly alienated from God ... has invaded the lands of those Christians and has depopulated them by the sword, pillage and fire; ... When they wish to torture people by a base death, they perforate their navels, and dragging forth the extremity of the intestines, bind it to a stake; then with flogging they lead the victim around until the viscera having gushed forth the victim falls prostrate upon the ground. Others they ... pierce with arrows. Others they ... cut through the neck with a single blow ... abominable rape of the women ... On whom therefore is the labor of avenging these wrongs ... if not upon you? ... Whoever, therefore, shall determine upon this holy pilgrimage ... shall wear the sign of the cross of the Lord on his forehead or on his breast ..."

(Pope Urban II's Speech Calling for the First Crusade)

Introduction

Following the September 11 attacks, an editorial in the *Journal of the American Psychoanalytic Association* stated,

> Future issues of JAPA will undoubtedly address September 11th in
> ways we might expect—papers on the psychological consequences of
> terror, loss, and bereavement, or on the psychology of international
> and cultural conflicts—as well as in ways we cannot predict. (Edi-
> torial, *Journal of the American Psychoanalytic Association*, 2001, p. 1107)

In this editorial, they cited Martin Bergmann's prophetic remarks: "It
is conceivable, although it may be too early to know for certain, that
September 11, 2001, will go down in history as one of those dates that
change the flow of history . . ." (Bergmann, 2004). While there have
been a number of publications, from what I could see there were
substantially fewer than I expected. They peaked between 2003 and
2005. For example, there was an article by Cabaniss, Forand, and
Roose (2004) that surveyed analysts and a relaxing of technique
following September 11 that quantified what Gensler and colleagues
described of their experiences in an article in *Contemporary Psychoanalysis* (Gensler et al., 2002). There was an article by Wurmser (2004)
on terrorism and genocidal prejudice. There was a book review by
Simon (2010) on therapy after September 11, as well as a book review
by Apfel and Simon (2005) reviewing Varvin and Volkan's book,
Violence or Dialogue? (2003) that, among other things, had a fascinating
paper by Thomson that viewed the attacks from an evolutionary
perspective describing them as ". . . male bonded coalitionary violence
with lethal raiding against innocents . . ." (Thomson, 2003, p. 73).
Their book review also covered the important text edited by Coates,
Rosenthal, and Schecter, *Trauma and Human Bonds* (2003). In their
review, Apfel and Simon observe the perennial avoidance of atrocities
and social catastrophe:

> We have found in both the psychoanalytic literature and clinical teach-
> ing little guidance on the more general questions of how we can be
> better at admitting patients' political concerns and allegiances into the
> analytic discourse. Is there denial or minimization on the part of
> patients, on the part of analysts, or some interaction between the two?
> (Apfel & Simon, 2005, p. 196)

The question of this difficulty is seen in our daily clinical work
when patients avoid addressing issues related to trauma and issues
related to socially sanctioned trauma, which was discovered decades
ago by pioneer researchers on the Holocaust (Bergmann & Jucovy,

1982). If it was not directly asked about, it just might never come up. Resistance and counter-resistance could conspire to exclude the reality of incalculable loss, grief, and man's capacity for unspeakable cruelty. While the other journals available on the PEP Web and a number of other distinguished authors have made significant contributions to this topic, the overall number of articles specifically addressing September 11 seemed to be remarkably limited. For example, there were publications of research on infants and their mothers (Pierce, 2006), personal reflections (Hirsch, 2003), and the complications in termination (I. Brenner, 2006c). While there are 155 allusions to September 11, only ten, including editorials and book reviews, were published in the *Journal of the American Psychoanalytic Association*. Overall, there seem to be only fourteen original articles in total. However, I do realise that I only accessed those with this date in their title, and there are more that have not been recognised, such as the work of the Section on Social Responsibility of the Division of Psychoanalysis of the American Psychological Association.

Nevertheless, if this observation is valid, it suggests a parallel institutional process to our individual tendency to avoid or not be able to process fully such utterly overwhelming experiences. This is an area of particular interest to me, as it occupies what I call the "dark matters of the mind". Dark matter, as noted earlier, is a reference to the mysterious, invisible matter in the universe that astrophysicists now realise comprises much of the universe and has an enormous effect on everything that the human eye can see as well as what it cannot see. I would contend that in the human mind, our dark matter consists of dissociation and its vicissitudes.

After 9/11

Especially on the anniversaries of those unimaginable airline crashes into the Twin Towers and the Pentagon that took so many lives, affected so many others, destroyed so much property, and continue to exert their repercussions, I suspect that most, if not all of us, have indelible memories of where we were, what we were doing, and who we were with when we heard the news or were personally involved in the atrocities of that day. The patient who first told me the news immediately realised that she would forever be associated in my mind with this catastrophe, which she dreaded relaying to me. She was correct. This *in vivo* illustration of the particular quality of traumatic memory does not need scientific proof. Moreover, as Freud pointed out, the opposite effect on memory may occur also: ". . . that nothing of the forgotten traumas shall be remembered and nothing repeated" (Freud, 1939a, p. 75). As we learn more and more about peri-traumatic dissociation, we see that disruptions of perception, memory, processing, consciousness, and even identity may occur during shocks of this nature. In addition, knowing and not knowing, being here and not being here, and being me and not being me are dissociative states of mind.

So, it is my hypothesis that, to some degree or other, most of us have experienced dissociation with regard to the events of September 11. While each of us may have slightly different ideas as to what dissociation might mean, I think we all would essentially agree that there is a particularly effective division in the mind as a means of keeping things separate. As Breuer and Freud said, there may be a splitting of consciousness, splitting of a personality, and a splitting of the mind (Freud, 1895d). The latter, as noted earlier, is especially significant, as it refers to the simultaneous existence of conscious and unconscious mental content that challenges classical theory and underlies the mental structure in DID. In this mental organisation, the dissociative defences are characterised by amnesia, different selves, denial of reality, disavowal of internal reality, and disowning of mental contents. Intentionally as well as automatically, things get put out of the mind for dynamic reasons and, as noted above, such a defensive altered state without a disturbance in self-constancy might underlie the "psychopathology of everyday life" (Freud, 1901b) in parapraxes and bungled actions (I. Brenner, 2009a). And if some aspects of September 11 have been unmetabolised and warded off, an event that occurred in the spring of 2011 might have helped bring it back into our awareness.

Finding Bin Laden

The dramatic announcement of the long-awaited and doubt-that-it-would-ever-happen capture and killing of Osama bin Laden on 1 May 2011 brought forth an immediate collective sigh of relief and a sense of jubilation in the USA. From impromptu crowds around the White House, Times Square, and Ground Zero to the cheers of the fans at a Phillies game, citizens eagerly listened as President Obama firmly told us that "Justice has been done." An elite group of approximately two dozen Navy SEALs in stealth helicopters, UH-60 Black Hawks, crossed into Pakistan just under the radar, as it were, from neighbouring Afghanistan in order to storm bin Laden's fortified mansion. The world's most wanted and hunted man was living with his three wives and thirteen children not in a cave in the mountainous, no-man's border land where he was suspected to have been protected by fiercely loyal tribesmen, but in a sedate, well-patrolled suburb within a kilometre of the elite Pakistan Military Academy located in Abbottabad, a short drive from the country's capital of Islamabad. During this daring and already legendary mission, bin Laden and several others, including a woman, were shot dead. Amid ever conflicting accounts of this raid, one of bin Laden's three wives reportedly was used by him as a human shield during his struggle before he was shot in the head. Others were handcuffed and spirited away, along with bin Laden's corpse, less than forty minutes later. Documents, CD-ROMs, and hard drives were collected by Special Forces while the inner circle of the White House watched the spectacle on a huge television screen in real time. An iconic photograph of this group includes Secretary of State Hillary Clinton, whose wide-eyed expression while holding her mouth with her hand evokes the tension and gravity of this situation.

Questions and controversies immediately arose: how was bin Laden located? Why did it take so long? What is the value of torture in eliciting the reliable information that might have led to his discovery? What were the role and the possible complicity of the Pakistani military? What about the decision to bury bin Laden at sea and the refusal to show photographs of the alleged mastermind of 9/11 with a gaping, bloody bullet hole in his head to "prove" he was actually found and killed? What about the legality of killing an unarmed man and not bringing him to trial? Occurring shortly after the fiftieth anniversary of the capture and trial of Adolph Eichmann, a comparison of the historical parallels and differences was quickly made.

The story changed so often that we quickly discovered that we would know, but never really know, what had happened. Knowing and not knowing is a dissociative state of mind that, on a societal level, was enacted by the Administration's response and intentional or unintentional leaking of reports. Moreover, this type of disinformation lends itself to conspiracy theories and societal paranoia. An absurdist version of the assassination of Osama bin Laden demonstrates an attempt to cope with this uncertainty through humour. A satirical article in *The New Yorker* describes different versions of what happened through several fictional accounts of Navy SEALs. Here are two excerpts:

> We flew in low and fast. Moonless night. Heavy gunfire from compound. Responded in kind. Lead copter provided cover. Second copter deployed two ropes, and sixteen SEALs were on the ground in four minutes. Took house. Searched the three floors. Engaged hundreds of enemy combatants, all of whom were firing, but we did this special dance move so they kept missing us. Main target was on top floor and used female as shield, though maybe "shield" is the wrong word, as she just happened to be standing in front of him. He was trying to fire a rocket-propelled grenade from a shoulder mount, but it kept slipping off his shoulder. His wife said he wasn't doing it right. He said he was and that it was broken. They argued. We left.

> Flying low, we approached from the west, and initially met enemy fire from the compound. Then we realized it wasn't gunfire. It was a campfire. A little one. I think some kids were camping. Or maybe homeless guys. Or it might have been one of those outdoor fire pits, which I love because you can just sit and talk and enjoy friends, no cell phones or computers. Anyway, we landed and stormed the house and were met by gunfire, but then realized it was coming from the TV. The bin Ladens were up late watching the Bruce Willis movie "Die Hard", which, how ironic is that? At first, they were confused, but then Mrs. bin Laden asked if we could leave our guns outside, which we did, and then we watched the rest of the movie, and then Mr. bin Laden died of a heart attack. (Kenney, 2011, p. 39)

What set the stage for this riveting conclusion to finding the "bad guy" was Mr Bush's reactivation of images of the "Wild West". He vowed to "hunt down" the perpetrators. When al-Qaeda was linked to the attack, he declared that bin Laden was "Wanted: Dead or Alive" and almost immediately posters in the style of that era began to proliferate. After the raid on his compound, we then learnt that the code name of this mission was "Geronimo", which paid homage to the last great Apache leader, who defiantly battled United States troops and hid out in the Sierra Madres, the North American analogue of the Tora

Bora Mountains where bin Laden eluded United States forces. Parenthetically, military historians note that Geronimo's name was first invoked in an earlier time when the first United States paratroopers, in order to muster up the courage to jump from an open plane with parachutes, would yell out his name in an effort to incorporate his bravery: "Geronimo!" Growing up in the post-war era of the 1950s, we baby boomers feasted on films which immortalised and glorified the Second World War, where more than one paratrooper was portrayed on the silver screen screaming "Geronimo!" From an anthropologic perspective, since it has long been a custom among certain warring tribes to cook and ingest certain body parts of their bravest enemies defeated in battle in order to incorporate and acquire their characteristics, perhaps these early jumpers spat out the name "Geronimo" as a reversal of this cannibalistic heritage.

Meanwhile, back at the celebrations, as though they were Munchkins in the *Wizard of Oz* singing "Ding Dong! The witch is dead!", spontaneous merrymaking burst forth over the demise of the founder of al-Qaeda, who helped usher in and then personified the era of terrorism for America and her allies. We saw and heard the degradation of his image from an elusive mastermind to a weak old man in a blanket, rocking in a chair, holding the remote control of an old television set watching videos of himself. We saw images of him dyeing his beard and rehearsing his lines. We were told that he had an extensive library of pornography and that he died a coward as he shoved his wife towards the Navy SEALs in order to protect himself. Bin Laden's deterioration and irrelevance in today's geopolitical world was proclaimed. Indeed, the Arab Spring, facilitated by social media— Facebook, Twitter, and YouTube—empowered a younger generation more interested in democracy than re-establishing the Caliphate. Yet, even among those who felt a sense of belated relief over his killing, many also experienced a sense of uneasiness over such jubilance in places like Times Square, which portrayed to the world the bloodlust and barbarous, vengeance-seeking nature of Americans. At the very least, it raised an ethical question about celebrating the death of another human being, even a mass murderer. So, the debate over the right to party in the streets *vs.* having a more sober, national moment of reflection came to the fore as we were reminded of our identities as citizens of America, whose fellow citizens and sovereign spaces were destroyed by a seemingly preternatural arch-enemy.

On a personal level, survivors of the attacks and those whose family members were murdered made public statements of relief, gratitude, and being able to sleep better at night but, as psycho-analysts and those who have had first-hand experiences there, we know the story is infinitely more complex. This suffering has taken many forms, including an almost invisible type, as seen in this not unfamiliar story.

Case report

A young man was training in a building next to the World Trade Center before being sent to London for a job in investment banking. He was in the middle of a lecture in a large auditorium when the first plane hit. It sounded like a huge explosion and his building shook. Some went to a window to look while he cautiously stayed back for fear of flying glass. Many in the group thought it was an explosion on the street, so they hesitated exiting the building. While they were waiting for information, the second plane hit. Again, there was an explosion and the whole building shook. Then, someone said a plane had hit the World Trade Center.

Finally, people started to exit in an orderly fashion down six or seven flights of stairs on to the street. By the time he got outside, bodies were already falling from the World Trade Center inferno. Some froze in horror and just looked upwards at the inconceivable sight, but he moved as quickly as possible uptown, walking all the way up to his company's mid-town lodging for the trainees. He then called his mother to say he was safe, but in his confused state of mind he called her at an office at which she had not worked for many years. He then stayed indoors watching television for the rest of the day. The next day he went to a female relative's house out of town and stayed for several days. He did not leave her side and was anxiously attached to her. He avoided contact with his parents, perhaps in the service of trying to suppress his memories, knowing how worried they were and how they would have encouraged him to talk about it.

The company sent him to the UK early. He chose an apartment near his office, always walking a half-hour to work regardless of the weather. He never took the subway or public transportation in his first years there and only rarely took a cab. It took him more than five years to take the subway in a non-rush hour. Then, one fateful summer morning, he got on a bus because he was late for work, and that was the day that one of the London subway bombers got on a bus and blew it up. He was very shaken up and tried to joke about how he felt like a jinx because he broke his rule once and on that day there was an attack. In a black humour-type way, he lamented that he would have to notify any city before he moved there.

When confronted with a career-determining decision to stay in the UK or return to the USA, he chose to return to the USA but did not want to live in New York City. Unfortunately, his only option was New York City and he ended up returning to the "scene of the crime". Again, since he had to live within walking distance of his office because of his fear of mass transportation, not surprisingly he ended up a few blocks from Ground Zero.

It was not until 2009 that he took his father to Ground Zero, showed him the building that he was in, and disclosed anything at all about that day.

When his brother called him in early May 2011, to alert him that President Obama would be on television late that Sunday night to announce bin Laden's death, he stayed up to watch the announcement. He could not sleep afterwards.

The unnamed day

This man, after more than a decade, has yet to be able to really talk to anyone about his experience. Instead of sleeping more soundly, he became plagued by what he tried not to think about and put out of his mind. He could not escape his trauma by moving to London and, indeed, uncannily repeated it after breaking his rule not to use public transportation. Now he is back in New York City, the last place he wanted to be, living within walking distance of the World Trade Center. The repetition compulsion is alive and well in his mind.

Is he desensitising himself as the cognitive therapists would want to do in order to treat his trauma? Or is he being so over-stimulated and re-traumatised that his mind needs to shut down and continue to wall off what he remembers as well as what he has not been able to remember and metabolise? If so, how might we understand what mental processes are involved? Denial? Disavowal? Repression?

Splitting? Dissociation? What is going on his mind, and what is going on in our minds as we experience each anniversary of the events of September 11?

Most of our holidays and remembrance days have names: Christmas, New Year's, Valentine's Day, Martin Luther King Day, Easter, Memorial Day, Independence Day, Labor Day, Pearl Harbor Day, Kennedy's Assassination, D-Day, VJ Day, etc. Those that commemorate secular events are fixed on the calendar, whereas others are based on a formula, for example, the fourth Thursday of November for Thanksgiving. The fact that September 11 has not acquired such a name and that most people simply refer to that day by its date, or simply "9/11", is perhaps quite significant. Does that lack of a name tell us that this national trauma has yet to be symbolised, formulated, mentalised, metabolised, or processed? In our minds, 9/11 easily merges into 911, the all-purpose emergency number, and that is exactly what that day was: a national emergency of the highest order.

It was striking to me that the only other commemorative day that immediately came to my mind that is referred to solely by its date is the Jewish holiday of Tisha B'av, or the 9th of Av. That day also memorialises enormous tragedy—the destruction of two Temples 565 years apart that have traditionally been thought to have occurred on the same day. It has been described as the saddest day in Jewish history. It is an annual day of fasting, prayer, and asking for forgiveness for not following God's laws and being punished, resulting in severe repercussions for the Jewish people. Recall the retrospective prophecies of the radical Islamic clerics and fundamentalist Christian preachers who declared that the destruction of the Twin Towers was also due to the wrath of God. Here, it was for sinful sexual practices and debauchery in the USA, of which homosexuality was especially singled out. Ten years after September 11, on 24 June 2011, New York State became the sixth and largest state to legalise gay marriage. Could this development be seen as a societal undoing of this religious curse from ten years earlier?

I wonder how long it took for our country to name 7 December 1941, the day that Roosevelt solemnly announced ". . . will live in infamy", as Pearl Harbor Day. How long did it take for it to be symbolised? The attacks on September 11 occurred in Washington, DC, and in New York City, both hugely populated areas, and the abortive attack on the White House ended in a plane crash in Shanksville, PA.

The heroic uprising of those passengers, whose last harrowing moments we could listen to from recordings, came to symbolise our determination to mobilise and fight back. But this act of war was different from the surprise attack on our military installations in Hawaii.

Societal regression

From the eyewitnesses, the survivors, those emotionally connected to the victims, and those exposed to the relentless images in our mass media, we have all been affected. Changes have been observed to occur in our society, and they are consistent with the symptoms of regression in traumatised societies that have been described by Volkan. He has described more than a dozen features (Volkan 1981, 1997, 2004) when large groups are under severe stress. For example, they might revert to fixation points in that group's history to times of both positive and negative events of major importance in that group's formation. The motivation for such a regression is to regain a sense of cohesion of their large-group identity, which Volkan likens to a large tent. Under this metaphorical "big top", millions of people who do not know each other may share the same ethnic, religious, ideological, and/or national sense of sameness. Under this canvas, the large group shares a developmental representation of its history, so that under threats to its existence—a societal sense of annihilation anxiety, as it were—it takes whatever steps are deemed necessary for its survival in order to regain its integrity and sense of identity. In a sense, the group's threatened fragmentation and disintegration can be seen as a dissociative process in which formerly functioning aspects of the society become disconnected and lose their overall sense of co-ordination and identity and separate along inherent lines of cleavage, such as ancient tribal loyalties or religious affiliations as was seen during the disintegration of the Soviet Union. The major signs of large-group regression identified by Volkan are:

1. Group members lose their individuality;
2. The group rallies blindly around the leader;
3. The leadership ruins "basic trust" within the family and creates a new kind of family hierarchy and morality that interferes with

roles within the family (especially women's roles), with normal childhood development, and with the adolescent passage;

4. The group becomes divided into "good" segments—those who obediently follow the leader—and "bad"—those perceived to oppose the leader;

5. The group creates a sharp "us" and "them" division between itself and "enemy" groups;

6. The group's shared morality or belief system becomes increasingly absolutist and punitive towards those perceived to be in conflict with it;

7. The group uses extensive introjective and projective mechanisms and may experience accompanying massive mood swings from shared depressive feelings to collective paranoid expectations;

8. The group feels "entitled" to do anything to maintain its identity;

9. Group members experience increased magical thinking and reality-blurring;

10. The group experiences new cultural phenomena or adopts modified versions of traditional societal customs;

11. The group's chosen traumas and glories are reactivated, resulting in a time collapse;

12. The leadership creates a break in the historical continuity of the group and fills the gap with elements such as "new" nationalism, ethnic sentiments, religious fundamentalism or ideology, accompanying "new" morality, and sometimes a "new" history of the group purged or unwanted elements;

13. Group members begin to experience the group's shared symbols as "protosymbols";

14. Shared images depict enemy groups with symbols or protosymbols associated with bodily waste, demons, or subhuman traits;

15. The group experiences geographical or legal boundaries as a "second skin";

16. The group focuses on minor differences between itself and enemy groups;

17. Group members become overly concerned with the notion of "blood" and an associated homogeneous or purified existence;

18. The group engages in behaviors symbolizing purification;

19. Group taste has difficulty differentiating what is beautiful from what is ugly;

20. The group turns its physical environment into a gray-brown, amorphous (symbolically fecal) structure. (Volkan, 2002, pp. 458–459)

Following the attacks of September 11, Mayor Giuliani's leadership was inspiring, despite many New Yorkers' feelings about him prior to that day. Seeing President Bush at the ruins with a bullhorn rallying us and the troops was empowering as well. We all felt like Americans except for those of us who did not, and those of us who did not were not seen as patriots: you were either with us or against us. This polarisation is evidence of splitting. I would contend, however, that what underlies this splitting is an even deeper disconnection, which would be in the realm of dissociation and will be elaborated upon further. We experienced the rise of Islamophobia, dehumanisation through racial profiling, and increased fear, prejudice, and violence against those of Middle Eastern and Muslim backgrounds. I witnessed this phenomenon first-hand when returning from an international psychoanalytic conference with a dark-skinned colleague who has a decidedly Muslim-sounding name. After putting his his carry-on bag through the scanner, he was immediately surrounded by armed security personnel. He had forgotten to return his simultaneous translation device and it looked suspicious. When confronted with the alleged weapon, he exclaimed "Oh, shit!", which further incriminated him. In reality he was actually upset because he had lost his $300 deposit by failing to return the device.

Aggressively infused societal customs, such as more vehement campaign rhetoric, more threats, and literal violence levied against our leaders, have occurred. Pieces of the wreckage of the World Trade Center became linking objects and took on enormous value and psychological significance, especially as the remains of so many lost loved ones were hard to identify and retrieve. On an individual level, a man I saw a number of times at the Family Center at the pier in New York City had transformed the outgoing message of his girlfriend into an auditory linking object. She had been very upset with him over his ambivalence and reluctance to marry her and then, unfortunately, she was killed in one of the Towers. He was in total shock and disbelief over her death, waiting for her to return so he could make it right with her. He was unable to change the message many, many weeks later and listened to it furtively in great agony.

Mr Bush's invoking of the glorious old West with his reference to a "Wanted: Dead or Alive" poster was a reactivation of a "chosen glory", whereas reminders of Pearl Harbor were a reactivation of a "chosen trauma". There has been tremendous tightening of our borders between Mexico and Canada, with controversial deportation legislation for illegal immigrants in Arizona. There is more erosion of trust in our leaders, governmental institutions, and with our neighbours, as well as wholesale violation of our privacy through domestic surveillance of our citizenry. Recently leaked accounts of the scope of domestic spying corroborated earlier reports in which ThinThread, the software breakthrough employed by the National Security Agency, is reportedly capable of storing copies of everyone's emails, billing records, and phone logs (Bamford, 2008; Mayer, 2011). While we mental health professionals rail against the invasion of our patients' privacy and the releasing of records, all of our privacy may be on the verge of being a thing of the past in the name of national security. And, as seen in the last presidential election, tremendous interest has been shown in the personality of our presidential candidates. The question of Mr Obama's religion, the origin of his middle name, Hussein, and whether or not he was even a legitimate American citizen became campaign issues that have continued throughout his presidency. The rise of religious fundamentalism and the focus of pundits on red and blue states are further evidence of splitting in our society, all suggestive that we have experienced regression in our society.

Our myth of invincibility was shattered. Our illusion of safety was shattered. The fantasy that this is the best country in the world in which to live was also shattered. We know it and do not know it. For example, our infrastructure in many places has not kept pace with population growth and changes in technology, so it is deteriorating. Many roads, bridges, tunnels, and highways have not been kept in good repair or are frankly obsolete. Having worked for the Highway Research Information Service of the National Research Council of the National Academy of Sciences many years ago when I was working my way through college, I was a tiny cog in the machinery responsible for computerising all their files. Therefore, I had the opportunity to read about the projects that were under way or planned at that time in our country. I learnt all kinds of highway trivia, including the fact that in New Jersey there are more miles of highway per capita than any other state in the country. As a result, I took a deep interest in the phenomenon of pothole repair, which might be seen as an index of infrastructure maintenance. During a recent trip to Europe, I spent some time in Zurich, Switzerland, a city that is consistently rated one of the top cities in the world in which to live. One of the first things that one notices is that everything works there! Everything—from the tiniest appliances to the seamless integration of punctual, efficient, ecologically sensitive, mass transportation—works. Everything is clean and the people adhere to an honour system of payment of fares. Even the public water fountains have water of such clarity and safety that people fill their water bottles directly from the mouths of the gargoyles throughout the city.

Returning to dissociation: individual and societal

How do we cope with the deterioration in so many aspects of the quality of our living and still maintain a fiction that this is the best place in the world to live? How do we convince ourselves that we are eating real food when so much of it is processed, denatured, and then artificially coloured, flavoured, shaped, and injected with synthetic additives to conform to the nutritional analysis on the labels? And what about the epidemic of obesity as food manufacturers entice us with excessive fat, sugar, and salt? What kinds of psychological mechanisms are needed in order to maintain this duality? I would suggest that dissociation, which may encompass denial, disavowal, splitting, and motivated forgetting, would be the most parsimonious answer. In the relational view of the mind, the mind is seen as

> a configuration of discontinuous, shifting states of consciousness with varying degrees of access to perception and cognition. Some of these self-states are hypnoidally unlinked from perception at any given moment of normal mental functioning . . . while other self-states are virtually foreclosed from such access because of their original lack of linguistic symbolization. (Bromberg, 1996, p. 57)

Relational theorists have appropriated the term "dissociation" and maintain that it underlies all other defences. Many find this hypothesis untenable. In a conversation with Arnold Goldberg many years ago, he felt that the test of a good model of the mind is to take it and push it as far as one can to try to explain as much as possible (Goldberg, 1991). Ironically, however, he insisted that Kohut's model of the vertical split was not intended to explain DID. Dissociation was not a Kohutian concept. But, what really is the difference between the contradictory self-states in the Kohutian mind that are separated by the vertical split through disavowal and the self-states in the relational mind that are separated by their version of dissociation? Moreover, how similar is dissociation to Schafer's "disclaimed actions" (Schafer, 1973) or Green's "work of the negative" (Green, 1999)? When reviewing such definitions, one may fluctuate between the excitement of a metapsychological debate between great thinkers and the ennui of the narcissism of minor differences.

Nevertheless, the problem with DID is that it utilises dissociation to unprecedented levels, and with a pseudo-externalised displacement, there develop a cadre of selves with their own cohesion that ward off a deep sense of annihilation anxiety and separation anxiety as the overall patient lacks both self-constancy and object constancy. In addition, it has been discovered up to this point that there are five organising influences that contribute to the genesis of these personifications. They are: (1) perverse sexuality, (2) the dream ego and autosymbolic phenomena, (3) intergenerational transmission of trauma, (4) near-death experiences, and (5) the divisive effect of aggression and its vicissitudes (I. Brenner, 2001, 2004).

Case report

During her hospitalisation after a suicide attempt, Mrs H was recounting how oppressed and controlled by her husband she was feeling. She had regressed from being a functional professional and mother to a chronic mental patient. The patient had a history of severe early sexual trauma, as well as an incident in college that she was unable to talk about and after which she hid in her closet for many days. This assault came to light during her hospitalisation when, during an amnestic state, she began to talk like a very young girl and recounted hiding in her dorm room in fear. I had been seeing her five days a week as both an inpatient and an outpatient for about two years at this time.

In a dissociated state of mind, the patient identified herself by an androgynous first name and politely explained as best as possible what had happened. Mrs H, she noted in her rather objective, professional-sounding way, was overwhelmed with the ongoing conversation in therapy about her marital relationship and her sexual obligations as a wife. She also revealed great anxiety over her children's emerging sexuality, using that as a rationale for eavesdropping on their telephone conversations. She then narrated in the third person how, when the patient was in college, she was accosted on the street one evening, beaten severely, gang-raped at knifepoint, and left in a bloodied state in an abandoned field to die or fend for herself.

The memory of her attackers, a group of African-American men, was constantly being revived by the African-American men who were patients and who also worked as staff at the hospital. Unbeknown to Mrs H, on an unconscious level she was being triggered constantly and her internal helpers, such as the nurse-like self who emerged, were unable to help her stay in control. The result was a seizure-like reliving of the life-threatening rape in graphic, motoric detail in a dissociated state, after which the patient would recover with amnesia, almost indistinguishable from *bona fide* postictal confusion. Critical experiences like these—and the less medically dramatic but no less profoundly emotional phenomena in the transference working analytically with such higher-functioning patients—have led me to the conclusion that the role of dissociation and the nature of the selves in DID are more than "just a special case" (Kiefer, 2011) of the ubiquitous dissociated self-states described by the relational theorists. In the former, the therapists are prone to criticism for iatrogenically creating different alter personalities, whereas in the latter therapists are required to recognise and delineate the self-states that can only be accessed through enactment and self-disclosure.

Mrs H was a chronic intermittent suicide risk on a perpetual misplaced mission to avenge herself against her attackers in one state of mind, punish herself for letting it happen in another, and all the while, as "herself", desperately trying not to be flooded by intolerably painful memories of terror, humiliation, and utter helplessness over a surprise attack. She became hyper-religious and one of her selves even sought out exorcism by a fundamentalist clergyman in order to purge herself of Satan's influence. Meanwhile, in another self, she participated in sadomasochistic, heterosexual relations with a man in his van while a patient in the hospital. As part of her effort both to punish her body by depriving it of nutrients as well as in fantasy controlling her inner and outer dangerous worlds, she became suicidally anorexic, practising starving, binging, and purging to a point of medical emergency. Then, in a childlike state, she would retreat into a fantasy land, drawing pictures of idyllic landscapes and sunny days.

In an unsuccessful effort to hasten the therapeutic process and promote an integration of her disparate selves long before she was ready, I asked the patient if she would be agreeable to videotaping some of our sessions during hospitalisation about a year later. I had hoped that, by viewing herself on tape "while her alters were out", she would begin to recognise, accept, and, I hoped, own that, indeed, she was "sharing the body" with other selves during which time she was essentially amnestic. If she could take that step, then it would facilitate her becoming "co-conscious" to observe herself while in the dissociative state and begin to own more and more of her psyche. Her condition at that time was incompatible with survival as one self, a genderless, destructive force bent on destroying Mrs H had a quasi-delusional belief that in doing so it would be able to take over the body and prevent any future harm from the outside. In the process of trying to destroy Mrs H, "Fate" had already seriously self-mutilated but felt no pain during her self-inflicted surgery due to autohypnotic analgesic properties that the patient was able to induce in these profoundly dissociated states.

When Mrs H viewed herself in the video pacing around and talking about Mrs H in the third person in "Fate's" distinctive voice, she started to laugh, turned away, and exclaimed "That's not me! That's not me!" Shortly thereafter, she spontaneously lapsed into a trance and another self emerged, unable to tolerate what her eyes had seen.[7] This malignant form of gaze aversion resulted in a turning away from an overwhelming perception, resulting in denial of reality, disavowal of her internal reality, and a type of negation (Akhtar, 2011; I. Brenner, 2009a) whereby she disowned what was in her mind through a negative statement.

Conclusion: a model for a traumatised, dissociated society

Based on my work with such patients with DID, I have extrapolated from this model and, as in Chapter Seven, have applied it to traumatised societies as well, building upon Volkan's perspective (I. Brenner, 1996, 2009a). In our post 9/11 world, we might consider some of the same phenomena observed in our society as large-group manifestations of a dissociated mind. For Mrs H, her different personifications embodied the rage, pain, grief, guilt, fear, regressive flight, and sexualisation of her trauma in amnestic states. Mrs H, in her dissociated state of mind, fought off the wrong enemy who resembled her attackers, engaged in extreme religious practices, attempted to destroy her own body, depleted her valuable resources, engaged in life-threatening eating practices, spied on her daughter, mistrusted her husband, escaped into childlike fantasy, and regularly participated in sadomasochistic sexual behaviour while hospitalised. Although bound by the rules of the hospital, she bypassed them when she was in the van. In a sense, she was in the hospital and not in the hospital. While all this was happening, she was desperately trying not to remember what had occurred to her at an earlier time. Yet, she was repeating it and punishing herself for it at the same time in her dissociated, personified states of mind. With a little bit of poetic licence, one might extrapolate to our traumatised society—the un-United States of America—struggling with its legacy post 9/11, as listed below

1. The military fought "the wrong enemy", attacking Iraq under the pretence that Saddam Hussein was closely linked to al-Qaeda and had huge amounts of weapons of mass destruction earmarked for us and our allies.

2. There has been a rise of fundamentalism and religious extremism that has entered the political process in unprecedented ways, essentially rewriting the basic tenet of separation of church and state.

3. There has been an increase in home-grown hate groups and militias whose beliefs are bound to ridding the country of outsiders, foreigners, and minorities in order to save it from destruction. However, in the process of such mass murder and deportation, their wish to take over control of the government would be utterly destructive and suicidal to this country.

4. Through greed, mismanagement, and short-sightedness, our own economy is suffering greatly with unemployment and increased aggression in the populace. In the midst of all this, there is an epidemic of obesity from grossly unhealthy eating practices.

5. In the name of national security, the Department of Homeland Security and the National Security Agency have justified domestic spying on an unprecedented level, bypassing the constitutional rights of our citizens.

6.   Films and entertainment with escapist themes, such as fantasy worlds, science fiction plots, comedy, and nostalgic times became quite prevalent. Further study of this phenomenon is warranted to compare it to other times of trauma and great stress.

7.   In the name of national security, the capture, sequestering, and harsh interrogation of thousands of suspected terrorists were carried out in Guantanamo, a place that is not really the USA but was appropriated by the USA and manned by United States citizens in order to bypass legal constraints over torture. It has the quality of a dissociated, sadomasochistic enactment: it is here and not here. We have known about it and not known about it, and it has been owned and disowned by us.

8.   There had been considerable difficulty in creating a suitable memorial at Ground Zero, the crime scene, which was cordoned off with yellow police tape and barricades, the killing field for thousands of people. The problems of remembrance, mourning, and reconciling the murder of innocent people persist and have been mired in conflict, politics, and religion. The conflict over building a Muslim community centre near Ground Zero is an example. Like the controversy over Carmelite nuns building a convent in Auschwitz, such a plan was offensive and downright repugnant to those of different backgrounds and sensibilities.

While it is possible to overstate the legacy of September 11 and over-diagnose our difficulties as a consequence of this attack, it is also quite possible to understate its impact on our society. Just as longitudinal studies on mothers and their infants born a decade ago will reveal more and more to us over time, on an individual level so, too, will the passage of time teach us about the fates of our institutions after this national trauma. Considering that a dissociative process may be operative could expand our understanding.

PART IV
TECHNICAL REALM

CHAPTER NINE

Interpretation or containment?

"What if you slept
And what if
In your sleep
You dreamed
And what if
In your dream
You went to heaven
And there plucked a strange and beautiful flower
And what if
When you awoke
You had that flower in your hand
Ah, what then?"

(Anonymous)

Introduction

In the minds of more and more analytically orientated clinicians, the word "dissociation" is associated with trauma. In the past, this area has been thought to be beyond the domain of psychoanalysis, especially when the aftermath of actual experience competes with psychic reality for consideration in the treatment. Since the introduction of the term "disaggregation" by Pierre Janet more than a century ago (Janet, 1889), its English counterpart, dissociation, has had a rather "chequered history" (Glover, 1943) in the psychoanalytic movement. With Freud's determination to create a totally new psychology with its own original terms (Makari, 2008), he discarded Janet's phraseology but incorporated and elaborated upon his notion of a split in the psyche. Despite its own unique history, the term "dissociation" has, nevertheless, suffered from the same malady of conceptual blurriness and ambiguity that afflicts other essential terms such as "splitting" (Lichtenberg & Slap, 1973; Pruyser, 1975). Indeed, different theoretical movements have adopted or appropriated certain terms for their central defensive operations, such as repression or horizontal splitting for the Freudians, primitive splitting for the Kleinians, vertical splitting for the Kohutians, and now dissociation for the relational theorists, which is becoming better appreciated in our overall understanding of the psyche. The term "dissociation" has seen a rise in popularity, as approximately one-half of the 115 articles on PEP Web with "dissociation" in the title have been published within the last decade.

The idea of a grand unifying theory that encompasses valid ideas from competing theories and has the most explanatory value has yet to be formulated. However, given the fact that this elusive goal has yet to be accomplished by more hard-core sciences such as physics, perhaps we should not be surprised. Certainly, with the explosion of knowledge in the neurosciences, the often-stated wish in the analytic community for an update of Freud's *Project for a Scientific Psychology* is like trying to hit a moving target. There is so much to assimilate. Yet, as we deal with the mental representations of these processes in our brains and, in particular, those related to psychic trauma, it is clear that the more we know about neural networks, memory systems, the amygdala and fear conditioning, the pleasure centres, and neuro-humoural influences, the closer we come to connecting the dots between observable psychological phenomena and brain function.

When we read the literature pertaining to dissociation, we see a lot of related words that amplify and elaborate on various definitions of dissociation but also add to our sense of confusion. We have "dissociation" and "dissociative". We have "dissociated relational unconscious", "dissociative personality", "dissociative character", "dissociative self", "dissociated self-states" and dissociopath". And, in their effort to come up with a model to supplant the Freudian structural model and the object relations model of the mind in which splitting figures prominently, it has been suggested that perhaps relational theorists have gone a little too far in one aspect of their thinking. The idea of a shared relational unconscious, or a two-person psychology, then becomes yet another one-person psychology with a shared mind, which overemphasises the importance of interaction in the analytic dyad (Blechner, 2010). In another realm, however—that pertaining to DID—I do not think they have gone far enough.

My earlier thinking about dissociation focused on it as an auto-hypnotic defence against over-stimulation and trauma that could change in function and then be redeployed to ward off anxiety from internal conflict. As such, I became able to recognise the dynamic relationship between such states as they became mobilised in the transference. The so-called "mosaic transference" in DID that I had been working with for years enabled me to do meaningful analytic work with this population as long as I had a safe-enough holding environment. While this population is indeed enactment prone and traumatised, my experience refutes the shibboleth of the relational theorists that these dissociated self-states are totally disconnected and have no relationship to one another. For example, the phenomenon of co-consciousness between certain personifications is of crucial clinical importance and merits careful exploration in dynamic treatment. Moreover, it can be shown that these dissociated personifications may have explicit memories of formulated experience, a distinction commonly made to contrast dissociated memories from repressed memories. As a result, I have found that not only can such individuals be worked with through enactment, disclosure, and the intersubjective matrix, but also through a more classical approach. In fact, the countertransference pressures might be so great when working with those who are extremely impulse ridden that regression and blurring of ego boundaries may quickly occur and impede the analyst's capacity to develop a healthy therapeutic alliance, so a hybrid approach seems most useful. Because the personifications in DID may be so complex, enduring, and capable of high-level functioning, such as practising law, medicine, and politics, as well as being enormously creative, they warrant psychoanalytic exploration as to their genesis, which, in turn, facilitates their integration into the psyche.

In an effort to join these perspectives on dissociation with the very important findings in child development and relational theory, I then considered a pathodevelopmental line for dissociation (see Chapter Three). Highlighting when and how mental states and content are divided and kept separate, one may begin with, as Freud (1926d) and, later, Bion (1989) described, the caesura of birth. It is that dramatic moment when the newborn takes her first breath, cries, and her cardiac circulation dramatically changes to accommodate terrestrial life. The embryonal hole in the heart, the foramen ovale, closes and the brain becomes fully oxygenated for the first time. The supply of placental peptides and other hormones bathing the foetal brain, which kept it in a near comatose state (Mellor, Diesch, Gunn, & Bennett, 2005), is suddenly stopped by the cutting of the umbilical cord. The hazy mental functioning of the foetus suddenly shifts after her liberation from the claustrum and the oxygenation of her brain. Then, as Winnicott pointed out, the actual sleep–wake cycle of the newborn is another important, natural dissociation (Winnicott, 1988). Individual variations in the twilight state (Weil, 1970), that fuzzy time between sleep and wakefulness when hypnogogic and hypnopompic hallucinations can occur, may also be observed in the newborn. Since it is a naturally occurring time of altered states of consciousness, early dyadic experiences, such as feeding, become incorporated. The hypnotic induction techniques used in adults seem to mirror and reactivate this phenomenon. Then we may observe the gaze aversion of the infant as a rudimentary defence against over-stimulation, a turning away from reality (Fraiberg, 1982), as well as disorganised, disorientated attachment and avoidant attachment (I. Brenner, 2009a; Liotti, 1992; Lyons-Ruth, 1999, 2003).

The transmission of fear occurs early on, and, if it continues, has lifelong implications. In this context one may see what I term the dissociogenic mother, who cannot know or recognise her child and his or her body because the mother is unable to know about herself. This maternal pattern has been described by many writers, such as Bion, Kohut, Mahler, Bromberg, and Fonagy. From here, we may consider an internalisation of this disturbed dialogue as a defence (Whitmer, 2001). Keeping and making things separate and unknowable, along with the intrapsychic precipitate of the disturbed relationship, might continue throughout life in this form, but can also be a precursor to what we call repression. This form of motivated forgetting is usually not seen before the age of three.

Years later, during puberty, should there be a crisis during adolescence due to the failure of integration of the sexually maturing body with the psyche, dissociation might be quite prominent. In addition, there is the dissociation of early childhood from later childhood as well as the dissociation between childhood and adulthood with that transitional period of adolescence that, in and of itself, might be seen as a prolonged dissociative episode. Adolescent breakdown, as described by Laufer and Laufer (1984), has lifelong implications for this severe manifestation of an adolescent crisis. In such situations, dissociative defences, in my experience, may be even more evident.

On a more benign level, one might also consider the dissociation of everyday life, which I contend is associated with everything from parapraxes to obsessional doubting to compulsive rituals. In situations where people cannot quite remember whether they have locked the door, turned the gas off, taken the food out of the oven, or where they have put their keys, careful observation of these phenomena often reveals that one is in a mini-trance when such events occur (I. Brenner, 2009a).

I would therefore suggest that dissociation might indeed underlie and incorporate denial, disavowal, splitting, and motivated forgetting. In the relational view of the mind, the mind is seen as

> a configuration of discontinuous, shifting states of consciousness with varying degrees of access to perception and cognition. Some of these self-states are hypnoidally unlinked from perception at any given moment of normal mental functioning . . . while other self-states are virtually foreclosed from such access because of their original lack of linguistic symbolization. (Bromberg, 1996, p. 57)

While I do have a different conceptualisation of dissociation than the relational theorists, I am intrigued by the notion that the appearance of its precursors is so early in development that, indeed, it may underlie all other defences. Of course, many find this hypothesis untenable, but, as Arnold Goldberg once told me, the test of a good model of the mind is to take it and push it as far as one can to try to explain as much as possible (Goldberg, 1991).

Ironically, however, Goldberg insisted that Kohut's model of the vertical split was not intended to explain DID, as dissociation was not a Kohutian concept. But, what really is the difference between the contradictory self-states in the Kohutian mind that are separated by the vertical split through disavowal as opposed to the self-states in the relational mind that are separated by their version of dissociation? Moreover, how similar is dissociation to Schafer's "disclaimed actions" (Schafer, 1973) or Green's "work of the negative" (Green, 1999)? When reviewing such definitions, one may fluctuate between the excitement of a metapsychological debate between great thinkers and the ennui of the narcissism of minor differences.

Nevertheless, the problem with severely traumatised individuals with DID, as I understand it, is that they utilise dissociation to unprecedented levels and then employ a pseudo-externalised displacement, resulting in a cadre of selves with their own cohesion. This constellation wards off a deep sense of annihilation anxiety and separation anxiety, as the overall patient lacks both self-constancy and object constancy. In addition, it has been discovered up to this point that there are five organising influences that contribute to the genesis of these personifications. They are: (1) perverse sexuality, (2) the dream ego and autosymbolic phenomena, (3) intergenerational transmission of trauma, (4) near-death experiences, and (5) the divisive effect of aggression and its vicissitudes (Brenner, 2001, 2004).

The analytically orientated treatment of such patients may be schematically thought of in five stages.

1. Development of the therapeutic alliance. It is essential to have a rapport with the patient in all stages of consciousness.
2. Definition of the "mosaic transference". Each self may perceive the analyst differently, project different internalised objects, and enact different traumatic scenarios. Appreciating these particular differences as well as the overall mosaic picture is essential. Given the overall lack of self-constancy in the patient, an overall lack of object constancy is prevalent, so that the composite transference is typically at a pre-oedipal rapprochement level of development with disturbances in attachment.
3. Challenging the "It's not me!" self. There appears to be a unique "alteration of the ego" (Freud, 1937c), resulting in a defensive disowning, that is, dissociation, of intolerable affects, drives,

memories, and fantasies. As a result, the patient, when finally confronted with the clinical evidence of dissociated selves and amnesia, will often say, "That's not me!", because the amnesia and different experiences of the body and mind are so alien to the patient. The shift from this Type I to Type II "It's not me!" self, whereby the patient ultimately recognises that "It must be me" even though "It's not me", is a crucial insight.

4.   On the road to integration. As with other patients in analysis, the ultimate resolution of conflict, healing of splits, and configuration of the psyche is part of the process and up to the patient. It cannot and should not be legislated by the analyst, although trauma therapists aim for the integration of all the disparate parts into a unified self. Integrative experiences may occur at unplanned and unexpected times in the course of analysis.

5.   Consolidation and working through (I. Brenner, 2004). As in other analyses, this aspect of the treatment may occur in the late-middle and termination phases (I. Brenner, 2004).

In the following case, I will describe this process in a profoundly traumatised, high-functioning young woman over about a six-month period of time. The patient, in the middle phase of analysis, may also be considered to be in Stage 3 of the treatment—challenging the "It's not me!" self.

Case report

Christine begins her Monday analytic session by reporting a dream she had on Saturday night, which she remembered clearly since it made a big impression upon her:

> "I was in a conference room or auditorium and there were a lot of psycho-analysts there!—or at least it seemed that way. I was in front playing the piano and you were there too! You were off to the side watching me and talking. I think you looked on approvingly."

For a patient in analysis four times a week on the couch for over four years, such a dream might at first glance seem quite comprehensible, even transparent, and not particularly extraordinary. After all, one would expect that in a well-enough-conducted analysis with a suitable patient, the transference would have been well developed enough and she would be somewhere in Stage 3 of treatment. Indeed, it would be timely to interpret the repressed wish represented in the dream symbolism unless, of course, the patient was able to interpret it herself. If properly timed, this interpretation, according to Strachey (1934), would be mutative and further the treatment. In such a classical psychoanalytic scenario, we might interpret that Christine had an oedipal wish to be my star patient, represented by her piano recital for her proud psychoanalyst while being admired by him and his colleagues. Such an exhibitionistic wish, in contrast to her usual shy, deferential, apologetic, and, at times, obsequious demeanour, was surely lurking in her unconscious mind and defended against by her characterological reaction formation. We might be on solid Freudian ground and Christine, when confronted with the creation of her dreaming mind, would no doubt have giggled anxiously and ultimately agreed.

At this point in the analysis, such derivatives were, at most, preconscious and, while still anxiety-laden and not linked with specific erotic material, would certainly have been much more accessible to her conscious mind than early on. So, while I imagined that she might have felt moderately pleased with such a piece of psychoanalytic work if I had guided her in that direction, I sensed it would also have come as a relief for her to stay at that level. It might have even stalled us in our work, perhaps the way an "inexact interpretation" (Glover, 1931) might increase one's resistance.

Unbeknown to Christine at that time, I had been thinking about a presentation during the weekend in question and was wondering what clinical material to present six months later at the conference. While reviewing my cases, I began to seriously think about presenting her case and pondered the issue of getting her permission and disguising the material. I was considering what effect preparing such a paper might have on the analytic process as well as the pros and cons of her actually knowing about my making such a presentation. I was, therefore, struck by the synchronicity of her having reported this dream as she, on a number of occasions, had reported having uncanny experiences where she seemingly knew things about others through "impressions" that would seem to enter her mind from nowhere, rather suddenly. This phenomenon was experienced by her most acutely with regard to her relationship with her estranged mother, where, on at least two occasions during her analysis, she became over-whelmed with anxiety, physical sensations, and an overwhelming sense of dread that something was seriously medically wrong with her mother. On both occasions, that was the case. She was rather shaken up by these experiences of "extraordinary knowing" (Mayer, 2007), but having had them intermittently for many years, she felt more concerned about disclosing them in analysis for fear of being thought of as "really crazy". Having encountered such reports and experiences in well over half of my patients with severe dissociative psychopathology, I was not surprised by all this and kept analysing (I. Brenner, 2001).

She had had "impressions" about me previously, which I neither confirmed nor denied, and, in an effort to analyse her conviction that she was entitled to know whether or not they were accurate, she was left with very hurt feelings of rejection and exclusion by me in the transference. To her credit, however, she also formed a deeper appre-ciation of the childhood determinants of her narcissistic vulnerability around such issues. All of these themes were going through my mind when she reported this dream. So, I wondered about the value of handling the situation differently this time, in the light of the reality demands of the conference, but while I was doing so, other crucial elements needed to be considered before I could comment.

Christine had once aspired to become a concert violinist but had abruptly stopped playing at about age eleven after a devastatingly traumatic experience. Although she always kept a violin and music stand in her home, it stood as a broken dream and a fixture that was never touched by her or, at least, that's what she believed . . .

Christine had told me early on that she used to love playing violin as a child and had been told she was rather talented. In her young girl fantasy of what she wanted to be when she grew up, she often imag-ined becoming a professional musician. However, something had happened—she was not quite sure what—and she stopped playing. She kept her rare and valuable violin in her home where it served as a monument and would exude a sense of dread and sadness if she got near it. She had hoped that someday she would overcome her mysterious inhibition and start to play again. Maybe analysis would help her, but she could not imagine how it might, especially since that was not the reason that she sought treatment in the first place. It was her uncontrollable stage fright over public speaking that was becoming an ever-increasing part of her job that made her seek help. She could not imagine that these inhibitions had any connection with one another, and I heard no more about the violin until about one-and-a-half years into analysis.

At that time, the patient made a startling revelation in a way that I had become somewhat accustomed to when working with those who had been severely traumatised in childhood. A seemingly separate self emerged, possessing knowledge, memory, affects, insight, and a different perspective on things. In this case, a personification with a coquettish, younger tone of voice, who identified herself as Tina, seemed to have the capacity to know everything Christine was talking about and saying without being noticed by her. Like viewing somebody through a one-way mirror, Tina had a "co-consciousness" with Christine but not *vice versa*. Therefore, she bragged in a giggly tone that she would get up in the middle of the night and play the violin without it ever being known to the grown-up. To the observer, such nocturnal behaviour would probably look like somnambulism. Oh, and, by the way, did I want to hear her play? Tina had a mischievous quality, knew that Christine wanted to keep her hidden from me, and desperately wanted to be recognised. She could not wait to come out and never wanted to leave. After a number of months of this surreptitious, nocturnal practising, she tape-recorded the music and a cassette was brought in. It became a huge issue because it was concrete evidence of her dream-like other life.

By this time, Christine had come to acknowledge what she had known and not known since she was a young child, that is, there were times when she would simply lose track of time and find herself minutes or hours later absorbed in a task or an activity in another location and had no idea how she got there. Having done her best to convince herself that it was just how it was for her—no big deal—and that she could usually bluff her way through the gap through a variety of means due to her otherwise excellent memory and considerable powers of reason, she found it least anxiety-provoking to simply forget that she had forgotten. In analysis, however, through our frequent meetings and the growing intensity of the transference, it became evident that these peculiar absences did occur and were most worthy of exploration and treatment.

Very disturbing memories of bizarre and painful weekly sexual rituals performed by her mother's sister, who did much of the caretaking, started to emerge. In addition, flashes of terrible violence on trips with her grandfather, a leader of an organised crime family with ethnic ties, started to plague her as well. When she was affected, she would often drift off in a session, a sensation that she ruefully admitted was, indeed, quite familiar. She referred to this defensive flight as going to hide in the toy closet, an autohypnotic phenomenon that other such patients have variously described as "taking a walk in the woods", "playing with my Barbies", "singing songs", "talking to the boy on the paint can" (as one woman recounted how, during painful abuse by her uncle in his workshop, she would fixate on the picture of the Dutch boy on the paint can on the shelf and become autohypnotically absorbed and anaesthetised) (I. Brenner, 2001).

At these times, Tina would emerge in the sessions recapitulating her earlier, traumatically induced, dissociative flight now apparently precipitated by anxiety in the here-and-now in the transference. Christine, fearing that she would overwhelm and damage me, also worried that I would have second thoughts about having accepted her into treatment and tell her not to come back. Her identification with her murderous grandfather filled her with self-loathing and fear of her own destructiveness and was embodied in another elusive personification. At times when she felt neglected or wronged by me over, for example, her confusion in the schedule, a menacing, angry, and thoroughly mistrusting self would emerge. This "dark" self refused to identify herself or participate in analysis.

The patient's very deep abandonment fears were linked not only to early maternal issues, but also to having been sadistically left behind by her grandfather at the scene of carnage during a gangland rampage. But, on the other hand, he loved her playing the violin and celebrated her talent to all within his sphere of influence. He even set up a special concert for her that was the pinnacle of her young life. However, afterwards he came to her bedroom that night and raped her. So, she hated her beloved grandfather afterward and prayed to Jesus Christ to make him die. She fixated on the cross hanging on the wall during this life-altering assault on her young body. Incredibly, later that week, he was assassinated by his rivals right in front of her but in his last seconds when he realised what was going to happen to him, he motioned to her to stay away, thus saving her from the same fate in his last moments. Thus, she was left in a totally confused state about not only all that had happened, but also how she felt about him.

Profound, idealised love alternated with profound fear and loathing. As this story was emerging piecemeal over time in terrifying flashbacks, somatic memories, nightmares, and altered states of consciousness, Tina tape-recorded her violin playing for me after many months of surreptitious practising in the wee hours of the night. "She" left the cassette on the music stand for Christine to bring the next day. Then, as though responding to a post-hypnotic suggestion—in this case, an autohypnotic suggestion—the patient dutifully handed it over to me and in a perplexed voice declared that she thought she was supposed to bring it. For many days afterwards, there were many such questions, such as, what was on the cassette? How was it made? How did she know to bring it? Did I listen to it? And, most importantly, did I like it? So, all this was going on in my mind when the patient reported her dream that Monday morning.

After a bit of deliberating, I decided to tell Christine that her dream was curious not only in its content, but also in the light of something that has been on my mind over the weekend.

The patient was quite familiar with my "analytic attitude" (Schafer, 1983) by now, in that I rarely spontaneously introduced my own ideas except to make announcements pertaining to the frame, such as changes in our schedule. Therefore, she took great interest in my disclosure that I had a conference and was thinking about what it would be like to present some elements of our work to the group. Having internalised aspects of the analytic dialogue by now, her first response was to ask me why I decided to reveal what was on my mind this time when in so many other instances when she had asked a question I was silent. I asked myself at that time how much of an analysand did I, myself, wish to be at that moment and realised once again how desperately hungry she was to analyse me, know about my inner thoughts, and how I really felt about her. I then told her that, given the apparent synchronicity between us, I wondered if it would be helpful for her to have known it as it might further our process.

The patient brightened immediately and expressed surprised delight to hear directly that she was in my thoughts over the weekend, as she regularly felt that she was such a burden, that she had inflicted herself upon me, and had periodically given me opportunities to discharge her. "I'd be fine!" she would say cheerily but disingenuously, to assure me as she tried to assuage her guilt over feeling she was damaging me with her toxicity by prolonged exposure to her suffering. Evidence of an avoidant attachment could be seen at weekends and during vacations where she would appear to be un-affected and "fine". So, to hear without any prodding on her part that she was on my mind and in my mind was not only gratifying but also a statement that she had a place in my mind (Spezzano, 2007). I demonstrated that I had object constancy even if she did not. Her realisation of my capacity to hold her and those disowned, dissociated aspects of her mind in my own mind apparently came as quite a pleasant shock to her.

I realised that she would then re-internalise my containment of her projected disparate selves, which could become for her a nidus of integration of her own psyche. At that moment, however, what was most pressing was that she told me that she felt that if I were to tell her story to a group of professionals, it would make her past feel all the more real for her. Having been deprived of parental reflecting of her early experience and literally punished by her mother when she tried to tell her what had happened to her when she was abroad with her grandfather, Christine could hardly believe her own ears when she heard her own self speak about her forbidden memories for the first time. She became uncharacteristically excited and enthusiastic about the idea and asked me when I would decide and whether I would tell her. She even started to pester me about it over the next several weeks. She was eager for the enactment to occur.

As the hour proceeded, we returned to her dream and the musical performance. She then brought up the issue of the audiocassette tape that she had automatically delivered to me, wondering about the qual-ity of her playing. Would I let her hear it? How else would she know if she still had talent? Was it all a delusion? She felt that she would have a breakthrough in analysis if she could just listen to the music that she had performed in those amnestic states of mind in the middle of the night.

As tempted as I was to believe with her that she might have an epiphany and be cured were she to hear the tape—the way such an intervention might be portrayed in the cinema—my experience had taught me otherwise. For example, in one extreme case (see Chapter Eight), I videotaped sessions with a patient as she was "switching" and carefully studied the subtle and at times dramatic changes in her facial musculature, eyes, levels of consciousness, speech, syntax, autobio-graphical self, body language, and transferences. At the time, she had total amnesia for these shifts in her self-states and was in total denial of her dissociative disorder. During this chaotic, frightening regression, there were life-threatening self-mutilation, multiple hospitalisations, refractoriness to medication, and a downhill, deteriorating course as her free-floating, instinctually laden material was coalescing in the complex transferences that had developed. Her rage, guilt, and need for punishment of herself and me was manifesting in self-amputation of her fingers in retaliation for my going away on vacation, so it was a very precarious time in treatment. Like a perverse sadomasochistic parody of the forlorn teenager pulling petals off a flower and saying, she loves me, she loves me not, the patient, in autohypnotic, amnestic, and anaesthetised states, sawed off several fingers and was working on the whole hand when I tried a desperate intervention.

I had hoped by encouraging her to watch the videotapes with me she could finally see that she was not being attacked by some mysterious assailant from the outside, but by her own mind. If she could accept the medical reality that was clearly shown on video that it truly was her own body and her own words acknowledging such deeds, then she could begin to own her mental content, work on gaining control of herself, and neutralise her aggression. If she could say, "Maybe it doesn't feel like it's me but it is me after all", this recognition could herald a new phase of treatment. However, such an acknowledgement would also require her to consider that all the unspeakable assaults on the body and mind actually did happen to her and not someone else. Unfortunately, she was nowhere near ready for such a reconciliation, so when she viewed the tapes of herself, she burst into raucous laughter and blurted out, "That's not me! That's not me!" She then lapsed into a dissociative stupor, clearly overstimulated, and unable to digest what she had seen with her own eyes.

So, when Christine asked to hear the tape, even though it was at her initiative, I resumed a more familiar analytic posture. I encouraged her to analyse her wish, elicit her fantasies of what she might hear and how she might feel, and defer any decisions about such an "active" intervention until we could see how her own mind could learn about itself through our current method.

About two weeks later, the patient had a very disturbing night, awakening to nightmares she could not remember and suddenly developing the disturbing symptom of tinnitus. Having been impressed with the frequency of unusual neurologic and muscular symptoms in this population that one might have considered to be "hysterical" in nature, I was very curious about this putative conversion reaction. My associations took me to the many conversations I had had with my sister, an audiologist, who explained that, not infrequently, tinnitus is related to psychological issues and may present with a variety of different sounds. I also associated to the haunting soundtrack of the film *Psycho*, especially the shrieking, high-pitched violin sounds during the infamous shower scene. So, as I sat with the patient in her very anxious state, I was reminded that, as a once-gifted prodigy, she had perfect pitch. Therefore, I asked her what note she heard in her tinnitus. Completely startled, she then quickly answered that it was the C sharp, two octaves above middle C. After a period of silence, she then recalled one of her nightmares, which was of chickens shrieking in a high-pitched sound exactly like the tinnitus. They were shrieking before their heads were cut off and started running aimlessly in a panic. She giggled nervously and then lapsed in and out of altered states of consciousness, hyperventilating, crying, and haltingly describing the carnage and mutilated human bodies that she had witnessed who were victims of the bloody rampage perpetrated by her grandfather and his henchmen. Her tinnitus resolved as quickly as it began.

Christine's expressed interest in listening to the tape diminished, but her curiosity increased as well as her capacity to tolerate more of her disowned psyche. She even decided to visit her estranged mother again, expecting that, with her precarious medical condition, it might be for the last time. Here, the music connection was associated with another mystery, that of the true identity of her father, a merchant marine who was frequently away. One of the biggest heartbreaks of her life was her father's total disregard for her, his disdain, and even a sexual assault where he degraded, humiliated, and treated her as if a prostitute when she was in college. Hearing from her repeatedly that she felt as if she did not belong in the family, and hearing periodically about a strange man who would visit the mother occasionally, especially on the patient's birthday, I began to wonder about this man's relationship to the patient. Both her father and this man were musicians. She recalled sitting next to the man while he played music, how he would give her gifts on her birthday, and how strangely her mother behaved in his presence. The unthinkable began to formulate in her mind that perhaps she was treated the way she was treated because, among other things, she was not her father's biological child but the child of this man, perhaps her mother's lover.

It all began to make sense to her, but the assault on her already shaky identity and sense of self was quite destabilising. Anxiety, sleeplessness, mood fluctuations, and an inability to concentrate prevailed for weeks. She decided to visit her mother and ask. Knowing her mother's violent tendencies, even as an old, frail woman, she approached her cautiously and before she could even complete the sentence "Do you remember that man who used to come visit?" her mother hauled off and slapped her in the face, rage gleaming from her eyes. Totally stunned, very, very upset, and literally speechless subsequently, the patient left her mother's bedside and returned home. She was essentially mute in the subsequent hours, as though an inner force was constricting her vocal cords every time she tried to speak. We wondered about her original complaint about speaking in public, speaking her mind, speaking the truth, knowing the truth. She then felt relief in hoping I would speak the truth about her and essentially be her symbolic proxy in confronting her mother were I to present her case at that conference. As she reflected on this humiliating experience with her mother, it further confirmed her shocking suspicion that indeed her father was not her father and she mourned for weeks.

Her awareness of yet another self, a mute self, was a disturbing but ultimately liberating insight. As her observing ego increased and she was better able to stay "present" when her self-states switched, she acquired more self-constancy and was rather amazed to feel how she could lose her capacity to speak. She appeared to have an integrative experience in which her vision improved and everything seemed brighter and more in focus. Once again, an observer of just the symptomatology might diagnose it as a hysterical conversion reaction, if the underlying dynamic issues were not amenable to exploration. At this point Christine expressed relief that she had not listened to the tape, given the profound affective reactions she was having and the movement she was making in her own time to reconcile the splintering of her mind.

Discussion

During this small segment of an extensive and complex treatment, I have tried to illustrate that during one crucial junction, instead of interpreting an underlying instinctual wish, I opted for an intervention that was a form of containment. There seemed to be a lot happening both intrapsychically and in the intersubjective matrix that went beyond id impulses and presented a potential opportunity for an integrative experience. The almost uncanny coincidence of the patient's dream and my preoccupation over the weekend reopened the delicate issue of paranormal phenomena and a type of communication for which we as analysts do not have a model. Projective identification seems to be a factor. However, other influences may also be at play (I. Brenner, 2001; Mayer, 2007). In addition, the manifest content of the patient's dream alluded to her surreptitious night-time playing of her violin in an amnestic dissociated state, which was very difficult for the patient to symbolise and put into words at this point. Moreover, she was frequently overwhelmed with anxiety, abject fear, grief, guilt, and disbelief over recurrent intrusions of traumatic memories of sexual abuse as well as witnessing atrocities and frank murder. I was quite affected by her affective states and fragmentation being unconsciously recruited to take all this in and do "something" with it to help her.

As Bion described it,

> When the patient strove to rid himself of fears of death which were felt to be too powerful for his personality to contain, he split off his fears and put them into me, the idea apparently being if they were allowed to repose there long enough, they would undergo modification by my psyche and could then be safely introjected. (Bion, 1959, p. 312)

This process of containment enlists the analyst's mind to modify and render tolerable what is intolerable to the patient. As such, it is now considered an essential tenet of Kleinian interpretation and treatment (Hinshelwood, 2007). While originally derived from Bion's work with schizophrenics, this approach seems quite applicable to the severely traumatised, dissociated mind. Christine's enthusiastic seizing upon the idea of having me present her case was no doubt multiply determined (Wälder, 1936), and her hope that through this enactment I, as a good maternal object, would finally set the record straight and affirm her experience. Such basic repair of the grossly disturbed mother–daughter relationship seemed to be a prerequisite before she could come to own her own erotic desires and explore their vicissitudes.

It would appear that a crucial role the analyst serves in working with such a patient is of becoming a particular type of container. I served as an auxiliary memory bank during her amnestic states, taking in and accepting her psychic reality of different selves inhabiting the mind and taking over the body at different times, and tolerating her intolerable affects associated with traumatic memories and underlying drive tensions. Christine could not begin to openly acknowledge her desires for anyone, especially in the transference, until she could better differentiate between the past and present as well as question her irrational sense of guilt over what had happened to her as a young girl. Especially where trauma is involved, one needs to be especially delicate and tactful when exploring underlying instinctual wishes associated with infantile sexuality, being mindful of Oliner's warning that analysis may be experienced as an "accusatory" treatment (Oliner, 1996). With this caveat about the extent to which conscious and unconscious guilt fuels the overt and less obvious self-destructiveness that often accompanies the post trauma state, the interpretative work of analysis may, at times, be actually contraindicated. Containment seems more appropriate to the clinical situation.

There is a distinction between a holding environment, as per Winnicott, as opposed to the container as per Bion, so that, in the former, one does not challenge or confront the patient's psychic reality even if the distortions are of psychotic proportion. In the latter, however, the analyst is obligated to eventually point out the projections of disowned internalised self and object that become detoxified through the alpha function of the analyst in order to strengthen reality testing. This type of intervention can have a mixed effect of reducing catastrophic anxiety, but also of possibly increasing higher-level separation or castration anxiety as a result of improved object relations and a deeper appreciation of the other (Caper, 1999). Moreover, because of the nature of the dissociative defence and the creation of disowned selves that are experienced as "not me!", the pseudo-externalised displacement (I. Brenner, 2001) that maintains the sense of separateness is particularly refractory to interpretation. Therefore, the analysis seems best served if the analyst can empathise with the patient's inner sense of different selves. The resistance to accepting the medical reality of one brain, one mind, and one body can be enormous despite its obviousness to the outside observer. Therefore, the insight needed to make the transition from a Type I to a Type II "It's not me!" self exemplifies the third phase of treatment, that is, confronting the "It's not me!" self.

Conclusion

In the case described here, Christine originally disowned her states of mind as "not me!" Once she could see and accept that both Tina and the mute self must be a part of her even if it did not feel that way, that is, "It's me and it's not me!", it heralded a new phase of the treatment. The analyst's capacity to tolerate uncertainty, ambiguity, psychic pain, helplessness, guilt and, at times, frank worry about the patient's welfare without giving up or giving out seem essential to the process. Being able to compassionately listen to, suspend any judgement over the accounts being given, and to assist in finding words for the unspeakable are also essential.

Thus, it appeared that for the patient to know about and reconcile the divided and disowned aspects of herself, it was necessary for the analyst to be able to take them all into his own mind first and not be destroyed. Such an experience with a patient is uniquely psychoactive and potentially healing.

Addendum

The dissociated selves that were evident at this point in Christine's analysis seemed to serve different functions and have their own organisation. Christine, the industrious, deferential, socially compliant self, had the most sustained relationship with the object world. Her name was on her birth certificate and all legal documents. Although highly capable, she was tentative, self-doubting, and prone to idealisation of others. Terrified of being sent away at any moment, she was loath to complain about anything and was accommodating to a fault. She had limited affect tolerance unless she anaesthetised herself.

Tina, the mischievous, wilful, and battle-hardened child, was endlessly inquisitive and protected Christine by keeping most of the traumatic memories to herself, that is, dissociated from Christine's consciousness. She often spoke with a slight speech impediment, not detected when Christine was "out". Although she manifested child-like qualities, childlike demands, childlike stubbornness, and childlike behaviour, such as pulling out a stuffed animal from the oversized pocketbook brought to sessions and comforting herself with it, she was fully educated and helped Christine out at work, much to the latter's dismay. She often spoke about what Christine was afraid of or unable to articulate, such as the fear of being thought of as crazy. In a sense, she articulated and interpreted the patient's unconscious motivation and feelings.

The angry, mistrustful, and elusive teenage self was least known and nameless. She appeared to protect through withdrawal and constant surveillance. The patient's fear of her destructiveness owing to an identification with the aggressor seemed to be embodied in this personification.

The mute child self was terrorised into silence by a punishing mother self who inflicted pain upon her whenever she tried to speak. The mother self would seem to take over the vocal cords and prevent the patient from talking about family secrets and other anxiety-laden topics.

Each of the personifications had her own relationship with me, which comprised the mosaic transference. Deep object hunger fluctu-ated with deep fears of rejection, abandonment, and personal harm, as well as a veneer of nonchalance and indifference. The emergence of a given self in the course of an hour was dynamically influenced, highly significant, and subject to analytic exploration like any other defensive shift. Moreover, the relationships among the selves, as well as the rela-tionship that the selves had with me in the transference, were of crucial analytic significance.

CHAPTER TEN

Handling the compulsion to repeat

"Only believers, who demand that science shall be a substitute for the catechism that they have given up, will blame an investigator for developing or even transforming his views"

(Freud, 1920g)

Introduction

Shaken as a result of the Great War himself, Sigmund Freud's opening remarks to the Budapest Congress in 1919 addressed the incompleteness of psychoanalytic knowledge as it related to the war neuroses. Dissatisfied with attributing the unimaginable carnage to repressed sexuality or anal sadism, he had to reconsider the ideas already put forth by colleagues such as Adler (1910), Stekel (1911), Spielrein (1912), and Reik (1911) about the role of aggression in the human psyche. He needed to expand his theory so "Rather implausibly, Freud also posited a 'war-like 'I' that created a lust for destruction" (Makari, 2008, p. 315). This line of thought evolved into "...the third step in the theory of the instincts, which ... cannot lay claim to the same degree of certainty as the two earlier ones—the extension of the concept of sexuality and the hypothesis of narcissism" (Freud, 1920g, p. 59).

Having recently published his thoughts on sadomasochism as they pertained to the Wolf Man (Freud, 1918b) and nearing completion of his work on masochism in "A child is being beaten" (Freud, 1919e), Freud started a new essay with what he described to Ferenczi as a "mysterious" title—*Beyond the Pleasure Principle* (Falzeder & Brabant, 1996, p. 355). In so doing, he appeared to be reversing himself and greatly disturbed his loyal followers by undermining the primacy of libido theory and the pleasure principle. This radical shift was stimulated by what he described as a separate class of dreams that did not adhere to the theory of wish-fulfilment, the recurrent traumatic dreams of soldiers that revisited the horror of the battlefield. Seeking an explanation, he revisited Fechner's constancy principle and conceptualised that the quest for stability and constancy required a need for mastery of an overwhelming stimulus that was not only a valid aspect of motivation, but also "beyond" the pleasure principle. The major mental principle that he had previously described, known as the compulsion to repeat (Freud, 1914g), was therefore fuelled by an innate drive for mastery, sameness, reduction of inner tension, and a movement towards ultimate peace—the eternal sleep of death. Thus, the "nirvana principle"—a term coined by Low (1920)—could explain how our species could wage war and bring about unspeakable destruction: it was now conjectured by Freud to be out of an unconscious drive towards permanent inner peace.

This theory appeared to be the ultimate paradox that many analysts, such as those espousing "modern conflict theory" (Abend, 2007), found, and continue to find, not only difficult to accept but also unnecessary for clinical work (I. Brenner, 2001). Notable exceptions are the Kleinians and a number of analysts working with traumatised individuals (Laub & Lee, 2003). However, even among those who endorse the concept, it is not unusual to issue a disclaimer, such as downgrading it to a less than basic aspect of all psyches. For example, Kernberg has recently stated,

> The death drive, I propose, is not a primary drive but represents a significant complication of aggression as a major motivational system, is central in the therapeutic work with severe psychopathology, and as such is imminently useful as a concept in the clinical realm. (Kernberg, 2009, p. 1018)

Almost a century later, contemporary analysts may not be able to fully appreciate the confusion and uproar over Freud's dismantling of his own orthodoxy. The faithful followers of libido theory were in a huge quandary. Perhaps we psychoanalysts practising today experienced an echo of this phenomenon when the late Charles Brenner questioned the value of the structural theory after devoting all of his professional life to conflict theory and the promulgation of Freud's ideas (C. Brenner, 2003b). Interestingly, Brenner's challenge to the very theory he espoused for decades went undiscussed in both his recently published memoir (C. Brenner, 2009a) and his interview with Robert Michaels (C. Brenner, 2009b). In his obituary, however, Jacobs emphasises the maverick quality that Brenner possessed despite having been seen as the quintessential standard bearer of classical psychoanalysis (Jacobs, 2009). As a younger man, his earlier challenge to the prevailing views on psychosis because they did not fit the data of clinical experience earned him this reputation with his elders. Interestingly, he was roughly the age Freud was when he put forth his theory of *Thanatos*. It is too soon to know whether Brenner's proposed revision will be forgotten about or even dismissed as an aberrant flight of fancy by his loyal followers, just as many loyal Freudians today choose to refute his forays into the "death instinct" as being too theoretical or, perhaps, autobiographically motivated. While Freud also expressed his own uncertainty about these radical ideas, the reader nevertheless gets the impression of his subtle enjoyment in being the provocative "*advocatus diaboli*" (Freud, 1920g, p. 59).

In over three decades of my own clinical work with traumatised individuals, I, too, have had experiences that have not conformed to prevailing theory, and I have felt the need to revise and ultimately extend some ideas about the effects of overwhelming life experience on the psyche (Akhtar & Brenner, 1979; I. Brenner, 2001, 2004, 2009a; Kestenberg & Brenner, 1996). The mutual influences of both external reality and internal psychic reality remain at the centre of the question as the latest developments in neurobiology, genetics, cognitive psychology, and trauma studies deepen our understanding of the mind–brain–body–environment question. It is in this very exciting climate where new discoveries made outside the consulting room might threaten to eclipse insights gleaned from the psychoanalytic situation unless the latter are revisited and integrated into a multi-disciplinary approach to depth psychology. It is in this context that I would like to underscore the clinical importance of the repetition compulsion, which was so carefully explicated by Freud in *Beyond the Pleasure Principle*. While the extensive debate over its metapsychology and neurophysiology continues, the fact of its existence and relevance to treatment is not in question. Indeed, an appreciation of its presence, especially where trauma is concerned, has helped this author make sense of those conditions currently known as dissociative disorders, especially "multiple personality". This realm has traditionally been seen as, at best, either "not psychoanalysis" or, at worse, an iatrogenic creation of over-zealous therapists (I. Brenner, 2001).

The dream and "waking dream" sequence

An unusual manifestation of the repetition compulsion may be observed in the mental life of someone severely traumatised in child-hood. It may only be observed where one is working analytically, because the extent of the patients' forgetting makes it impossible for them to see it on their own and because other forms of treatment would not allow the opportunity to examine the repeating relation-ship between dreams and altered states of consciousness. A typical scenario is as follows: the patient might report a disturbing dream or a recurring dream in which he/she is *watching another person—usually a child—get hurt in some specific way*. The dream often awakens the patient, who is left shaken up and confused about the manifest con-tent. The child who is being victimised by others may be vaguely recognised by the dreamer or seem to be a total stranger. Moreover, the degree of upset is quite variable, ranging from mild concern, such as might be seen with the recall of a screen memory, to outright panic. Associations to the dream may be, if the patient is able, to the day residue which, according to well-known classical principles, then enable the tentative conclusion to be drawn that some identifiable precipitant stimulated the creation of a dream that incorporates child-hood determinants.

So far, all is well and good. At this point, the analyst feels on the same solid ground that generations of dream interpreters have trod before, rediscovering Freud's formula that eventually, in a "good-enough" conducted analysis, the earlier material will emerge, which will enable a construction of childhood fantasy/memory. However, in the situation under consideration, there is an additional component, and a most vexing one, that many clinicians might prefer to ignore or downplay, or they might simply fail to appreciate its profound significance. If they do take it seriously, then a whole host of uncomfortable questions may follow that could even challenge some of our basic assumptions about psychic structure and the centrality of repression as the primary defence mechanism (I. Brenner, 2009a).

This second component of the sequence usually occurs within days of the dream. It could be as soon as the next analytic session or possibly up to a week later. At this time, the patient either presents in a different state of consciousness or undergoes an alteration in ego functioning or self-state during the session. It may be sudden and dramatic or subtle and imperceptible, especially if the patient is lying on the couch and the analyst is not aware of this phenomenon. It is referred to as "switching", in the jargon of those who typically treat dissociative disorders. Anxiety in the transference or a very dysphorically affect-laden topic might precede this shift (I. Brenner, 2004). At such times, the patient might talk in a different way—that is, use different words or use words in a different way, with a different inflection, syntax, or cadence. The voice itself might sound different—perhaps as if it were coming from a younger person or from a person of the opposite gender. In addition, there might be fluttering of the eyelids, as seen in an autohypnotic state, or a dramatic change of facial expression in which the facial musculature is used differently. Body language could also be different, as hand gestures and movements seem out of character. There might even be a sense of unfamiliarity or disorientation with the surroundings as the patient might come across as having just materialised in the analyst's office for the first time.

During this shift in the patient's demeanour, he or she may then relate a memory of being subjected to a horrendous situation that sounds very similar, or even identical, to the ordeal in the dream. This expression would appear to be an elaboration of the "night residue" (Leveton, 1961), where, according to the Morris hypothesis (Akhtar, 2009; Kelman, 1975b), the manifest dream gets lived out in the waking state. In contrast, however, the recounting of the memory is in the first person, as opposed to it being observed as happening to someone else in the dream. It could have the quality of an overpowering narrative or a psychological reliving of the trauma (Laub & Auerhahn, 1993), as the immediacy of the experience and the associated affect might have an abreactive quality to it. In addition, should the analyst happen to enquire about the aforementioned dream at this time, or in any way try to make a connection or invite any connections between the two phenomena while the patient is in this mental state, he would typically hear that the patient has no knowledge, memory, or perhaps even any connection whatsoever with the process of dreaming. It is almost as though *someone else* had the dream and was responsible for that realm of mental functioning that is of no concern to the patient at this time. One might even say that the patient's lack of curiosity has a quality of indifference to it, not unlike *la belle indifférence* ascribed to hysteria.

What might be ascribed to unusually deep repression for this apparent "disconnect" becomes even more mystifying if, at some point in the not-too-distant future, the dream is revisited. If the patient is asked about the subsequent abreaction in his/her aberrant state of mind, he/she denies any knowledge or recollection of having such a childhood memory, let alone having revealed it in a session. This denial appears sincere and genuine. At this point, the analyst might experience his own momentary doubt over the accuracy of his memory and may either enquire further from the patient or simply let it pass as yet another inexplicable moment in the space–time continuum of analysis. I would contend, however, that such a clinical event is in the realm of dissociation and is of the greatest importance, as it belies a type of forgetting or defensive not knowing that goes beyond repression and perhaps even precedes it developmentally (I. Brenner, 1994, 2009a, 2009b). It should also be noted that this sequence could also occur in reverse, meaning that the first-hand account in an altered state of consciousness might precede the reporting of the dream.

In a clinical example that represents some aspects of this situation in reverse, Reiser describes a woman in analysis who, as a preteenager many years earlier, had a "hysterical dissociative" episode following the accidental burning of her younger brother (Reiser, 1994). She was sent to the pharmacy to procure a medicine for the badly scalded boy but went into an amnestic altered state for several hours, became lost, and was found in a park in a daze hours later. She had been haunted by this mental lapse ever since and was obsessed with trying to remember the name of the burn preparation she never picked up. During a time when this material entered the treatment, she had a dream of *consulting a travel agent about wanting to go to*

Germany but was not able to remember the name of the town she wanted to visit. In addition, someone oddly complimented her on her "tan". Through the analyst's empathic listening to her associations, the patient was then able to recall that the elusive name of the burn medicine was "*tan*nic acid"—which Dr Reiser had already suspected by then. Significantly, *the travel agent* (analyst) in the dream *was not able to help her plan the full itinerary for her travels throughout Germany* (German was Freud's native language), which appears to be a symbolic allusion to her frustration in analysis over not being able to recall what was going on in her mind during this fugue state many years earlier. A link between her dissociative episode and the dream, catalysed by analysis, then became evident to this perceptively attuned analyst, who helped the patient to remember and integrate her traumatically induced flight into an altered state of consciousness many years earlier. It appears that the psychological ingredients in this vignette are included in a more complex sequence where reciprocal amnesia (Janet, 1907) and a disturbance in identity are present.

Case report: Cindy/Candy

In one such case, a patient in analysis was experiencing considerable anxiety over the prospect of a major surgical procedure for a very painful condition (I. Brenner, 2001).

The patient, Cindy, was asked by the surgeon, while she was giving her consent to the operation, whether she would also give her permission for photographs to be taken. It was an academic teaching hospital and, because of the exploratory nature of the operation, it was unclear what would be revealed inside the body as the cause of this condition. Eager for relief, she naturally focused on the risks of the surgery and was rather blasé about the request to be photographed. However, when she mentioned it during the session, she seemed to hesitate a bit and could not identify whether anything was, in fact, bothering her about it. The next hour, she reported a puzzling dream from the night before, which left her with a vague uneasiness. In that dream, *she was watching a young girl being taken to a barn by grown-ups to see the animals, but once she got there it was very strange, and there were many bizarre lights.* She awoke feeling disturbed by the images but could not elaborate. Then, several days later, during a session, the patient spontaneously underwent a mental transformation, "switched", and began to speak in a younger, more affect-laden, coquettish voice.

Having had some familiarity at this point in the treatment with these shifts, I recognised that at such times she insisted that she was not that "boring" other person, Cindy, who went to work every day, paid the bills, and was so very serious all the time. In great contrast, she loved to go out at night and dance and have a good time party-ing. She even insisted that I recognise her as a separate person and call her Candy. In fact, Candy loved to recount how she recently "tricked" Cindy into planning a very expensive vacation to a resort. Cindy made all the arrangements, did all the packing, boarded the plane, but then had no memory of the vacation until she got back on the plane to return home. From Candy's perspective, she "took over" and had the time of her life. From Cindy's perspective, however, she essentially went into a fugue.

However, it was not all fun and games for Candy: she had a crucial psychological job to perform. Candy was the one who protected Cindy from bad memories, and this time in the session she wanted to tell me about another time Cindy was tricked. It happened a long time ago, when "they" were young, when she went into a barn with her sneaky uncle and a friend of his that she did not know. They asked her if she wanted to see the farm animals and told her that she would even be able to pet them. Cindy was very excited about this idea and went with them, but when she got there it was not as it was supposed to be. Cindy became terrified and "hid" somewhere inside the mind; Candy then took over control of the body. There were many bright lights inside the barn, and the man wanted her to take her clothes off while he took pictures of her as she was touching the animals' private parts. The animals were also made to do painful things to her bottom. Although she was scared, too, and did not like it, she knew that Cindy would not be able to deal with it at all, and so she, Candy, was the one who usually "came out" when these bad things were happening. In that state of mind, the patient, as Candy, had no knowledge of Cindy's dream. Then, when Cindy "returned" to the session, she had no mem-ory of the time that Candy was out, describing this ordeal.

During this time, Cindy's anxiety over the impending operation increased as her pain escalated. As "Candy", she could not compre-hend the medical necessity of the procedure and was afraid that the "bad people" were tricking them again. Cindy experienced another such repetitive sequence of a dream followed by a waking dream, as it were. As her fears of disfigurement came to the fore, Cindy reported a disturbing dream in which she was watching a teenage girl being held down on a table. The girl was naked and was being restrained by a woman who was a stranger while a man, whom she also did not know, savagely cut the girl's body. The girl screamed in pain while the people laughed and were totally indifferent to her suffering.

Several days later, Candy again reappeared in a session. This time she appeared quite paranoid, explaining that the "bad people" had intended to cut her completely open if she were to tell anyone what was going on. Since she had "heard" about the operation, she feared that "they" were the ones behind it and were going to really punish her this time. It seemed that talking to me was the reason she feared they were going to get her again. She then described a time when she was held down on a kitchen table by the mean girlfriend of her uncle while he inserted a knife into her vagina and cut her. Terrified, overwhelmed, and doubled over in pain as she relived this scenario, she was sure that he would make good on his promise to complete the job. There appeared to be a collapse of time in this "Candy" state of mind so that she could not appreciate the passage of time and feared that these perpetrators from childhood many years ago were still around to harm her. Furthermore, as with the previously mentioned sequence, Candy had no knowledge of Cindy's uncannily similar dream, and Cindy had amnesia for that part of the session when Candy took over.

It is known that such patients appear to be in a "waking dream" (Mark, 2009; Marmer, 1980, 1991) during their dissociative episodes. In my own observations of this dream-like state (I. Brenner, 1995a, 2001), I have come to appreciate the importance of the so-called "functional phenomenon" (Silberer, 1909) as a mechanism to understand some of the symbolism seen in the accompanying dream imagery. Although alluded to by Freud (1900a), expounded upon by Rapaport (1949), and later rediscovered by Silber (1970, 1979), this aspect of dreams has been largely overshadowed by the classical theory of wish-fulfilment. This under-appreciated phenomenon refers to the ego's capacity to create imagery to symbolise its own various states of consciousness in metaphorical and very often anthropomorphic terms. In other words, this autosymbolic function may result in the creation of people to represent its own different levels of alertness or awareness. A somewhat elusive quality of the human mind, Kohut (1977) apparently recognised its significance, applying it to his concept of self-state dreams in narcissistic patients. Here, the dream represents the attempts of the psyche to ward off threats of loss of cohesion. Even earlier, Fairbairn recognised the link between the endopsychic structures of the mind—that is, ego and internal objects—and the personae in dreams (Fairbairn, 1944). For a number of reasons, however, the functional phenomenon, Fairbairn's "state of affairs" dreams, and the self-state dream have received limited attention in the literature (Slap & Trunnell, 1987), and any possible connection with the repetition compulsion has been obscure.

Autosymbolism: a self-report

Silberer (1909) described his own mind's creations in his efforts to stay awake in order to think and do his work. These creations included images of other people. For example, his conflict over maintaining his concentration was once represented as an unfriendly secretary in a library who ignored him and would not help him with his request for help, whereas, another time, a helpful assistant did await his orders. In my own experience, a recent dream in the early morning just before awakening further illustrates this phenomenon, which often occurs in hypnogogic/hypnopompic states: I had been up unusually late the night before trying to complete a project to meet a publishing deadline and was concerned about waking up on time the following morning. After my alarm went off, I drifted back to sleep for a few moments and dreamt that

> I was crossing an international border back to the United States. The border guard asked me whether I had anything to declare. I said, "No". He then asked if I had been exposed to any diseases, such as the swine flu, that might be contagious and spread to others if I were let back in. Again, I said, "No". He seemed satisfied and was about to let me pass through. Just as I was proceeding, he suddenly sprayed a liquid into my eyes, which he said was a new procedure because of the pandemic. It surprised and annoyed me as I was not aware of this new protocol. I was also concerned that the disinfectant might burn my eyes, but I hardly felt it. I was relieved. I was more focused on having been let back in and was

ready to proceed because I had somewhere to go and was on a tight schedule. Then, just as I was passing through the checkpoint, I woke up and my eyes were stinging.

I was immediately aware of my dream, which amused me, as it seemed to symbolise my plight over having fallen back into a light sleep when I knew I had to get up. The conflict over my states of consciousness was apparently personified by the border guard who took his time doing his job of "guarding" my sleep and letting me rest a few more moments but who did eventually let me pass through to United States territory, my homeland, so I could wake up back in my home. The sudden action of the guard spraying me with the disinfectant, which I had expected to burn my eyes, seemed to represent the experience of my suddenly waking up with sore eyes due to lack of sleep, which I wished would not happen this time.

In the larger reality at this time, the global anxiety over a swine flu/H1N1 pandemic and the precautions that were being implemented seemed to be part of the day residue in forming my mind's choice of scenarios. A determinant from childhood also came to mind during my self-analysis of the dream. An apocryphal story related to my ancestors' immigration to the USA was of a great-uncle who, as a boy, had endured the hardship of transatlantic passage in the bowels of an overcrowded ship, only to be refused entry at Ellis Island because his eyes were red. The immigration authorities were worried that his bloodshot eyes were indicative of a very infectious disease, and he had to return to Eastern Europe with his father while his mother and siblings were admitted. The uncertainty of being permitted to pass through the borders to safety became a cautionary tale in my growing up. It appeared, therefore, that the classical elements of dream formation, such as wish-fulfilment, day residue, and childhood factors, were also operative in this type of dream, which symbolised my passing through different states of consciousness—that is, from sleep to wakefulness.

Despite such "personification of . . . drowsiness" (Rapaport, 1949), Rapaport reports that in normative circumstances ". . . distinguishing between I and not-I is preserved . . . [whereas] [I]n other states of consciousness parts of the self may not be as perceived. Multiple personalities . . . are commonly known examples" (p. 200). Under certain circumstances, therefore, this universal phenomenon may contribute to, or reinforce, a sense of multiple selves. It is, therefore, a very important clinical opportunity for the analyst to be able to point out to the patient the common origin of the content of both the dream and the altered state. Becoming aware of this manifestation of the compulsion to repeat could be a decisive moment for the patient to begin to accept formerly disowned aspects of the mind. When confronted with the possibility of a common origin to both the remembered dream and the dissociated self-state, the patient might experience this intervention as a well-timed interpretation.

Dreaming of defensive altered states

The representation in post-trauma dreams of the defensive altered states employed by the patient in response to the traumatic experience itself is that obscure aspect of the repetition compulsion under examination here. It was illustrated by a patient in analysis, Karen, who was desperately warding off the belief that she had been sexually abused by her aunt, a most trusted relative who had taken care of Karen when she was young. Karen emphatically insisted that she had no memories of molestation and, therefore, could not verify it in her mind. Nevertheless, her exceedingly refractory symptoms of memory loss, fluctuating levels of consciousness, psychogenic pain, genital hallucinations, self-mutilation, eating disorder symptoms, alcohol abuse, precocious sexuality, and recurrent dreams of penetration by trusted women in authority had raised the question of abuse in a number of previous treating clinicians. In addition, she described hallucinatory experiences of "others" in her mind who could take over for periods of time after which point she would then "come to" in the middle of an activity.

While she was in the throes of a crisis in treatment where she induced the kind of helplessness in me that she regularly lived with herself, she reported a dream where

> her aunt suddenly jumped out from behind a curtain and stated that a prominent medical specialist had finally diagnosed her condition as a hormonal disturbance. The patient then replied that no one really thought that this was the case any more. The aunt then exclaimed that she knew what was causing her problem. The patient, who then became self-conscious because others were around, asked if they could talk about it more privately elsewhere. The aunt, however, persisted and declared that it was because the patient wanted to surpass everyone else but was really

unimportant in her family and was neglected. At that point, the patient then started to cry and refuted the aunt, saying that her explanation could not cause her to feel pain so severe that it was as if her bones were ripping through the skin and coming out of her body. Then the aunt became quite angry and approached the patient in a menacing and mechanical way, like a character in a horror movie. The patient could not move and then found herself sitting in a chair across the room. The aunt continued to approach her and said that the patient did not think that she could do something like this, at which point the aunt sat atop her with her legs wrapped around her. The aunt's breasts then came closer to the patient's face and felt like dangerous, disgusting weapons as Karen became overwhelmed with panic. These words formed in her mind: "It's true! It's true! I can't do this! How am I going to get through this?!?!"

Suddenly, it became very misty, everything became blurry, and everything in her body and mind began to feel fine. Then it was as though she were in a blackout.

Karen reported that she remembered nothing more until she awoke in tremendous physical pain; she felt too paralysed with pain to move, yet in too much pain to stay in bed. Her perpetual sense of being in a no-win situation was exemplified by the extent of her pain.

Significantly, one of the "selves" that the patient experienced as inhabiting her mind was known to her as the shadow, one who personified living in darkness. This "part" of her reportedly had memories of bad events and protected the patient by destroying her memory and inducing body pain in order to keep her from thinking and remembering too much. Thus, it appeared as though the patient's dream represented her defensive altered state of consciousness in response to the over-stimulating advances by her aunt. The dream imagery of mist, blurriness, and relief of both physical and mental pain suggested an autohypnotic flight from traumatic experience or experiences that might have been condensed into this one scenario.

Discussion

In severe dissociative psychopathology, where patients may shift between different levels of consciousness while awake, this mechanism also appears to be operative. In such cases, they may also employ a "pseudo-externalised displacement" in the service of negation. In so doing, they develop a quasi-delusional insight enabling them to say,

"I didn't think, say, do, feel, or dream that—someone else did!" Thus, anthropomorphisation of autohypnotic, dreamlike, hypnogogic, and hypnopompic states, a reflection of the functional phenomenon, seems to be a contributing factor to this psychological state. Under the influence of the repetition compulsion, a reciprocal amnesia between these dissociated states and post-trauma dreams may further reinforce this process of disowning what is in the mind, even as the themes keep repeating themselves. As a result, this complex form of negation cannot be reversed by a mere lifting of repression through simple interpretation. While the timing of any interpretative effort is always crucial, it is especially important in helping the patient recognise and own these mental contents. Recognition of these complex operations in response to severe early trauma is necessary in the understanding of this defence/symptom compromise formation, which may be catalysed by analysis of the transference (I. Brenner, 2001, 2004, 2009a). When successfully handled, such patients, who initially have no conscious memory of trauma at a young age, may, over time, come to be able to own what, in their "heart of hearts", they had known but did not *really* know was there all along (I. Brenner, 1997). As one patient on the verge of a breakthrough very succinctly and insightfully observed, "I cannot think about what I remember!"

My experience with hundreds of patients with severe dissociative pathology has shown that there is clinical value in viewing their recurrent dreams and their altered ego states from this perspective. In such cases, the striking similarities between the manifest content of traumatic dreams and the first-hand accounts of the personifications themselves suggest a common mental origin to both (Barrett, 1995; I. Brenner, 2001), as described above. These findings seem to suggest that the psychic fates of these altered states of consciousness, which originally occurred in response to severe early trauma, may be represented and repeated in the post-trauma dream and then reincorporated into repeated altered states.

A bridge from "hypnoid states" to psychic energy and Beyond the Pleasure Principle

One of the major theoretical contributions in *Beyond the Pleasure Principle* is based upon Freud's elaboration of Breuer's hypothesis of bound and unbound energy, where the former is quiescent and the latter is free and mobile (Freud, 1895d). As such, the conscious would contain energy with the potential to be discharged freely due to the nature of mental activity and excitatory processes occurring there. For protection against over-stimulation, however, a specialised function of the psyche develops, resulting in a psychological callous, as it were, in which ". . . its outermost surface ceases to have the structure proper to living matter, becomes to some degree inorganic and thence-forward functions as a special envelope or membrane resistant to stimuli" (Freud, 1920g, p. 27). Therefore, "By its death, the outer layer has saved all the deeper ones from a similar fate – unless, that is to say, stimuli reach it which are so strong that they break through the protective shield" (Freud, 1920g, p. 27). Freud then goes on to say that it would be

> ". . . 'traumatic' [if] any excitations from outside . . . are powerful enough to break through the protective shield . . . [and therefore] provoke a disturbance on a large scale in the functioning of the organ-ism's energy and to set in motion *every possible defensive measure*. (Freud, 1920g, p. 29, my italics)

In this case, a defensive altered state of consciousness would be an example of such a desperate defensive measure. As a result, the plea-sure principle is no longer in operation, and the major task of the psyche is to master, bind, and dispose of the excessive energy. This model of disposal is analogous to the function of metabolism in the liver, whereby one method of disposal of toxic substances that enter the digestive system is to attach certain molecules to the intruding materials to make them water soluble and easily excreted as a waste product. This process of chemical binding, known as conjugation, then enables the poison to be safely excreted in waste material in the faeces. In Freud's words, "The binding of an instinctual impulse would be a preliminary function designed to prepare the excitation for its final elimination in the pleasure of discharge" (Freud, 1920g, p. 62).

It then follows that the painful invasion due to the breach of the protective shell results in the deployment of high amounts of energy: "An 'anticathexis' on a grand scale is set up . . . [for the purpose] of converting it into quiescent cathexis, that is of binding it psychically" (Freud, 1920g, p. 30). Here, Freud's ". . . principle of the insusceptibil-ity to excitation of uncathected systems . . ." (Freud, 1917d) suggests that the amount of quiescent cathexis is directly proportional to the psychic capacity for binding. As a result, the

> ... importance [of] the element of fright ... [which] is caused by [the] lack of any preparedness for anxiety [results in] those systems ... not [being] in a good position for binding the inflowing amounts of excitation ... (Freud, 1920g, p. 31)

Therefore, the "... preparedness for anxiety and the hypercathexis of the receptive systems constitute the last line of defence ..." (Freud, 1920g, p. 31). In order "... to master the stimulus retrospectively, by developing the anxiety whose omission was the cause of the traumatic neurosis ... [traumatic dreams occur] in obedience to the compulsion to repeat ..." (Freud, 1920g, p. 32). So,

> If there is a 'beyond the pleasure principle', it is only consistent that there was also a time before the purpose of dreams was the fulfilment of wishes ... [that is] the psychical binding of traumatic impressions ... [which] obey the compulsion to repeat ... (Freud, 1920g, p. 33)

Strachey noted that, surprisingly and repeatedly, Freud makes an "... unexpected attribution to Breuer of the distinction between bound and unbound psychical energy and between the primary and secondary processes" (Freud, 1895d, p. xxvii). Originally, Freud did not elaborate on these ideas, but he was clearly influenced (Holt, 1962). Interestingly, Breuer's discourse on hypnoid states, which Freud never totally endorsed (I. Brenner, 2009a), follow shortly after his comments on energy. His observation on these altered states of consciousness, which have all been forgotten by psychoanalysts, has particular relevance to the discussion here and serves as a starting point of an alternative pathway to understanding. Breuer conjectured that

> ... if the split-off mind is in a constant state of excitation, as it was with Janet's hemi-anaesthetic patients ... so little cerebral functioning is left over for waking thought that the weakness of mind which Janet describes and regards as innate is fully accounted for. (Freud, 1895d, p. 238)

Moreover, he wonders what happens while in a state of autohypnosis:

> If during such a state of absorption, and while the flow of ideas is inhibited, a group of affectively-coloured ideas is active, it creates a

high level of intracerebral excitation which is not used up by mental work and is at the disposal of abnormal functioning, such as conversion. (Freud, 1895d, p. 218)

While Breuer's ideas remain in the more physiological realm than in the psychological, the similarity to Freud's later ideas is quite evident. Regarding the debate over whether the hypnoid state precedes the traumatic excitation or is, in fact, caused by it, Freud concluded that ". . . the affect itself created a hypnoid state . . ." (Freud, 1895d, p.128), whereas Breuer suggested that "Auto-hypnosis has, so to speak, created the space or region of unconscious psychical activity into which the ideas which are fended off are driven" (Freud, 1895d, p. 236). Therefore, the sharp distinction between hypnoid hysteria and defence hysteria, which Freud preferred, might have not been so clear-cut, but more in the service of his effort to claim originality of his ideas. Regardless, Breuer describes how

> . . . pathogenic auto-hypnosis would seem to come about in some people – by affect being introduced into a habitual reverie . . . [and] [O]nce this has happened, the hypnosis-like state is repeated again and again when the same circumstances arise . . . (Freud, 1895d, pp. 218–219)

Breuer then suggests that the ". . . recollection of the affective idea, which is constantly being renewed, keeps on re-establishing this state of mind, [and] 'hypnoid fright' . . . [is] . . . the incubation stage of 'traumatic hysteria' . . ." (Freud, 1895d, p. 220). Breuer's way of explaining the compulsion to repeat is also based on energic considerations such that ". . . fright inhibits the flow of ideas at the same time at which an affective idea (of danger) is very active . . . [and] offers a complete parallel to a reverie charged with affect . . ." (Freud, 1895d, pp. 219–220).

Through Breuer's clinical observation and reasoning, therefore, he appears to conclude that the hypnoid state, an altered state of consciousness identical to an autohypnotic state, is what we would now consider a compromise formation that can be pathological or defensive and allow some gratification of an impulse that he described as a repetitive affectively charged idea. Furthermore, it is an ego-weakening mental state unable to bind the excessive stimulation entering the psyche and, in his oft-quoted words,

> . . . the splitting of psychical activity which is so striking in the well-known cases in the form of 'double conscience' is present to a rudimentary degree in every major hysteria [and that] the liability and tendency to such a dissociation is the basic phenomenon of this neurosis. (Freud, 1895d, p. 227)

Perhaps, in an effort of the overwhelmed ego to bind the putative psychic energy that Breuer and then Freud described, the massively traumatised child has recurrent dreams at night of his defensive altered states during the day and might become confused by the mutual influences of one on the other. The result might be the formation of dissociated quasi-identities that attempt to keep mental contents separate and bind the psychic energy.

The sense of separateness in such patients' minds appears to be related to, but also extend beyond, the lack of integration of libidinally and aggressively derived self- and object representations. It is the quintessential expression of the lack of self-constancy, which is enhanced by the subjective experience of separate selves with their own cohesion. These personifications appear to be created with the help of a number of so-called "organising influences", such as perverse sexuality, intergenerational transmission of trauma with identification with the aggressor, the divisive effects of aggression itself, near-death experiences, and the employment of these dream-like and "hysterical" mechanisms (I. Brenner, 2001, 2004).

There was reciprocal amnesia between Cindy's personifications with their monoideic fugues (Janet, 1907) and her dreams, which seemed to symbolise the anthropomorphisation of her disturbance of consciousness (Silberer, 1909) during the original trauma. In other words, when Cindy switched into different alters, she had no memory of her dreams; as Cindy, she had no memory of what her alters knew, but did remember her dreams. Through pseudo-externalised displacement, she attributed her impulses, affects, fantasies, and memories to her cadre of "inside people". This way, she could disown what was intolerable and thereby experience her intrapsychic conflicts as interpersonal conflicts. Her narcissistic investment in her separate selves (Kluft, 1987b) posed a most powerful resistance which, if confronted too soon, could have had suicidal implications.

The onset of Cindy's medical symptoms, which developed at a time of great intensity in the transference, resulted in further dissociative symptoms and absences as well as a regressive impasse. Her recurrent dreams at this time bore an undeniable resemblance to the first-hand accounts of the childhood sexual trauma reported by her as another self. With the help of treatment, the patient's eventual awareness of the internal consistency of those accounts enabled her to "feel it in her bones" and allowed her to become convinced that it was truly herself who had been victimised. Similarly, the other patient, Karen, had a feeling in her bones, too. She dreamt of bones literally ripping through her flesh, which was so painful that she, too, had to finally consider that something unthinkable must have happened to her in order to create so much pain.

Concluding comments

In order for the realisation and acceptance of ownership of the mind to occur, it seems crucial to help such a patient realise how it may have operated during such intolerable experiences. By doing so, Cindy could begin to consider that the creation of her alters might indeed have been, in part, due to the spilling over of what usually remains in the realm of post-trauma dreams. In the dreams, the symbolic representation of defensive altered states at the time of the original trauma may take the form of a child being violated while the patient enters such an autohypnotic state and "leaves" her body, or experiences a "blackout". There seems to be a reciprocal influence on the dreams, self-perception, and identity, as this cycle may apparently repeat itself for years. This phenomenon may then manifest itself through "switching" to other dissociated selves. Containment and interpretative work on how a patient's mind functions under these conditions might enable a movement toward a healing of the rifts in the psyche. Thus, the interrelationship between trauma, recurrent dreams, and defensive altered state(s) presents an unusual manifestation of the compulsion to repeat.

Freud's difficulty in explaining unconscious guilt via the topographic theory required him to revise his thinking and devise the structural theory (Freud, 1923b). Then, the problem of repetitive traumatic dreams required him to go "beyond the pleasure principle" (Freud, 1920g) and postulate the death instinct. Similarly, I would suggest that phenomena such as the relationship between dreams and amnestic self-states warrant a reconsideration of the role of dissociation in mental functioning. It is, therefore, ironic and, as Fliess suggests, puzzling (Fliess, 1953b) that Freud omits the death instinct in the "Revision of dreams" lecture in his *New Introductory Lectures* (Freud, 1933a, pp. 28–30). While he does discuss the role of the death instinct in the compulsion to repeat later on in his lecture on "Anxiety and instinctual life" (Freud, 1933a, pp. 107–108), he merely states that the function of the dream as the guardian of sleep has failed and that, essentially, a psychical overload has occurred. It is the fate of this overload that is the subject of exploration here. Regardless of the ultimate validity of the death instinct *per se*, the power of the repetition compulsion as a fact of mental life enables the analyst to help certain patients come to terms with very disturbing traumatic experiences.

CHAPTER ELEVEN

Psychoactive therapy

"Trust your wound to a teacher's surgery.
. . .
Don't turn your head. Keep looking
at the bandaged place.
That is where the light enters you.
And don't believe for a moment
you are healing yourself"

(Rumi, 2006, p. 307)

W hy would I consider describing the therapeutic relationship with a severely traumatised individual as being "psychoactive"? After all, the term came into prominence during the early 1960s and was associated with mind-altering drugs such as LSD. More recently, it has been used to describe the class of medications that are prescribed for psychiatric conditions, such as anti-depressants, anxiolytics, mood stabilisers, and antipsychotics. So, the idea that a powerful, therapeutic agent is neither a pill nor an electric current but, rather, another human being, is both ancient and futuristic at the same time. Yet, what exactly it is about the nature of such a relationship that facilitates lasting change in the psyche has been the subject of intense scrutiny since the beginning of the analytic enterprise. Most analysts today would agree that the recommendations that Freud gave to those entering our field over a century ago were rather "sterile" and perhaps a bit of an over-correction to the counter-transference pitfalls that were already well known at the time. He stated that clinicians should

> ... model themselves during psycho-analytic treatment on the surgeon, who puts aside all his feelings, even his human sympathy, and concentrates his mental forces on the simple aim of performing the operation as skilfully as possible . . .The justification for requiring this emotional coldness in the analyst is that it creates the most advantageous conditions for both parties: for the doctor a desirable protection for his own emotional life and for the patient the largest amount of help that we can give him *to-day*. (Freud, 1912e, p. 114, my italics)

As the "classical" approach became further codified, more than twenty years later Strachey's delineation of the "nature of the therapeutic action" through interpretation was extremely influential in its comprehensive description of the prevailing attitudes at the time:

> What, then, *is* interpretation? and how does it work? Extremely little seems to be known about it, but this does not prevent an almost universal belief in its remarkable efficacy as a weapon: interpretation has, it must be confessed, many of the qualities of a *magic* weapon. It is, of course, felt as such by many patients . . .

> But I believe it would be true in general to say that analysts are inclined to feel interpretation as something extremely powerful whether for good or ill . . . Thus, we are told that if we interpret too soon or too rashly, we run the risk of losing a patient; that unless we interpret promptly and deeply we run the risk of losing a patient; that interpretation may give rise to intolerable and unmanageable outbreaks of anxiety by "liberating" it; that interpretation is the only way of enabling a patient to cope with an unmanageable outbreak of anxiety by "resolving" it; that interpretations must always refer to material on the very point of emerging into consciousness; that the most useful interpretations are really deep ones; "Be cautious with your interpretations!" says one voice; "When in doubt, interpret!" says another. (Strachey, 1934, pp. 140–141)

These seemingly contradictory attitudes about interpretations certainly lend themselves to having increased the mystique of the power of such interventions, as well as having increased the anxiety of psychoanalytic candidates who, when presented with the promise of wielding such a powerful weapon, have often felt quite unprepared and diffident. Through such efforts to elevate psychoanalysis to the realm of science, formulas for therapeutic action via this procedure minimised the role of the analyst *per se*, his own psychology, and the life circumstances of the patient:

> This modification of the patient's super-ego is brought about in a series of innumerable small steps by the agency of mutative interpretations, which are effected by the analyst in virtue of his position as object of the patient's id-impulses and as auxiliary super-ego. (Strachey, 1934, p. 158)

Twenty years later, Stone, in his most influential paper on the widening scope of indications for psychoanalysis, advocated flexibility and modification of technique in order to accommodate the psychological needs of patients who do not meet the theoretical, ideal, and, essentially, non-existent neurotic patient so elegantly described by Eissler (Eissler, 1953) in his classic paper on parameters. Stone concludes,

> I believe that any number and degree of parameters can be introduced where they are genuinely necessary to meet special conditions, so long as they all directed to bringing about the ultimate purposes and processes of the analytic end requirements, as we have just described them . . . (Stone, 1954, p. 575)

The mobilisation of the transference neurosis and its maximal dissolution were indeed the analytic end points. He also emphasised the person of the analyst himself:

> Another consideration in our field is the analyst himself. In no other field, save surgery, to which Freud frequently compared analysis, is the personal equation so important. It is up to us to know our capacities, intellectual and emotional, if we cannot always know one another so clearly in this respect. Again, special predilections, interests, emotional textures may profoundly influence prognosis, and thus—in a tangible way—the indications. I suppose one might generalize

crudely to the effect that, apart from skills, a therapist must be able to love a psychotic or a delinquent, and be at least warmly interested in the "borderline" patient (whether or not this feeling is *utilized* technically), for optimum results. (Stone, 1954, p. 592)

In today's psychoanalytic world, the ascendancy of the relational model has taken the position that the shared relational unconscious and the enactments that inevitably occur in the analytic dyad provide the main source of data in which meaning is co-constructed. In this more egalitarian system, both analyst and analysand work together to understand the contribution of their psyches in identifying those aspects of the mind in dissociated self-states that have not been accessible to consciousness. In Bromberg's paper, "Stumbling along and hanging in: if this be technique, make the most of it! (Bromberg, 2012), he makes a plea for the total loosening of ties with the idea of analytic technique and favours a freer exchange. In practice, however, I think most contemporary analysts employ a variety of techniques and psychoanalytic models based on different models of the mind and develop their own so-called hybrid approach. I offer a vignette to illustrate such an approach taken in the treatment of a severely traumatised woman with a lower-level dissociative character, that is, DID, in which classical and relational aspects were utilised. In this case, the analysis of an enactment facilitated a profound "integration" of her selves.

Case report

A curiously timed error by my billing company and how I handled it—or mishandled it—became the focal point of a very painful clinical moment that ultimately furthered the treatment. The intensity and range of feelings in the transference–countertransference matrix illustrate the, dare I say, "highly charged" nature of the therapeutic relationship and the enormous power it has for intrapsychic change. I will describe the circumstances surrounding this enactment and provide enough background information about this rather complex case to put the situation in context.

After several years of four-times-a-week analysis on the couch, I announced to Margaret that I was planning a rather modest fee increase in my practice and wanted her to be aware of it. I then asked her how she felt about it. After all, even a small fee increase per session can add up if one is in analysis and, knowing that she had already taken on an additional financial responsibility for an ailing relative who was in desperate need and had no one else to turn to, I anticipated that the patient might have been dismayed at my announcement. Since I had not levied a fee increase across the board in a number of years, I felt a sense of healthy entitlement, especially since my expenses had steadily risen during that time. I sensed, however, that Margaret might react strongly to this announcement, especially since she had made recent overtures about needing to "take a break" because of her new financial commitments. Even prior to that, she was struggling. On a deeper level, however, she was at a point in analysis where she was overwhelmed by the emergence of very disturbing material pertaining to a perverse and vicious sexual assault by her estranged step-brother, a man much older than she who was essentially a father surrogate.

I considered whether to "protect" her by making her an exception to the fee increase and sparing her the stress of such additional pressure, but then wondered whether I would be doing such a thing out of fear that our therapeutic alliance could not withstand an intensification of the sadomasochistic perpetrator–victim aspect of the transference, which had periodically emerged and then quickly subsided. Moreover, she was aware that I was willing to allow her to defer some payment of the fee, but she, nevertheless, felt very uneasy about such indebtedness. Having escaped her family to study abroad in the USA and having never returned to the UK, she had been destitute for several years, surviving on very meagre means and with the help of the kindness of some older people who took a parental, protective role towards her. She had periodically experienced me that way, but was terribly afraid to feel too deeply about what she would truly want.

With these considerations in mind, I gently made the announcement about the fee increase only to hear what I already knew of her terrible financial straits and her petulant insistence that her feelings about it would not make any difference anyway. In her mind, I would do whatever I was going to do and that was that. What was the point of "analysing" her feelings about it and indulging in fantasies? She would just react to whatever I did and that would be that. Throughout the month, she would get to the "fee issue" periodically, tearfully recalling that time in her life when she was essentially homeless were it not for the generosity of several benign, parental figures. It would have been most despairing now to let herself ask for anything lest she be rejected—or perhaps even worse—were her unspoken wish to be granted . . . So, the issue was left hanging in the air. As the end of the month was approaching and bills needed to be prepared, I was quite aware that this topic was not very well "analysed". I sensed that, for a complex set of reasons, it would probably not be able to be analysed further until she received the forthcoming bill. Rather ambivalently, I decided to proceed with the fee increase and trusted that we would be able to arrive at some compromise about deferring the increase and/ or some of the payment if necessary. However, I felt just a bit uneasy about the patient's overt, quiet "surrender" to my will.

Meanwhile, one of the main reasons that our further exploration of the fee did not occur—at least directly—was because many of the sessions at that time were characterised by the re-emergence of an unusual form of communication, the nature of which I had already become quite familiar with. Margaret would often arrive several minutes late and enter the office rather formally and very seriously. She would then quietly lie on the couch and be silent for a minute or two. She would often say that she had nothing on her mind and ask me to talk to her or ask her a question. She was tense and quite internally preoccupied, but seemed rather blocked verbally. After a few associations related to the day residue and her difficulties navigating the traffic in order to get to the office, I would then notice subtle changes in the muscle tension of her arms as well as her neck and head. In addition, I sensed a change in the nature of her silence, so that through my reverie—as Bion described it (Bion, 1962a,b)—I felt a difference in her, a difference in the nature of her silence. Shortly afterwards, she would begin speaking but in a different, more clipped, staccato way, picking up on where we had left off on a very different dialogue which had been ongoing but intermittent. In this dialogue, of which Margaret had no memory, another, seemingly separate, self—one who was very angry, totally mistrustful, and deadly serious—would confront and grill me over basic questions such as what was the purpose of Margaret's visits and why should she continue.

This other self's "emergence", as it were, was a signal that the patient was experiencing very deep anxiety in the transference and utilised dissociation and pseudo-externalised displacement

(I. Brenner, 2009a,b) as a defence. Furthermore, her wish to interrupt treatment for financial reasons, no matter how valid her external reality was, apparently legitimised her urge to flee out of a deep sense of danger. The "dark one", as this self became known, began to reconstruct the disastrous meeting with her step-brother amid her constant interrogation of me and my purpose. In the patient's flight from the here and now, it was apparently preferable to dredge up the past in an altered state of consciousness than own her own desires in the transference. The story, as it was further pieced together, eventually went like this:

After several years of virtually no contact with her family and assuming she was totally forgotten about after she left home and worked her way through college, her step-brother unexpectedly called her. He was in the USA and actually in her city on business. He invited her to dinner. She was overcome with joy at what felt like a dream come true and instantly accepted his invitation. Preparing herself for the best surprise of her life, she put on her best dress, make-up, jewellery, and even wrote a poem of exultation to read to him. Perhaps he really did love her after all and this was a chance for him to prove it after years of her essentially being ignored and believing her absence was not even noticed. She hurriedly met him at the hotel, expecting they would go to a very nice restaurant for a wonderful reunion dinner. She was a bit dismayed when he directed her to a dingy coffee shop adjacent to the hotel, but she did not let this disappointment register in her mind for long and they sat down. Throughout their meal, her stepbrother at times seemed distracted and paid little attention to her heartfelt poem recited to him at this auspicious time, yet he seemed impressed afterwards as he asked her if she had really written it herself. A left-handed compliment to be sure, the patient did her best to extract whatever positive aspects of this comment she could. Desperately hungry for affection from him, when their brief repast was completed, she wanted to spend more time with him and perhaps take a walk.

During those awkward moments at such a time when the uncertainty of parting or continuing with someone is in the air, Margaret got a very odd sensation as they stood looking at each other. It was a fleeting, momentary, eerie, creepy feeling that she quickly suppressed and hastily ejected from her consciousness. In fact, she recalled, as she replayed the events in her mind in analysis decades later and struggled to find the words for her visceral reaction, that she had had the same fleeting sensation for a moment at dinner. A flash—so totally incongruous and ludicrous that she immediately suppressed it—in which she felt as though he were looking at her, eyeing her up and down, as though she were in a bar and he were a man having lewd thoughts about her. But how could that be? It was her step-brother after all, the only man who did not abandon or abuse her when she was young, at least as she remembered it. She had always thought, at least consciously, that he was a protector.

Convincing herself that it was an aberrant perception, no doubt the product of her love-starved mind, when he looked at her this way again and asked her if she wanted to see his hotel room, she hesitated for a moment but then agreed. Squelching a queasy feeling as they silently waited in front of the elevator, she recalled how she almost automatically dismissed these doubts and ascended to his floor. (Significantly, the location of the elevator and the door to my office in the hallway resembled the arrangement at the hotel room.) When they exited and approached his door, she halted again and once again renounced her mounting anxiety until she felt him pushing her into his room and heard him locking the door behind them. It was only at that moment that she gave full attention to her plight—trapped and terrified in a locked hotel room with a man she thought she knew who had been leering at her during their icy reunion.

Trying her best to mask her abject fear, she excused herself and scurried to the bathroom where she locked herself in for an indeterminate period of time. Her head was pounding, her heart was racing, and her mind was racing. Trying to pry open a window and imagining escaping that way, her hopes for an exit from the intolerable fate awaiting her back in the bedroom were dashed when she could not pry it open. Even if she could, she was not sure whether or not there was a fire escape that she could reach or merely a sheer drop to the pavement many storeys below. She contemplated that fate for a very long moment. Then, at that point, she apparently lost track of time and her surroundings and, despite her attempts over the years to reconstruct every detail of their meeting, things became blurred. As she could not escape with her body, she apparently escaped with her mind by detaching from it psychologically. Earlier in analysis, in piecemeal fashion and terror-filled, abreactive utterances in altered states of consciousness, she sketched out a brutal rape and utter humiliation afterwards, but many gaps remained. She relived aspects of this trauma with little or no observing ego or a sense of it having been a past event. Having walked down my hallway countless times over the years and not having made any conscious connection between the arrangement of this hallway and the hallway of her step-brother's hotel, when she finally became aware of the connection, her fear in the transference escalated greatly.

The patient's hesitation and subsequent dismissal of her vague uneasiness was a source of lifelong regret, despair, and self-loathing. Something broke and died inside of her that day. She lamented how the events of such a short period of time could have such lasting effects on the rest of her life. She vowed to herself that never again would she let herself get into a situation where her desire for recognition, affirmation—or dare she say, "love"—would make her feel vulnerable to another sadistic betrayal. The words "desire" and "wish for love" were permanently deleted from her vocabulary. She did not think that she could ever recover from another betrayal and, as the pressures of the transference increased, so did her panic. Fuelled by her terror, which was frequently just out of her awareness, she created a most convincing rationalisation that she needed to take a break from treatment for her "real" financial reasons.

During such a crucial moment in the process, the patient frequently "switched" during sessions, and the personification who clearly "knew" what the step-brother had in mind had emerged but did not stop Margaret from going to his room. She asked me to keep this revelation a secret from Margaret. In other words, I was being asked not to reveal to the patient in her usual state of consciousness what I was about to learn from her in a dissociated, amnestic state. I was, essentially, speaking to her unconscious mind and was basically being warned that it would be too much for her to know, that is, that deep down inside she did know what would happen. So, from a classical, technical perspective, I was being supervised by this self not to make a premature interpretation to the patient lest it overwhelm her.

It is generally recommended by DID trauma therapists not to "take sides" or play favourites with the alters because of the possible negative repercussions in the alliance, so I felt in a bind in this situation. Would keeping a secret about Margaret's mind from Margaret hurt her, adversely affect her trust, and feel like a dreaded betrayal? Would it reflect a patronising, parental, overprotective, countertransference enactment? Or would it be respecting a plea from the patient in the only way she could do so that she was simply not ready to hear all of this in her usual state of mind? Conversely, would telling this self that I could not make such a promise backfire also, as in this state of mind the patient experienced and remembered much of the details of what had transpired and was already extremely angry and mistrustful in the transference?

Earning the patient's trust in this component of the mosaic transference (I. Brenner, 2004) was quite difficult and was taking place over many weeks in brief instalments, as it were, during her intermittent, spontaneous appearances during the treatment hours. Therefore, I sensed that such a request had enormous significance and also sensed that I had become a repository for her own conflict over this matter, which had been deposited into my psyche. Sensing the patient's great anguish at the moment, as well as her need to reveal something of great importance in confidence, I decided to keep her "secret" about her from her. I conceptualised that to do otherwise would be tantamount to making, indeed, a premature interpretation to a patient who masochistically might be "asking for it" (again) before she was ready to assimilate it.

The "dark self" uncharacteristically became tearful and said that she was so sorry that she did not impose her will upon Margaret, as her instincts told her in no uncertain terms there would be trouble. The "dark self" prided herself on being a protector and had let everybody down by allowing Margaret's desperate wish for her stepbrother's love to prevail and being "pushed out of the way". The "dark self" felt a deep sense of shame and did not want Margaret to know just yet how badly she had failed her. This admission of vulnerability had eroded the self's veneer of toughness in the transference, and she was shocked to have trusted me enough to have divulged it. My technical handling of her request seemed appropriate in the moment, but I was left with a vague, nagging sense of doubt, wondering how Margaret would feel when we met next time. I also wondered whether she would enquire about what had transpired during her most recent absence, as she had become much more aware of her amnestic lapses during the hours.

With the impending three-day gap in the sessions due to the weekend, as well as the end of the month approaching, I received my bills from my billing company and intended to give the patient hers at our next session on the following Monday. Interestingly, the bill did not reflect the very modest increase that I had asked them to factor into her statement. I reflected upon this error and was faintly amused to realise that the company, despite my instructions, seemed to have enacted my own conflict over the increase by keeping the original amount! Indeed, our analysing the meaning of the increase was incomplete, and I was confronted with another technical dilemma over how to handle this problem with Margaret. I could have stayed with my original conscious intent and have the bill redone, giving it to her on Tuesday, or I could have delayed giving her any bill until we had more adequately explored the issue, or I could have reversed my position, make a unilateral decision to maintain her fee for the time being, and hand her the bill as it stood. However, for reasons that were not totally clear to me at the time, I decided to give her the bill as it stood, disclose what had actually happened, and take it from there.

I had mistakenly thought that our rapport at that point was such that she could appreciate the irony of the situation, especially since she not infrequently found humour to be a way of reducing the heaviness of her moods. That was not the case here.

Unbeknown to me at the time, as she walked down the increasingly disturbing hallway that day for the session, she had a fleeting idea that I had changed my mind about the fee increase and would not change anything. She experienced a sudden rush of happy giddiness over this private fantasy of her wish fulfilled and squelched her mood immediately, dismissing it as fanciful, absurd, and childish. By the time she entered the office, she had sobered up and did not reveal any of these associations. Therefore, when she saw the unchanged bill, her heart soared again immediately; even though I believed I had announced the dilemma as soon as she received the statement, it was too late. Another disaster had just taken place and, just like with her step-brother, all of her excited anticipation and hopes had been shattered by a ruthless betrayal. She was devastated and enraged, never expecting such cruelty from me. She clearly experienced my attempt at a collaborative sharing of the problem that we could mutually work on together as a sadistic teasing. Despite the fact that she often asked me to talk to her about my experience of being with her and had seemed to appreciate such moments of disclosure, such was not to happen this time. The suddenness and the intensity of the rupture of our alliance were shocking to me at first as I sensed her impulse to get up and run out.

I wondered if this would become a moment where she would indeed have to "take a break", having been gripped by fear and mistrust, never, ever expecting such behaviour from her analyst, of all people. An "Et tu, Brute?" moment filled the air and, as much as I wanted to exonerate myself from her accusation, I listened quietly and empathically. I had the sense that if "we" could tolerate the intensity of her affect—and indeed analyse what was going on in each of us in order to understand the enactment—then perhaps we could avert an interruption. At the time, I did not realise just how potentially psychoactive this moment was, but I did realise that I needed to understand my part in it very quickly and hopefully before the next hour.

In my self-analytic reflection after the session, I realised that the intensity of the moment completely eclipsed—in my mind—the other dialogue that had been ongoing with Margaret's dissociated self about her sexual assault by her step-brother. In a sense, I, too, had temporarily dissociated that aspect of the process, which made me curious about a concordant identification (Racker, 1953, 1957). With this awareness, my mind then became freed up so I could wonder if any aspect of that dialogue had been unconsciously pressing upon my psyche and influencing my handling of the billing situation. Certainly, her reaction of intense betrayal was a moment of affective congruence with her past. I then realised that my thought about sharing my dilemma over the company's error was motivated by a wish to share a deeper conflict with her. I discovered that I was more troubled than I appreciated by my pact with her "dark self" to keep the secret from Margaret that she "knew" what was going to happen to her, but went into the hotel room none the less. Evidently, the content of the secret was one issue, but the fact that I had made a secret pact with her— evidently without her conscious knowledge—was also troubling to me. So, I apparently displaced that wish to reveal that a pact had been made on to the billing problem, which I then convinced myself would have been amusing to her as well. Unconsciously, I must have thought that working out that dilemma would have been preferable, but that substitute obviously failed and I could not avoid being the target of her explosive wrath. A scorned woman, whose deep desire for love was brutally exploited and whose trust was so hard to earn and so quickly broken, Margaret was on the warpath in the transference. I knew that the forthcoming hour could be decisive and felt relieved that my mind could now integrate the two dialogues. But could she?

The state of mind of the analyst at the onset of any given hour has been the subject of great importance to clinicians from Freud's "evenly-suspended attention" (Freud, 1912e) to an analytic attitude (Schafer, 1983) to Bion's "no memory or desire" (Bion, 1962a,b). Essentially, however, most would agree upon having a stance of being open-minded, non-directive, receptive, and curious. One of the significant aspects of the Tuesday hour was that it was not possible for me to clear my mind in anticipation of the session. I knew that Margaret was expecting to hear from me, and the way I felt was not dissimilar to how I would feel prior to testifying in court as an expert witness. Expecting a tough cross-examination, I would review my material, imagine certain questions being asked, expect my credibility to be challenged, and also be on the lookout for being intentionally provoked. In addition, there was an element of theatre involved in such a performance, as I had seen in a recent experience with a prosecuting attorney. He made an off-handed remark about my reports not being timely, definitely wanting to give the impression to the jury of my being unreliable. When given the opportunity at a later time, I non-defensively commented on the regularity of my write-ups, and nothing more was said about it during cross-examination. During recess at the hearing, I approached this attorney, who had cross-examined me numerous times in the past. After exchanging formal pleasantries, I quietly said to him that I made a point of getting reports to him regularly and that if he truly was not getting them, would he please contact me in advance so I could make sure that he got another copy. At that moment, he smiled ever so briefly and simply said, "I know." Such vindication "off the record" further confirmed the importance of not losing one's composure on the stand. Here, the notion of applied psychoanalysis (Freud, 1933a) is useful as the analytically trained expert witness strives for "neutrality" in this non-clinical setting.

I suspect that such a detour into forensics came to my mind as I recognized that Margaret was the victim of a criminal, sexual assault and that she had never had her day in court. The upcoming session would be a trial in every sense of the word, and Margaret would be the aggrieved party, the prosecuting attorney, and the jury. I would be both the perpetrator and the expert witness.

When Margaret arrived for the next hour, her face was sternly set and she walked tentatively over to the couch, carefully placed her keys and glasses on the corner of the desk as usual, and hesitated before lying on the couch. As though her daily ritual had been performed in slow motion, she lay motionless and in stony silence, her façade of implacability showing no emotion whatsoever. I waited. She waited. After several minutes, I broke the silence and quietly spoke to her, telling her how I recognised what an effort it must have been for her to have returned to the office after such a shock the day before. I acknowledged that I had indeed given the situation a lot of thought and, while I was certainly interested in what was on her mind at the moment and was very receptive to her speaking, I had no intention of using her associations to avoid telling her what I myself had learnt the day before. I essentially explained what I had described above, which was that two dialogues were taking place. Moreover, I felt more of a loyalty bind between her and her dissociated self than I had realised, and this conflict was displaced on to the billing error, which I was more than willing to share with her. In the context of that situation, her feelings of betrayal, fear, and rage from the covert dialogue broke through and found expression in the overt dialogue about the bill.

Gradually and definitively, she began to relax, letting out a deep sigh, having essentially held her breath since she entered the office. While I still sensed that she was very much on guard, I could see that I had re-engaged her in the analytic process as she became curious and less hostile. Tears began to stream down the sides of her face while she tried to wipe them away as quickly as they came but to no avail. A meeting of her minds began to take place.

Several days later, she gingerly reported a hallucinatory-like experience while walking down the hall for the session: she quietly "heard" a young woman's voice whispering, "I'm sorry." It shook her up as she did not ever report having had such a clear auditory perception of this other self within her. Then she calmed down and became less anxious overall. Shortly afterward, she reported a profound change in her visual perception. Colours seemed brighter and clearer. Her visual acuity for distance actually improved, as she could now read the titles of my books on the shelves across the room without her glasses. Also, she felt a peculiar sense of loss of some heavy presence in a corner of her mind. It was as though something had left her and she felt sadness and almost an empty feeling that coexisted with a sense of lightness. She could not account for this seeming contradiction. It was a sensation that she had never before experienced and would take some getting used to, but she thought she could like it. She even felt a bit freer. Dare she ever reveal that she felt possessed at times by this other presence that now seemed to have vanished? She felt almost giddy with a new sense of buoyancy and sharpened visual perception. Could it truly be that an "integration" of her dissociated self had occurred? And if so, how and why?

Discussion

Margaret appeared to have had a profound psychophysiological experience that had an enduring effect upon her psyche. Her visual acuity improved and colours were brighter. She felt relieved of a deep burden after describing the voice of her other self apologising for not protecting her from the assault. She had increased clarity and continuity of memory of the assault, as well as an increased sense of continuity of self—her self. She could now own more of her experience and her dangerous desire to be loved at apparently almost any cost.

The phenomenon of "integration" in patients with severe dissociative psychopathology has been extensively described in the psychiatric literature but less so in the psychoanalytic realm (I. Brenner, 2001, 2004, 2009a; Kluft, 1993; Rothschild, 2009). "On the road to integration" has been considered a pivotal stage in the analytic treatment of such patients (I. Brenner, 2004, 2009a), and this clinical event seemed to herald its onset with Margaret. DID therapists have viewed the integration of alter personalities as the goal of an active treatment, whereas analysts have been less doctrinaire and more "analytic" in their approach. Elaborate imagery and hypnotic interventions after processing of traumatic memories were seen as the route to integration. During such times, a variety of somatic sensations such as Margaret reported has been described and has left an indelible impact upon patients. When it occurs spontaneously in trauma-focused therapy utilising hypnotic techniques, however, a dangerous decompensation might occur because of the premature collapse of dissociated defences before the patient is ready. As a result, new alters might then be created by the patient to re-establish the autohypnotic amnesia, a situation analogous to symptom substitution known to occur in hysteria. Therefore, a more controlled strategy was developed that titrated the patient's level of anxiety and ego strength. The fractionated, abreaction technique described by Kluft is one of these examples (Kluft, 2013).

In contrast to this active approach, the relational model of dissociation favours not so much an integration and melding of selves as much as an "interstate intersubjectivity" (Howell, 2005). From this perspective, the patient remains aware of other various dissociated self-states, but the shifting from one to another is much smoother and one "stands in the spaces" of these selves (Bromberg, 1996). What is significant in Margaret's case is that through a modified psycho-analytic technique that allowed for the free expression of her selves and an appreciation of the dual nature of dissociation as a defence, a structural change seemed to occur that incorporated elements of both of the approaches. Here, dissociation was seen to be utilised as a defence against both the anxiety of remembering a horrendous assault by a loved one as well as defending against anxiety in the transference over her desires for the analyst's recognition and love. My counter-transference self-analysis after the enactment of the billing situation enabled me to see how I, too, had essentially dissociated the two concurrent dialogues with the patient. By empathically disclosing to the patient how my own mind worked in such a situation, I offered it as a container for hers. In so doing, I enabled her to then reinternalise her own psyche after it had been integrated by mine. As a result, her dissociated selves then apparently joined, and she acquired self-constancy and continuity of the self.

Powerful moments in psychoanalytic encounters resulting in psychic change have been the subject of considerable research recently, such as has been reported by the Boston Change Process Study Group (2010). To my knowledge, however, such methodology has not been applied to patients with profound dissociative psycho-pathology. In my work with such patients, the impact of such nodal moments might be so profound that they may be considered the result of a psychoactive relationship. However, the findings of the Boston Group, although helpful, might be insufficient to explain the complex phenomenon occurring here.

The Boston Change Process Study Group, which comprised adult and child specialists, extensively studied the mechanisms of change during psychotherapy (Boston Change Process Study Group, 2010). Utilising a developmental perspective in studying non-interpretative interventions, they saw the mother–infant dyad as the template for the therapeutic relationship and emphasised the centrality of implicit knowledge and relational meaning. This implicit relational knowing (IRK) is defined as "knowing how to do things with others, how to be with them . . . [and this capacity] operates outside focal attention and conscious experience" (Boston Change Process Study Group, 2010, p. 166). Through attunement in the dyad, which is internalised by the patient, an improved capacity for self-regulation may then occur. The Group's research efforts focused on the *present moment*, which enabled them to identify what they called *moments of meeting (MOMs)*, times of important meeting of the minds where such change could occur. A *present moment* is defined as a "unit of dialogic exchange that is relatively coherent in content, homogeneous in feeling and oriented in the same direction towards a goal" (Boston Change Process Study Group, 2010, p. 14). Such an exchange "is embedded in an emotional, lived story with a narrative-like format that is grasped intuitively while it is unfolding, even though it lasts only between 1 and 10 seconds" (Boston Change Process Study Group, 2010, p. 170).

By invoking dynamic systems theory, or DST, the Group viewed the interaction in the therapeutic dyad as "a complex system with multiple variables" (Boston Change Process Study Group, 2010, p. 172) in which "new properties emerge that were neither predicted nor expected" (Boston Change Process Study Group, 2010, p. 173). But, while the element of unpredictability is very important here, the relational history of each member of the dyad exerts its influence, and the meaning of such past experiences becomes reorganised in this new context. Such a conceptualisation about psychic change has been thought to be quite helpful "to create organization . . . in the face of uncertainty, ambiguity, and/or dissociation" (Knoblauch, 2008, p. 154).

In the vignette of Margaret described above, it would be difficult to understand what had transpired by this paradigm alone because of the dual dialogue and the manifestations of "splitting of the mind" (Freud, 1895d) that reflected altered states of consciousness and unconsciousness for dynamic reasons. Moreover, the meeting of minds seemed to occur both within the patient's fragmented psyche between her selves, resulting in an integration, and in the dyad itself. Moreover, our articulation of what was going on was essential in this case. The Boston Group's work has been criticised for marginalising the importance of a dynamic unconscious and also for apparently

downgrading the importance of verbalisation. In this case, my countertransference fuelled a miscalculation about the patient's interest
in the "back story" of the billing error and led to my erroneously
believing that through our implicit relational knowing (IRK) we could
have shared a moment of ironic humour, which might have furthered
the treatment. In fact, it produced a rupture, which, through my
reverie, self-analysis, and subsequent explicit verbalisation, seemed to
be essential to re-establishing an equilibrium between us. While, no
doubt, non-verbal communication of my concern, empathy, and more
took place alongside my words, I feel rather convinced that without a
clear and open expression of my internal process the treatment
process itself would probably have stalled. There is much to be
learnt about the nature of such a psychoactive relationship with this
patient population and, one hopes, future research will provide more
elucidation.

A better appreciation of how this approach fits in with more
mainstream thinking may be derived by putting it in context. For
example, the "bifurcation" in analytic theory regarding the technical
handling of the patient's associations has been eloquently delineated
by Akhtar (Akhtar, 2000). He organises this dichotomy along classical
and romantic lines (Strenger, 1989), conflating an emphasis in the
former on a one-person psychology, the centrality of the Oedipus
complex, conflict, the importance of repressed impulses, utilisation of
interpretation of resistance, defence, and transference, sceptical
listening for hidden meaning, neutrality of the analyst, and the
disruptive attunement of the developing child's father (Herzog, 1984).
In contrast, the "romantic" viewpoint privileges an intersubjective,
two-person psychology: the preoedipal, the transitional space
(Winnicott, 1960), a deficit model of psychopathology (Kohut, 1977),
empathic listening, the analyst as a new object (Loewald, 1960),
non-verbal communication, safety (Sandler, 1960), acceptance, affirmation, and the homeostatic attunement of the developing child's
mother. He makes a convincing plea for a synthesis of these
approaches into an "informed oscillation" of the analyst's interventions, an erudite elaboration of Killingmo's ideas (Killingmo, 1989).
His recognition of the need for open-mindedness and flexibility is
quite consistent with the contemporary practices of analysts who
employ a "hybrid" approach "between empathy and interpretation"
(Josephs, 1995).

As useful as this conceptualisation is, it might inadvertently give newly trained analysts the impression that this "healing of a split" is sufficient to master all that is known about treatment. In my view, it is necessary but not sufficient. Such an integration of theory and technique may be better understood as merely a step in the evolution of our understanding of how one human may heal another through their relationship.

The idea of such a schism is particularly limiting when it comes to the challenge of working with those who have sustained severe early trauma. An integrated approach is a given, but additional factors need to be taken into consideration. The clinician's attunement to defensive altered states of consciousness, the recognition of dissociated self-states, and the tolerance of disturbing symptoms of quasi-psychotic proportion require not only ongoing self-analysis, but also a serious reappraisal of the implications of the historic collaboration between Breuer and Freud. In this way, the therapeutic relationship with this patient population may be greatly enhanced.

PART V
EPILOGUE

CHAPTER TWELVE

From darkness to light

"... a light heart lives long"

(Shakespeare, 1593)

S cientists believe that they are closing in on discovering the mystery of dark matter in the universe (*Science Daily*, December 18, 2012). However, they were disappointed by recent findings that contradict pre-existing theory about the subatomic particles in question (Hogenboom, 2013). Nevertheless, they are persisting. And in the realm of genetics, where another form of dark matter has been recognised, here, too, advances are being made. Formerly thought to be an inert part of the instruction manual for human life known as non-encoding RNA and comprising an amazing ninety-five per cent of the genome, scientists now suspect that it is very important. While not actually encoding the manufacture of proteins, this "genomic dark matter" is nevertheless now thought to play a significant role in complex, polygenic patterns of inheritance (Venters & Pugh, 2013).

In the field under consideration here, we clinicians and researchers are also hoping to further unravel the mysteries of dark matter that occupies much of the mind. While there is much to learn on an underlying neurophysiological basis, therapeutically it is best studied under the specialised conditions created in an analytic relationship. Yet, in this era of outcome studies and evidence-based medicine, the long-term, intensive, psychoanalytically orientated treatment model has been notoriously difficult to defend. But, those of us whose lives have been saved and who have been fortunate enough to be able to "pay it forward" by becoming analysts ourselves do not need any further proof of its healing power. Unfortunately, the rest of the world simply cannot take our word for it on faith. More research is needed and more clinical exploration is needed. Hopefully, publications such as this volume, which illustrate the value of the single case study approach, will add a bit more to our collective data.

To be able to facilitate such a process whereby one human being is able to make a substantial difference in the health, quality of life, and longevity of another is truly a gift. While the debates in the field rage on over what exactly constitutes psychoanalysis, what the optimum technique is, and how it actually works, most analysts would agree on one thing: it does indeed help. For those of us who have presided over such truly life-altering and transformative experiences in our patients, we would say that there is no substitute for it. Indeed, we should strive to improve ways of helping people more effectively through our own life-long efforts at understanding our own minds in order to better tolerate our patients' intolerable mental states (Coen, 1997).

Our minds and hearts are the essence of the "analyzing instrument" (Isakower, 1938), which is most effectively employed in the context of a sustaining, consistent relationship capable of observing and metabolising potentially life-threatening affects and impulses. Certainly, in the case of those who have been profoundly affected by trauma, it is absolutely essential for the clinician to become as comfortable as possible with his own demons, as it is almost certain that they will be summoned by the forces in the dark matter of the patient's mind. It is especially true in those who have been subject to sadistic abuse and torture in childhood, when their internalised persecutors become activated in the treatment process because the analyst dares to help free them from their lifelong mental imprisonment. This dictum was illustrated to me—yet again—in a sudden, dramatic, and unexpected moment the day I returned from a vacation and discovered that I had two patients expecting to see me at the same time.

Not realising my error initially, I greeted Mr J (Brenner, 2009a), who had arrived first, and we started the session. A very troubled, very provocative, and very self-defeating man, Mr J could not tolerate the strides he had made in treatment. He had had a severe regression associated with an exacerbation of multiple addictions and had subjected family members to degrading and dangerous situations. Moreover, he interrupted therapy and then resumed at a sub-optimum frequency while he proceeded to owe me more and more money. Chipping away at the bill very slowly while losing enormous sums at the gambling casinos and flaunting it, Mr J essentially dared me to throw him out of treatment. At times, I felt that I was being forced to helplessly observe his inexorable decline, which felt like a sadistic torture as I felt as though I were witnessing an atrocity.

Knowing that I was quite aware of his death wish, in large part due to unresolved guilt associated with profound sexual abuse by a male relative and callous neglect by his maternal care-taker, Mr J put his fate in my hands. Were I to finally give up on him after more than a decade of a heroic treatment, including five-times-a-week therapy for a number of these years, he would then know he was a lost cause who deserved the same fate as his sister, who had committed suicide prior to the beginning of his treatment.

Often citing lyrics from the song "There's a doctor" from the rock opera *Tommy*, in which a very disturbed, sexually abused young boy finds a doctor who will "remove his sorrows" (The Who, 1969), the patient's idealising transference was merely part of a larger mosaic transference in which various, dissociated self-states experienced me and treated me quite differently. The "crew", as his inner world was dubbed, manifested an avoidant attachment style as his desperate, younger self-states were silenced, and he would have pretended he did not know me if we ran into each other outside the office. However, dreams of young children crying, which awakened him in a confused state with tears streaming from his eyes, gave him enough subjective evidence of his deeper longings, which he tried to ward off through mockery, practical jokes, sarcasm, and, at times, cruelty.

During my break, the patient's gambling, drug abuse, and high-risk sexual acting out intensified. His first words to me were "I'm dying". As we settled in for the session and his impaired efforts at reconnecting with me proceeded, we were interrupted by very loud, insistent knocking on the consulting room door. Mr J became quite startled and shaken up. My sense was that this knocking would continue and further disrupt us, so I informed the patient that I would see who was at the door and handle the problem. He nodded in relief, and I opened the door slightly, expecting to send away an obtuse mail delivery person who could not read the "Do Not Disturb" sign. Instead, I was confronted by an irate patient, who had arrived moments after I had started the session and was waiting impatiently for the door to open so he could have his long-awaited hour as well. I was taken aback and was rather unprepared to confront this agitated individual. As I stepped into the foyer to talk with him, he triumphantly presented an appointment card on which I had clearly written the time that he had arrived, which was the same time as Mr J, and he demanded his hour.

Knowing this man's low frustration tolerance, irritability, paranoid tendencies, and impulse control problems, when I asked him if he could wait until the next hour, I was doubtful that he would be able to endure it. He had already been waiting several weeks during my break and had very pressing issues also. When I re-entered the office, Mr J had a peculiar smirk on his face. He was quite aware that there was a scheduling problem and relished my obvious discomfort with this quandary. Being in physical pain that day and taken by surprise, I clearly was not at my best. In the past, Mr J had tried to trick me in a variety of ways, such as reporting other patients' dreams that he had read about in my writings and claiming they were his own. He also paid me with two notes taped together so I would miscount the amount, only to have him then secretly untape them and vindicate himself for actually paying the correct amount. Knowing that his enjoyment of such pranks easily merged with his sadomasochism and penchant for sexual humiliation, he, too, was unable to wait until the next hour, which should have been his hour in the first place. He told me several weeks later that if I had only informed him that there was a younger man with a severe rage problem banging on the door, which reminded him of his younger self, he would have "worked with me" and waited. Instead, he reminded me that when he called the day before to confirm his appointment, I had hurriedly told him the incorrect time.

So, at that moment, I felt that I needed to make a "Sophie's choice" decision. Knowing that Mr J and I had worked together for more than a decade and that we had a second appointment two days later, I rationalised this decision and hoped that the strength of our alliance would prevail. Therefore, I told him that I needed to see the patient waiting outside and asked him again if he could wait for what should have been his actual time. I also knew that after our appointments he often went to the casino in a dissociated state, losing both time and money, so I thought that realistically he could have waited. Mr J smiled generously, abruptly got up, and said that he would see me in two days. After he left, I then invited the other patient into the consulting room.

Needless to say, I was disturbed by this turn of events and had a progressively sickening feeling that there would be problems with Mr J. He called several hours later and very curtly said that he was cancelling his appointment for later in the week and cancelling all future appointments, as he was going to be on the road for several weeks. Knowing that in his disturbed family people would refuse to talk to one another for years after being insulted, I realised how deeply I had hurt him. While I had wanted to believe for the moment that he could "take it" better than the angry younger man, in fact, this played into his masochistic transference fantasy. In my self-analysis of my error and my handling of the situation, I realised that the sudden, unexpected surprise may have provided an opportunity for an unconscious wish for retaliation to find its expression against Mr J.

Mr J. would not answer any of my return calls to him. He found my email address and sent me a story about Dr Mengele, the "Angel of Death", the notorious SS Nazi doctor who performed selections at Auschwitz. Mr J had previously discovered that I had a connection to the Holocaust and revealed that he had been preoccupied with Holocaust fantasies for much of his life. One of his favourite fantasies was imagining how he could hide from the Gestapo, how many people he could protect in his house, and how he could help them escape. His morbid fascination with the Holocaust intensified in the transference as he identified with the doomed prisoners who were selected to go to the gas chambers, as they were "life unworthy of life" (Binding & Hoche, 1920; Glass, 1997). Simultaneously, he took sadistic pleasure in being able to name me as a Nazi persecutor, hoping it would hurt me.

It took us many weeks to repair. During that time, I made it quite clear to him that, indeed, it disturbed me to have displaced him that day. I also confirmed his awareness of how challenging and how difficult it was to maintain equanimity with someone of his profoundly provocative nature. In addition, I pointed out to him that this enactment gave license to his "crew" to then break off treatment and continue to sabotage and destroy himself. As a result of this very tense, emotionally trying, and very "real" several weeks, a deeper recommitment to his treatment resulted in our being better able to address the serious life-and-death issues at stake. Such moments when the patient becomes the interpreter of the analyst's aggression in the countertransference (Hoffman, 1983) are inevitable when working with this population.

A question

Given all the pressures to bear in such situations, can the explosion of knowledge from related fields in the neurosciences, which have been alluded to throughout the previous chapters, be truly incorporated in ways that might enhance or expedite our clinical efforts? After the location of brain function with advanced imaging techniques such as functional MRI and PET scans to the discoveries in the fields of genetics and epigenetics, there is a wealth of exciting new findings to take in. Yet, their direct clinical relevance and applicability to the treatment situation are not so clear as yet (Pulver, 2003). The emerging field of personalised medicine, the next "revolution" (Collins, 2010), is of particular interest here, and a strong plea has been made for psychoanalysts to be open to collaborate with other specialists on behalf of the patient (Emde, 2012). While it could be argued that good care has always been personalised, the new meaning of the term refers to utilising knowledge of the individual's genome to determine vulnerability to disease and to prescribe specific treatments that would be most effective for the patient's genetic package. With an emphasis on health, prevention, and longevity (Friedman & Martin, 2011), it requires an appreciation of patients' unique genetics and their susceptibility to environmental influences, that is, the epigenetic changes in the genome in the creation of illness. For these reasons, the term "precision medicine" is becoming preferred by many.

New findings in those who have been subjected to significant child abuse and sexual abuse in childhood have actually been able to demonstrate changes in the genome due to methylation of certain alleles (Klengel et al., 2013). While the clinical implications are still being worked out, these discoveries demonstrate that on a sub-cellular level, our DNA is actually affected by early traumatic experience, which, among other things, might contribute to disturbances in immunity. In a previous book, *Dissociation of Trauma: Theory, Phenomenology, and Technique* (I. Brenner, 2001), I shared the observation that on the Dissociative Disorders Unit at the former Institute of Pennsylvania Hospital at any given time, roughly half of the patients were suffering from autoimmune diseases in various forms and degrees of severity. This was a percentage significantly higher than other units in the hospital. The possibility of a traumatically induced genetic susceptibility to autoimmune diseases due to the patients' early trauma is highly significant and, perhaps, just one of many manifestations of the problems that may arise.

Interestingly, in the history of psychoanalytic theory, one of the metapsychological assumptions about mental functioning is the so-called genetic approach. From this perspective, the patient's developmental history, early conflicts, ego strengths, fixations, etc., are assessed in order to come up with a psychogenetic formulation about the patient's symptomatology. So, here we see that on a metaphorical basis, the field of psychoanalysis has foreshadowed the exciting new developments in personalised, or precision, medicine. It has always emphasised the uniqueness of each person's dynamics.

What, then, are the implications of all this for today's practising clinician working with severely traumatised individuals who employ defensive altered states of consciousness and have significant dissociative psychopathology? And what does the future hold? The integration of the mind, as well as the integration of mind and body, are central tenets of treatment. To these ends, physical health, self-care, and diet—crucial prognostic factors—can be easily hijacked by dissociated, self-destructive forces. Once an illness develops, be it an eating disorder, an addiction, a gastrointestinal disturbance, an autoimmune condition, etc., treatment becomes more complicated, as these problems often develop their own autonomous clinical courses that warrant their own specific remedies. In addition, advances in one's therapy can be accompanied by medical regressions that may necessarily slow down the process or warrant additional considerations such as pharmacologic intervention or adjunctive treatments. The more we learn about the mutual influences of mind and body, as well as external factors impinging upon the human experience, the more we psychoanalysts will, I hope, be able to treat the effect of these dark matters of the mind. Having said all this, the basic equation remains: there are two minds in the two people in the room with one noble purpose, but with all of the forces of human nature converging, coalescing, and conspiring to undermine our efforts.

NOTES

1. Ferenczi's own contribution to splitting and trauma are enormous, as exemplified by his observation that

   If the shocks increase in number during the development of the child, the number and the various kinds of splits in the personality increase too, and soon it becomes extremely difficult to maintain contact without confusion with all the fragments each of which behaves as a separate personality, yet does not know of even the existence of the others. (1933, p. 165).

2. Freud's formulation regarding his depersonalisation while in Rome (Freud, 1936a) is relevant here in that he created an intrapsychic illusion that it was not he who was actually there lest he surpass his father and risk the retribution from his superego.

3. The eyes and their surrounding structures are quite reactive to affective states. Changes in eye colour have also been observed. One such patient whom I treated in the hospital insisted upon meeting in a darkened room lest I know that a change had occurred and another self was "out".

4. Visitors to this camp which, since the reunification of Germany is much more accessible to the West, now enter a modern visitors' centre and may rent audiophone guides, as in an art museum. With these self-guided

tours, they will hear stories about such notorious criminals as Iron Gustav.

5.   This legacy of suffering is succinctly expressed in the well-known Yiddish saying: "*Shver tsu zayn a yid*", or "It's hard to be a Jew."

6.   An Associated Press release on this subject came out in a number of papers, interestingly within two weeks of Rabin's assassination.

7.   She became overwhelmed by viewing something intolerable on television, illustrating how we may become traumatised simply by viewing terrible images such as the attack on the Twin Towers.

REFERENCES

Abend, S. M. (2007). Therapeutic action in modern conflict theory. *Psychoanalytic Quarterly, 76S*: 1417–1442.

Abraham, B. (1986). *The Angel of Death: The Mengele Dossier*. São Paulo, Brazil: Sherit Hapleita, Brazilian Association of the Survivors of Nazism.

Abse, D. W. (1974). Hysterical conversion and dissociative syndromes and the hysterical character. In: S. Arieti, & E. B. Brody (Eds.), *The American Handbook of Psychiatry* (2nd edn), *Volume 3* (pp. 155–194). New York: Basic Books.

Abse, D. W. (1983). Multiple personality. In: S. Akhtar (Ed.), *New Psychiatric Syndromes: DSM III and Beyond* (pp. 339–361). New York: Jason Aronson.

Adler, A. (1910). Beitrag zur Lehre vom Widerstand. *Zentrallblatt für Psychoanalyse, 1*: 214–219.

Adler, A. (1989). Transitional phenomena, projective identification, and the essential ambiguity of the psychoanalytic situation. *Psychoanalytic Quarterly, 58*: 81–104.

Akhtar, S. (1992). *Broken Structures: Severe Personality Disorders and Their Treatment*. New York: Jason Aronson.

Akhtar, S. (2000). From schisms through synthesis to informed oscillation: an attempt at integrating some diverse aspects of psychoanalytic technique. *Psychoanalytic Quarterly, 69*: 265–288.

Akhtar, S. (2001). From mental pain through manic defense to mourning. In: S. Akhtar (Ed.), *Three Faces of Mourning: Melancholia, Manic Defense and Moving On* (pp. 95–113). Northvale, NJ: Jason Aronson.

Akhtar, S. (2003a). Mentorship. In: *New Clinical Realms: Pushing the Envelope of Theory and Technique* (pp. 201–210). Northvale, NJ: Jason Aronson.

Akhtar, S. (2003b). Things: developmental, psychopathological, and technical aspects of inanimate objects. *Canadian Journal of Psychoanalysis, 11*: 1–44.

Akhtar, S. (2009). *Comprehensive Dictionary of Psychoanalysis*. London: Karnac.

Akhtar, S. (2011). Introduction. In: M. K. O'Neil & S. Akhtar (Eds.), *On Freud's "Negation"* (pp. 1–10). London: Karnac.

Akhtar, S., & Brenner, I. (1979). Differential diagnosis of fugue-like states. *Journal of Clinical Psychiatry, 40*: 381–385.

American Psychiatric Association (2013). *Desk Reference to the Diagnostic Criteria From DSM-5*. Arlington, VA: American Psychiatric Association.

American Psychoanalytic Association (2006). *Psychodynamic Diagnostic Manual (PDM)*. Silver Spring, MD: Alliance of Psychoanalytic Organizations.

Anonymous. *What If You Slept?*

Apfel, R. J., & Simon, B. (2005). Trauma, violence and psychoanalysis. *September 11: Trauma and Human Bonds*. Edited by S. W. Coates, J. L. Rosenthal, & D. S. Schechter. Hillsdale, NJ: Analytic Press (Relational Perspectives Book Series, Vol. 23), 2003. 312 pp. *International Journal of Psychoanalysis, 86*: 191–202.

Apprey, M. (1993). The African-American experience: forced migration and transgenerational trauma. *Mind and Human Interaction, 4*: 70–75.

Arlow, J. A. (1966). Depersonalization and derealization. In: R. M. Loewenstein, L. M. Newman, M. Schur, & A. J. Solnit (Eds.), *Psychoanalysis—A General Psychology* (pp. 456–478). New York: International Universities Press.

Arlow, J. A. (1969). Unconscious fantasy and disturbances of conscious experience. *Psychoanalytic Quarterly, 38*: 1–27.

Arlow, J. A. (1992). Altered ego states. *Israel Journal of Psychiatry and Related Sciences, 29*(2): 65–76.

Asendorpf, J. B., Warkentin, & Baudonnière, P.-M. (1996). Self-awareness and other-awareness. II: Mirror self-recognition, social contingency awareness, and synchronic imitation. *Developmental Psychology, 32*: 313–321.

Associated Press (1995). Israel: survivors of Nazi holocaust locked in mental asylums, 27 November.

Auerhahn, N. C, & Laub, D. (1987). Play and playfulness in Holocaust survivors. *Psychoanalytic Study of the Child, 42*: 45–58.

Bach, S. (2001). On being forgotten and forgetting one's self. *Psychoanalytic Quarterly, 70*: 739–756.

Back To The Future (1985). Universal City, CA: Universal City Studios.

Bak, R. C. (1968). The phallic woman—the ubiquitous fantasy in perversions. *Psychoanalytic Study of the Child, 23*: 15–36.

Balint, M. (1959). *Thrills and Regressions*. London: Hogarth.

Bamford, J. (2008). *The Shadow Factory: The Ultra-Secret NSA From 9/11 to the Eavesdropping of America*. New York: Doubleday.

Barrett, D. (1995). The dream character as prototype for the multiple personality alter. *Dissociation, 8*: 61–68.

Bass, A. (1997). The problem of "concreteness". *Psychoanalytic Quarterly, 66*: 642–682.

Bassanese, F. A. (1997). *Understanding Luigi Pirandello*. Columbia, SC: University of South Carolina Press.

Bauer, Y. (1988). Personal communication.

Beebe, B., Lachmann, F. M., & Jaffe, J. (1997). Mother–infant interaction structures and presymbolic self- and object representations. *Psychoanalytic Dialogues, 7*: 133–182.

Bekerman-Greenberg, R. (2011). *I Am Carrying the Holocaust in My Pocket*. Documentary film given to Dr Brenner.

Bergmann, M. S. (2004). Reflections on September 11. In: D. Knafo (Ed.), *Living With Terror, Working With Trauma: A Clinician's Handbook* (pp. 401–413). Lanham, MD: Jason Aronson.

Bergmann, M. S., & Jucovy, M. E. (Eds.) (1982). *Generations of the Holocaust*. New York: Basic Books.

Berman, E. (1981). Multiple personality: psychoanalytic perspectives. *International Journal of Psychoanalysis, 62*: 283–300.

Binding, K., & Hoche, A. (1920). *Allowing the Destruction of Life Unworthy of Life*, C. Modak (Trans.). Tarlton, OH: Suzeteo Enterprises, 2012.

Bion, W. R. (1956). Development of schizophrenic thought. *International Journal of Psychoanalysis, 37*: 344–346.

Bion, W. R. (1959). Attacks on linking. *International Journal of Psychoanalysis, 40*: 308–315.

Bion, W. R. (1962a). *Learning From Experience*. New York: Basic Books.

Bion, W. R. (1962b). The psycho-analytic study of thinking. *International Journal of Psychoanalysis, 43*: 306–310.

Bion, W. R. (1989). *Two Papers: The Grid and the Caesura*. London: Karnac.

Blechner, M. J. (2010). Interpersonal and uniquely personal factors in dream analysis: commentary on paper by Susan H. Sands. *Psychoanalytic Dialogues, 20*: 374–381.

Blum, H. P. (1986). On identification and its vicissitudes. *International Journal of Psychoanalysis, 67*: 267–276.

Blum, H. P. (1987). The role of identification in the resolution of trauma: the Anna Freud Memorial Lecture. *Psychoanalytic Quarterly, 56*: 609–627.

Bollas, C. (1987). *The Shadow of the Object: Psychoanalysis of the Unthought Known*. New York: Columbia University Press.

Bollas, C. (1989). *Forces of Destiny: Psychoanalysis and Human Idiom*. Northvale, NJ: Jason Aronson.

Bos, J., & Groenendijk, L. (2007). *The Self-Marginalization of Wilhelm Stekel: Freudian Circles Inside and Out*. New York: Springer.

Boston Change Process Study Group (2010). *Change in Psychotherapy: A Unifying Paradigm*, New York: W. W. Norton.

Brenner, C. (1982). *The Mind in Conflict*. New York: International Universities Press.

Brenner, C. (2003a). Commentary on Ilany Kogan's "On Being a Dead, Beloved Child". *Psychoanalytic Quarterly, 72*: 767–776.

Brenner, C. (2003b). Is the structural model still useful? *International Journal of Psychoanalysis, 84*: 1093–1096.

Brenner, C. (2009a). In his own words: Charles Brenner (1913–2008). Personal memoir, 2007. *Psychoanalytic Quarterly, 78*: 637–673.

Brenner, C. (2009b). Interview with Robert Michaels, 2006. *Psychoanalytic Quarterly, 78*: 675–700.

Brenner, I. (1988). Unconscious fantasies of the selection in children of Holocaust survivors. Paper presented to the first International Conference on Children of Holocaust Survivors, Jerusalem, December.

Brenner, I. (1994). The dissociative character: a reconsideration of "multiple personality" and related phenomena. *Journal of the American Psychoanalytic Association, 42*: 819–846.

Brenner, I. (1995a). Reply to Brenneis. *Journal of the American Psychoanalytic Association, 43*: 300–303.

Brenner, I. (1995b). Revisiting the death instinct in a case of "multiple personality". Paper presented to the Annual Meeting of the International Society of Traumatic Stress Studies, Boston, MA, November 4, 1995.

Brenner, I. (1996). A psychoanalytic view of Israel's "split personality". *Mind and Human Interaction, 7*: 44–51.

Brenner, I. (1997). Letter to the editor. *Journal of the American Psychoanalytic Association, 45*: 1285–1287.

Brenner, I. (1999). Deconstructing DID. *American Journal of Psychotherapy,* *53*: 344–360.

Brenner, I. (2001). *Dissociation of Trauma: Theory, Phenomenology, and Technique.* Madison, CT: International Universities Press.

Brenner, I. (2002a). Trauma, transmission and time. Paper presented to P.A.N.Y./Melitta Schmidberg Lecture.

Brenner, I. (2002b). Reflections on the aftermath of September 11. *Philadelphia Interpreter—The Newsletter of the Psychoanalytic Center of Philadelphia,* February 2002, p. 4.

Brenner, I. (2003–2004). Remembering, forgetting and keeping separate: reflections on the "gospel" according to Freud. *Journal of the Indian Psychoanalytical Society, 57*: 25–35.

Brenner, I. (2004). *Psychic Trauma: Dynamics, Symptoms, and Treatment.* Lanham, MD: Jason Aronson.

Brenner, I. (2006a). Letter to the editor: More thoughts on dissociation. *Clinical Psychiatry News, 34*: 11–12.

Brenner, I. (2006b). Panel Report. Terror and societal regression: does psychoanalysis offer insights for international relations? *Journal of the American Psychoanalytic Association, 54*: 977–988.

Brenner, I. (2006c). Termination of psychoanalysis and September 11. *Psychoanalytic Quarterly, 75*: 753–781.

Brenner, I. (2007). Contemporary anti-semitism: variations on an ancient theme. In: H. Parens, A. Mafwouz, & S. Twemlow (Eds.), *The Future of Prejudice* (pp. 141–162) . Lanham, MD: Rowman & Littlefield.

Brenner, I. (2009a). *Injured Men: Trauma, Healing, and the Masculine Self.* Lanham, MD: Jason Aronson.

Brenner, I. (2009b). A new view from the Acropolis: dissociative identity disorder. *Psychoanalytic Quarterly, 78*: 57–105.

Brenner, I. (2010). Is that all there is? In: S. Akhtar (Ed.), *The Wound of Mortality: Fear, Denial and the Acceptance of Death* (pp. 171–186). Lanham, MD: Jason Aronson.

Britton, R. (1999). Getting in on the act: the hysterical solution. *International Journal of Psychoanalysis, 80*: 1–14.

Bromberg, P. M. (1991). On knowing one's patient inside and out: the aesthetics of unconscious communication. *Psychoanalytic Dialogues, 1*: 399–422.

Bromberg, P. M. (1994). "Speak! that I may see you": some reflections on dissociation, reality and psychoanalytic listening. *Psychoanalytic Dialogues, 4*: 517–547.

Bromberg, P. M. (1996). Hysteria, dissociation, and cure: Emmy von N revisited. *Psychoanalytic Dialogues, 6*: 55–71.

Bromberg, P. M. (2012). Stumbling along and hanging in: if this be technique, make the most of it! *Psychoanalytic Inquiry, 32*: 3–17.

Buck, O. D. (1983). Multiple personality as a borderline state. *Journal of Nervous and Mental Disease, 171*: 62–65.

Cabaniss, D. L., Forand, N., & Roose, S. P. (2004). Conducting analysis after September 11: implications for psychoanalytic technique. *Journal of the American Psychoanalytic Association, 52*: 717–734.

Caper, R. (1999). *A Mind of One's Own: A Kleinian View of Self and Object.* London: Routledge.

Carroll, L. (1871). *Through the Looking-Glass, and What Alice Found There.* New York: Macmillan, 1906.

Celan, P. (1948). Death fugue. In: *Poems of Paul Celan*, M. Hamburger (Trans.). New York: Persea Books.

Clary, W. F., Burstin, K. J., & Carpenter, J. S. (1984). Multiple personality and borderline personality disorder. *Psychiatric Clinics of North America, 7*: 89–99.

Coates, S. W., Rosenthal, J. L., & Schechter, D. S. (2003). *September 11: Trauma and Human Bonds.* Hillsdale, NJ: Analytic Press.

Coates, S. W., Schechter, D. S., & First, E. (2003). Brief interventions with traumatized children and families after September 11. In: S. W. Coates, J. L. Rosenthal, & D. S. Schecter (Eds.), *September 11: Trauma and Human Bonds* (pp. 23–49). Hillsdale, NJ: Analytic Press.

Coen, S. J. (1997). How to help patients (and analysts) bear the unbearable. *Journal of the American Psychoanalytic Association, 45*: 1183–1207.

Collins, F. S. (2010). *DNA and the Revolution in Personalized Medicine.* New York: HarperCollins.

Collins, L. (1995). Who really killed Yitzhak Rabin? *Jerusalem Post* (International Edition), 24 November.

Coons, P. M., Bowman, E. S., & Milstein, V. (1988). Multiple personality disorder: a clinical investigation of 50 cases. *Journal of Nervous and Mental Disease, 176*: 519–527.

Czech, D. (1990). *Auschwitz Chronicle 1939–1945: From the Archives of the Auschwitz Memorial and the German Federal Archives.* New York: Henry Holt.

Danieli, Y. (1980). Countertransference in the treatment and study of Nazi Holocaust survivors and their children. *Victimology, 5*: 355–367.

Danieli, Y (1998). *International Handbook of Multigenerational Legacies of Trauma.* New York: Plenum Press.

Davies, J. M. (2001). Erotic overstimulation and the co-construction of sexual meanings in transference–countertransference experience. *Psychoanalytic Inquiry, 70*: 757–788.

De Cervantes, M. (1605). *Don Quixote de la Mancha*, C. Jarvis (Trans.). London: Oxford University Press, 1998.

de Veer, M. W., Gallup, G. G., Theall, L. A., Van den Bos, R., & Povinelli, D. J. (2003). An 8-year longitudinal study of mirror self-recognition in chimpanzees (*Pan troglodytes*). *Neuropsychologia, 41*: 229–234.

Derrida, J. (1998). Geo-psychoanalysis ". . . and the rest of the world". In: C. Lane (Ed.), *The Psychoanalysis of Race* (pp. 65–90). New York: Columbia University Press.

Dickes, R. L. (1965). The defensive function of an altered state of consciousness: a hypnoid state. *Journal of the American Psychoanalytic Association, 13*: 365–403.

Dobroszycki, L. (Ed.) (1984). *The Chronicle of the Łódź Ghetto, 1941–1944*, R. Lourie, J. Neugroschel, & others (Trans.). New Haven, CT: Yale University Press.

Dwork, D. (1991). *Children With a Star—Jewish Youth in Nazi Europe*. New Haven, CT: Yale University Press.

Editorial (2001). September 11, 2001. *Journal of the American Psychoanalytic Association, 49*: 1107.

Eisen, G. (1988). *Children and Play in the Holocaust: Games Among the Shadows*. Amherst, MA: University of Massachusetts Press.

Eissler, K. R. (1953). The effect of the structure of the ego on psychoanalytic technique. *Journal of the American Psychoanalytic Association, 1*: 104–143.

Ellenberger, H. F. (1970). *The Discovery of the Unconscious*. New York: Basic Books.

Emde, R. N. (2012). Reviews. *Health and the Future of American Medicine: Opportunities and Challenges for Psychoanalysis: The Language of Life: DNA and the Revolution in Personalized Medicine*. By Francis S. Collins. New York: HarperCollins, 2010, 371 pp., $26.99. *Tracking Medicine: A Researcher's Quest to Understand Health Care*. By John E. Wennberg. New York: Oxford University Press, 2010, 344 pp., $29.95. *Next Medicine: The Science and Civics of Health*. By Walter M. Bortz. New York: Oxford University Press, 2011, 264 pp., $34.95. *The Longevity Project: Surprising Discoveries for Health and Long Life from the Landmark Eight-Decade Study*. By Howard S. Friedman and Leslie R. Martin. New York: Hudson Street Press, 2011, 273 pp., $29.95. *Journal of the American Psychoanalytic Association, 60*: 819–835.

Epstein, H. (1979). *Children of the Holocaust: Conversations With Sons and Daughters of Survivors*. New York: Putnam.

Erikson, E. H. (1950). *Childhood and Society*. New York: W. W. Norton, 1963.

Escoll, P. J. (2005). Man's best friend. In: *Mental Zoo: Animals in the Human Mind and Its Pathology* (pp. 127–159). Madison, CT: International Universities Press.

Eshel, O. (1998). "Black holes", deadness and existing analytically. *International Journal of Psychoanalysis, 79*: 1115–1130.

Estabrooks, G. H. (1945). Hypnotism in warfare. In: *Hypnotism* (pp. 185–205). New York: E. P. Dutton.

Faimberg, H. (1988). The telescoping of generations: genealogy of certain identifications. *Contemporary Psychoanalysis, 24*: 99–117.

Fairbairn, W. R. D. (1944). Endopsychic structure considered in terms of object-relationships. *International Journal of Psychoanalysis, 25*: 70–93.

Fairbairn, W. R. D. (1952). *An Object-Relations Theory of the Personality*. New York: Basic Books.

Falk, A. (1974). Border symbolism. *Psychoanalytic Quarterly, 43*: 650–660.

Falzeder, E., & Brabant, E. (1996). *The Correspondence of Sigmund Freud and Sándor Ferenczi, Vol. 2, 1914–1919*, P.T. Hoffer (Trans.). Cambridge, MA: Belknap Press of Harvard University Press.

Federn, P. (1952). *Ego Psychology and the Psychoses*, E. Weiss (Ed.). New York: Basic Books.

Fenichel, O. (1945). *The Psychoanalytic Theory of Neurosis*. New York: W. W. Norton.

Ferenczi, S. (1933). Confusion of tongues between adults and the child. In: M. Balint (Ed.), *Final Contributions to the Problems and Methods of Psycho-Analysis* (pp. 156–167), E. Masbacher and others (Trans.). New York: Brunner/Mazel, 1980.

Fernando, J. (2009). *The Processes of Defense: Trauma, Drives, and Reality—A New Synthesis*. Lanham, MD: Jason Aronson.

Flavius Josephus (1900). *The Works of Flavius Josephus*, W. Whiston (Trans.). New York: Siegel-Cooper.

Fliess, R. (1953a). The hypnotic evasion: a clinical observation. *Psychoanalytic Quarterly, 22*: 497–516.

Fliess, R. (1953b). *The Revival of Interest in the Dream*. New York: International Universities Press.

Fogelman, E. (1984). *Breaking the Silence: The Generation After the Holocaust*. University Park, PA: Penn State University Psychological Cinema Register.

Fogelman, E., & Savran, B. (1979). Therapeutic groups for children of Holocaust survivors. *International Journal of Group Psychotherapy, 29*: 211–235.

Fonagy, P., & Target, M. (1996). Playing with reality: I. Theory of mind and the normal development of psychic reality. *International Journal of Psychoanalysis, 77*: 217–233.

Fraiberg, S. (1982). Pathological defenses in infancy. *Psychoanalytic Quarterly, 51*: 612–635.

Frank, A. (1969). The unrememberable and the unforgettable – Passive primal repression. *Psychoanalytic Study of the Child, 24*: 48–77.

Freud, A. (1936). The ego and the mechanisms of defence. In: *The Writings of Anna Freud, Vol. 2*. New York: International Universities Press, 1966.

Freud, A. (1954). Problems of technique in adult analysis. In: *The Writings of Anna Freud, Vol. 4* (pp. 377–406). New York: International Universities Press, 1968.

Freud, A., & Burlingham, D. T. (1943). *War and Children*. New York: Medical War Books.

Freud, A., & Dann, S. (1951). An experiment in group upbringing. *Psychoanalytic Study of the Child, 6*: 127–168.

Freud, S. (1891d). Hypnosis. *S.E., 1*. London: Hogarth.

Freud, S. (with Breuer, J.) (1895d). *Studies on Hysteria. S.E., 2*. London: Hogarth.

Freud, S. (1900a). *The Interpretation of Dreams. S.E., 4–5*. London: Hogarth.

Freud, S. (1901b). *The Psychopathology of Everyday Life, S.E., 6*. London: Hogarth.

Freud, S. (1905e). *Fragment of an Analysis of a Case of Hysteria. S.E., 7*: 3–122. London: Hogarth.

Freud, S. (1910a). Five lectures on psycho-analysis. *S.E., 11*: 3–55. London: Hogarth.

Freud, S. (1912e). Recommendations to physicians practising psycho-analysis. *S.E., 12*: 109–120. London: Hogarth.

Freud, S. (1912–1913). *Totem and Taboo. S.E., 13*: 1–161. London: Hogarth.

Freud, S. (1914g). Remembering, repeating and working-through. *S.E., 12*: 145–156. London: Hogarth.

Freud, S. (1915d). Repression. *S.E., 14*: 143–158. London: Hogarth.

Freud, S. (1915e). The unconscious. *S.E., 14*: 161–215. London: Hogarth.

Freud, S. (1917d). A metapsychological supplement to the theory of dreams. *S.E., 14*: 217–235. London: Hogarth.

Freud, S. (1918b). *From the History of an Infantile Neurosis. S.E., 17*: 3–103. London: Hogarth.

Freud, S. (1919e). 'A child is being beaten': a contribution to the study of the origin of sexual perversions. *S.E., 17*: 179–204. London: Hogarth.

Freud, S. (1920g). *Beyond the Pleasure Principle. S.E., 18*: 7–64. London: Hogarth.

Freud, S. (1921c). *Group Psychology and the Analysis of the Ego. S.E.*, 18: 67–143. London: Hogarth.

Freud, S. (1922b). Some neurotic mechanisms in jealousy, paranoia and homosexuality. *S.E.*, 18: 221–232. London: Hogarth.

Freud, S. (1923b). *The Ego and the Id. S.E.*, 19: 3–66. London: Hogarth.

Freud, S. (1923c). Remarks on the theory and practice of dream-interpretation. *S.E.*, 19: 127–140. London: Hogarth.

Freud, S. (1924b). Neurosis and psychosis. *S.E.*, 19: 149–154. London: Hogarth.

Freud, S. (1925j). Some psychical consequences of the anatomical distinction between the sexes. *S.E.*, 19: 243–258. London: Hogarth.

Freud, S. (1926d). *Inhibitions, Symptoms and Anxiety. S.E.*, 20: 77–174. London: Hogarth.

Freud, S. (1926e). The question of lay analysis. *S.E.*, 20: 179–258. London: Hogarth.

Freud, S. (1930a). *Civilization and Its Discontents. S.E.*, 21: 59–145. London: Hogarth.

Freud, S. (1933a). *New Introductory Lectures on Psycho-Analysis. S.E.*, 22. London: Hogarth.

Freud, S. (1936a). A disturbance of memory on the Acropolis. *S.E.*, 22: 237–248. London: Hogarth.

Freud, S. (1937c). Analysis terminable and interminable. *S.E.*, 23: 209–253. London: Hogarth.

Freud, S. (1939a). *Moses and Monotheism. S.E.*, 23: 3–137. London: Hogarth.

Freud, S. (1940a). *An Outline of Psycho-Analysis. S.E.*, 23: 139–207. London: Hogarth.

Freud, S. (1940e). Splitting of the ego in the process of defence. *S.E.*, 23: 271–278. London: Hogarth.

Friedman, H. S., & Martin, L. R. (2011). *The Longevity Project: Surprising Discoveries for Health and Long Life from the Landmark Eight-Decade Study*. New York: Hudson Street Press.

Friedman, I. R. (Ed.) (1982). *Escape or Die: True Stories of Young People Who Survived the Holocaust*. Reading, MA: Addison-Wesley.

Furst, S. S. (1967). Psychic trauma: a survey. In: S. S. Furst (Ed.), *Psychic Trauma* (pp. 3–50). New York: Basic Books.

Gabbard, G. O., & Twemlow, S. W. (1984). The metapsychology of altered mind/body perception. In: *With the Eyes of the Mind: An Empirical Analysis of Out-of-Body States* (pp. 169–183). New York: Praeger.

Gampel, Y. (1982). A daughter of silence. In: M. S. Bergmann & M. E. Jucovy (Eds.), *Generations of the Holocaust* (pp. 120–136). New York: Basic Books.

Gay, P. (1987). *A Godless Jew: Freud, Atheism and the Making of Psychoanalysis*. New Haven, CT: Yale University Press.

Gensler, D., Goldman, D. S., Goldman, D., Gordon, R. M., Prince, R., & Rosenbach, N. (2002). Voices from New York: September 11, 2001. *Contemporary Psychoanalysis, 38:* 77–99.

Glass, J. (1997). *Life Unworthy of Life: Racial Phobia and Mass Murder in Hitler's Germany*. New York: Basic Books.

Glassner, M. I., & Krell, R. (Eds.) (2006). *And Life is Changed Forever— Holocaust Childhoods Remembered*. Detroit, MI: Wayne State University Press.

Glover, E. (1931). The therapeutic effect of inexact interpretation: a contribution to the theory of suggestion. *International Journal of Psychoanalysis, 12:* 397–411.

Glover, E. (1943). The concept of dissociation. *International Journal of Psychoanalysis, 24:* 7–13.

Glover, E. (1955). *The Technique of Psychoanalysis*. New York: International Universities Press.

Goldberg, A. (1991). Personal communication.

Gordon, E. (1995). Respect giving way to fear. *Jerusalem Post* (International Edition), 9 December, p. 3.

Gottlieb, R. M. (1997). Does the mind fall apart in multiple personality disorder? Some proposals based on a psychoanalytic case. *Journal of the American Psychoanalytic Association, 45:* 907–932.

Greaves, G. B. (1980). Multiple personality. 165 years after Mary Reynolds. *Journal of Nervous and Mental Disease, 168:* 577–596.

Greaves, G. B. (1993). A history of multiple personality disorder. In: R. P. Kluft & C. G. Fine (Eds.), *Clinical Perspectives on Multiple Personality Disorder* (pp. 355–380). Washington, DC: American Psychiatric Press.

Green, A. (1999). The death drive, negative narcissism and the de-objectalising function. In: A. Weller (Trans.), *The Work of the Negative* (pp. 81–88). London: Free Association Books.

Greenson, R. R. (1967). *The Technique and Practice of Psychoanalysis*. New York: International Universities Press.

Grubrich-Simitis, I. (1981). Extreme traumatization as cumulative trauma—psychoanalytic investigations of the effects of concentration camp experiences on survivors and their children. *Psychoanalytic Study of the Child, 36:* 415–450.

Grubrich-Simitis, I. (1984). From concretism to metaphor: thoughts on some theoretical and technical aspects of the psychoanalytic work with children of Holocaust survivors. *Psychoanalytic Study of the Child, 39:* 301–319.

Gruenwald, D. (1977). Multiple personality and splitting phenomena: a reconceptualization. *Journal of Nervous and Mental Disease, 164*: 385–393.

Guralnik, O., & Simeon, D. (2010). Depersonalization: standing in the spaces between recognition and interpellation. *Psychoanalytic Dialogues, 20*: 400–416.

Haaretz (2012). New Israeli study finds signs of trauma in grandchildren of Holocaust survivors, 16 April, 2012. Accessed at: www.haaretz.com.

Halpern, J. (1999). Freud's intrapsychic use of the Jewish culture and religion. *Journal of the American Psychoanalytic Association, 47*: 1191–1212.

Hart, K. (1981). *Return to Auschwitz: The Remarkable Life of a Girl Who Survived the Holocaust.* Saddle Brook, NJ: American Book-Stratford Press.

Hartmann, H. (1939). *Ego Psychology and the Problem of Adaptation.* New York: International Universities Press, 1958.

Hersh, S. M. (1991). *The Sampson Option: Israel's Nuclear Arsenal and American Foreign Policy.* New York: Random House.

Herzog, J. (1982). World beyond metaphor: thoughts on the transmission of trauma. In: M. S. Bergmann & M. E. Jucovy (Eds.), *Generations of the Holocaust* (pp. 103–119). New York: Basic Books.

Herzog, J. (1984). Fathers and young children: fathering daughters and sons. In: J. D. Call, E. Galenson, & R. Tyson (Eds.), *Foundations of Infant Psychiatry, Volume 2* (pp. 335–343). New York: Basic Books.

Hesse, E., & Main, M. (1999). Second-generation effects of unresolved trauma in non-maltreating patients: dissociated, frightened, and threatening parental behavior. *Psychoanalytic Inquiry, 19*: 481–540.

Heydrich, R. (1942). Speech at the Wansee Conference, Berlin, Germany (20 January, 1942). In: A. J. Mayer, *Why Did the Heavens Not Darken: The "Final Solution" in History* (p. 304). New York: Pantheon Books, 1990.

Hinshelwood, R. D. (2007). The Kleinian theory of therapeutic action. *Psychoanalytic Quarterly, 76*(S): 1479–1498.

Hirsch, I. (2003). Reflections on clinical issues in the context of the national trauma of September 11. *Contemporary Psychoanalysis, 39*: 665–681.

Hirschberg, E. (1995). Invoking the spirits. *The Jerusalem Report*, 16 November, 1995, p. 3.

Hoffman, I. Z. (1983). The patient as interpreter of the analyst's experience. *Contemporary Psychoanalysis, 19*: 389–422.

Hogenboom, M. (2013). Ultra-rare decay confirmed in LHC. *BBC Online News*, 24 July 2013.

Holt, R. R. (1962). A critical examination of Freud's concept of bound vs. free cathexis. *Journal of the American Psychoanalytic Association, 16*: 475–525.

Howell, E. F. (2005). *The Dissociative Mind*. Hillsdale, NJ: Analytic Press.

Isakower, O. (1938). A contribution to the pathopsychology associated with falling asleep. *International Journal of Psychoanalysis, 19*: 331–345.

Jabotinsky, Z. (1922). Jabotinsky to the Zionist Executive, 29 December, 1922. Central Zionist Archives, Jerusalem: File of the Central Office of the Zionist Organization, London, 4113. In: A. M. Lesch, *Arab Politics in Palestine, 1917–1939: The Frustration of a Nationalist Movement*. London: Cornell University Press, 1979.

Jabotinsky, Z. (1926). "Aharei hakamat he'il ha-sefar" (After the Establishment of the Border Patrol) in his *Ne-umim, 1905–1926*, p. 303. In: A. Shapira, *Land and Power: The Zionist Resort to Force, 1881–1948* (p. 157), W. Templer (Trans.). Stanford, CA: Stanford University Press.

Jacobs, J. (2009). Obituary: Charles Brenner, M.D. *International Journal of Psychoanalysis, 90*: 963–955.

Jacobson, E. (1964). *The Self and the Object World*. New York: International Universities Press.

James, W. (1890). *The Principles of Psychology*. New York: Dover, 1950.

Janet, P. (1889). *L'automatisme psychologique*. Paris: Ballière.

Janet, P. (1907). *The Major Symptoms of Hysteria*. New York: Macmillan.

Jones, E. (1953). *Sigmund Freud: Life and Work, Vol. 1*. London: Hogarth Press.

Josephs, L. (1995). *Balancing Empathy and Interpretation: Relational Character Analysis*. Northvale, NJ: Jason Aronson.

Jucovy, M. E. (1986). The Holocaust. In: A. Rothstein (Ed.), *The Reconstruction of Trauma: Its Significance in Clinical Work* (pp. 153–169). Madison, CT: International Universities Press.

Jung, C. G. (1902). *Ur Psychologie und Pathologie sogenannter okkulter Phänomene*. Leipzig: Mutze.

Kafka, F. (1914). *Letters to Ottla & the Family*, N. N. Glatzer (Ed.), R. Winston & C. Winston (Trans.). New York: Schocken Books, 1982.

Kaplan, S. (2006). Children in genocide: extreme traumatization and the 'affect propeller'. *International Journal of Psychoanalysis, 87*: 725–746.

Karpin, M. I. (2006). *The Bomb in the Basement: How Israel Went Nuclear and What That Means for the World*. New York: Simon & Schuster.

Karski, J. (1944). *The Story of a Secret State*. Boston, MA: Houghton Mifflin.

Ka-Tzetnik 135633 (1989). *Shivitti: A Vision*, E. N. De-Nur and L. Herman (Trans.). San Francisco, CA: Harper & Row.

Keinon, H. (1995a). A nation (sadly) like any other. *Jersualem Post* (International Edition), 11 November, 1995, p. 3.

Keinon, H. (1995b). A distrust of "other" ideologies. *Jerusalem Post* (International Edition), 23 December, 1995, p. 3.

Kelman, H. (1975a). Metapsychological analysis of a parapraxis. *Journal of the American Psychoanalytic Association, 23*: 555–568.

Kelman, H. (1975b). The "day precipitate" of dreams: the Morris hypothesis. *International Journal of Psychoanalysis, 56*: 209–218.

Kenney, J. (2011). What happened. *The New Yorker*, 23 May, p. 39.

Kernberg, O. (1973). Discussion of presentation by F. Coplan and E. Berman in S. Bauer (Chm.). Multiple Personality—A Reevaluation. Symposium at the Annual Meeting of the American Psychiatric Association, Honolulu, Hawaii.

Kernberg, O. (1975). *Borderline Conditions and Pathological Narcissism*. New York: Jason Aronson.

Kernberg, O. (2009). The concept of the death drive: a clinical perspective. *International Journal of Psychoanalysis, 90*: 1009–1023.

Kestenberg, J. S. (1972). Psychoanalytic contributions to the problem of children of survivors from Nazi persecution. *Israel Annals of Psychiatry and Related Disciplines, 10*: 311–325.

Kestenberg, J. S. (1980). Psychoanalyses of children of survivors from the Holocaust: Case presentations and assessment. *Journal of the American Psychoanalytic Association, 28*: 775–804.

Kestenberg, J. S. (1982a). A metapsychological assessment based on an analysis of a survivor's child. In: M. S. Bergmann & M. E. Jucovy (Eds.), *Generations of the Holocaust* (pp. 137–158). New York: Basic Books.

Kestenberg, J. S. (1982b). Survivor-parents and their children. In: M. S. Bergmann & M. E. Jucovy (Eds.), *Generations of the Holocaust* (pp. 83–102). New York: Basic Books.

Kestenberg, J. S., & Brenner, I. (1988). Le narcissisme au service de la survie. *Revue Française de Psychoanalyse, 6*: 1393–1408.

Kestenberg, J. S., & Brenner, I. (1996). *The Last Witness: The Child Survivor of the Holocaust*. Washington, DC: American Psychiatric Press.

Kestenberg, J. S., & Gampel, Y. (1983). Growing up in the Holocaust culture. *Israel Journal of Psychiatry and Related Sciences, 20*: 129–146.

Khan, M. M. R. (1963). The concept of cumulative trauma. *Psychoanalytic Study of the Child, 18*: 286–306.

Kiefer, C. C. (2011). The waiting room as boundary and bridge between self-states and unformulated experience. *Journal of the American Psychoanalytic Association, 59*: 335–349.

Killingmo, B. (1989). Conflict and deficit: implications for technique. *International Journal of Psychoanalysis, 70*: 65–79.

Kirchheimer, J. R. (2007). *How To Spot One of Us: Poems*. New York: CLAL: The National Jewish Center for Learning and Leadership.

Klein, H. (1973). Children of the Holocaust: mourning and bereavement. In: E. J. Anthony & C. Koupernik (Eds.), *The Child in His Family, Volume 2: The Impact of Disease and Death* (pp. 393–409). New York: John Wiley & Sons.

Klein, M. (1946). Notes on some schizoid mechanisms. In: *Envy and Gratitude and Other Works: The Writings of Melanie Klein, Vol. 3*. London: Hogarth Press, 1975 [reprinted London: Karnac, 1993].

Klengel, T., Mehta, D., Anacker, C., Rex-Haffner, M., Pruessner, J. C., Pariante, C. M., Pace, T. W. W., Mercer, K. B., Mayberg, H. S., Bradley, B., Nemeroff, C. B., Holsboer, F., Heim, C. M., Ressler, K. J., Rein, T., & Binder, E. B. (2013). Allele-specific *FKBP5 DNA* demethylation mediates gene-childhood trauma interactions. *Nature Neuroscience, 16*: 33–41.

Kluft, R. P. (1984). Treatment of multiple personality disorder: a study of 33 cases. *Psychiatric Clinics of North America, 7*: 9–29.

Kluft, R. P. (1986). Personality unification in multiple personality disorder: a follow-up study. In: B. G. Braun (Ed.), *Treatment of Multiple Personality Disorder* (pp. 29–60). Washington, DC: American Psychiatric Press.

Kluft, R. P. (1987a). First-rank symptoms as a diagnostic clue to multiple personality disorder. *American Journal of Psychiatry, 144*: 293–298.

Kluft, R. P. (1987b). Unsuspected multiple personality disorder: an uncommon source of protracted resistance, interruption and failure in psychoanalysis. *Hillside Journal of Clinical Psychiatry, 9*: 100–115.

Kluft, R. P. (1993). Clinical approaches to the integration of personalities. In: R. P. Kluft & C. G. Fine (Eds.), *Clinical Perspectives on Multiple Personality Disorder* (pp. 101–133). Washington, DC: American Psychiatric Press.

Kluft, R. P. (2013). *Shelter from the Storm: Processing the Traumatic Memories of DID/DDNOS Patients with the Fractionated Abreaction Technique*. North Charleston, SC: Createspace Independent Publishing Platform.

Knoblauch, S. H. (2008). "A lingering whiff of Descartes in the air": from theoretical ideas to the messiness of clinical participation. Commentary on paper by the Boston Change Process Study Group. *Psychoanalytic Dialogues, 18*: 149–161.

Kogan, I. (1995a). *The Cry of Mute Children: A Psychoanalytic Perspective of the Second Generation of the Holocaust*. London: Free Association Books.

Kogan, I. (1995b). Love and the heritage of the past. *International Journal of Psychoanalysis, 76*: 805–824.

Kogan, I. (2002). "Enactment" in the lives and treatment of Holocaust survivors' offspring. *Psychoanalytic Quarterly, 71*: 251–272.

Kohut, H. (1971). *The Analysis of the Self: A Systematic Approach to the Psychoanalytic Treatment of Narcissistic Personality Disorders*. New York: International Universities Press.

Kohut, H. (1977). *The Restoration of the Self*. New York: International Universities Press.

Korczak, J. (1967). *Selected Works of Janusz Korczak*, M. Wolins (Ed.). Washington, DC: National Science Foundation.

Kramer, S. (1985). Object-coercive doubting: a pathological defense response to maternal incest. In: H. P. Blum (Ed.), *Defense and Resistance* (pp. 325–351). New York: International Universities Press.

Kramer, S. (1993). Personal communication.

Kris, E. (1956). The recovery of childhood memories in psychoanalysis. *Psychoanalytic Study of the Child, 11*: 54–88.

Krystal, H. (1968). *Massive Psychic Trauma*. New York: International Universities Press.

Lacan, J. (1953). Some reflections on the ego. *International Journal of Psychoanalysis, 34*: 11–17.

Lacan, J. (1982). *Female Sexuality*. New York: W. W. Norton.

Laplanche, J. (1976). *Life and Death in Psychoanalysis*. Baltimore, MD: Johns Hopkins University Press.

Lasky, R. (1978). The psychoanalytic treatment of a case of multiple personality. *Psychoanalytic Review, 65*: 355–380.

Laub, D. (1998). The empty circle: children of survivors and the limits of reconstruction. *Journal of the American Psychoanalytic Association, 46*: 507–529.

Laub, D., & Auerhahn, N. C. (1993). Knowing and not knowing massive psychic trauma: Forms of traumatic memory. *International Journal of Psychoanalysis, 74*: 287–302.

Laub, D., & Lee, S. (2003). Thanatos and massive psychic trauma: the impact of the death instinct on knowing, remembering, and forgetting. *Journal of the American Psychoanalytic Association, 51*: 433–463.

Laufer, M., & Laufer, M. E. (1984). *Adolescence and Developmental Breakdown: A Psychoanalytic View*. New Haven, CT: Yale University Press.

Lesch, A., & Lustick, I. A. (Eds.) (2005). *Exile and Return: Predicaments of Palestinians and Jews*. Philadelphia, PA: University of Pennsylvania Press.

Leveton, A. F. (1961). The night residue. *International Journal of Psychoanalysis, 42*: 506–516.

Levine, H. B. (Ed.) (1990). *Adult Analysis and Childhood Sexual Abuse*. Hillsdale, NJ: Analytic Press.

Lewin, B. D. (1954). Sleep, narcissistic neurosis, and the analytic situation. *Psychoanalytic Quarterly*, 23: 487–510.

Lichtenberg, J. D., & Slap, J. W. (1973). Notes on the concept of splitting and the defense mechanism of the splitting of representations. *Journal of the American Psychoanalytic Association*, 21: 772–787.

Liotti, G. (1992). Disorganized/disoriented attachment in the etiology of the dissociative disorders. *Dissociation*, 5: 196–204.

Loewald, H. W. (1960). On the therapeutic action of psychoanalysis. In: *Papers on Psychoanalysis* (pp. 221–256). New Haven, CT: Yale University Press, 1980.

Low, B. (1920). A revived sensation-memory. *International Journal of Psychoanalysis*, 1: 271–272.

Luther, M. (1543). *On The Jews and Their Lies*. In: F. Sherman & H. T. Lehmann (Eds.), *Luther's Works, Volume 47: Christian in Society IV*, M. H. Berman (Trans.). Philadelphia, PA: Fortress Press, 1971.

Lyons-Ruth, K. (1999). The two-person unconscious: Intersubjective dialogue, enactive relational representation, and the emergence of new forms of relational organization. *Psychoanalytic Inquiry*, 19: 576–617.

Lyons-Ruth, K. (2003). Dissociation and the parent–infant dialogue: a longitudinal perspective from attachment research. *Journal of the American Psychoanalytic Association*, 51: 883–911.

Mahler, M. S., Pine, F., & Bergman, A. (1975). *The Psychological Birth of the Human Infant: Symbiosis and Individuation*. New York: Basic Books.

Main, M. (1993). Discourse, prediction, and recent studies in attachment: implications for psychoanalysis. *Journal of the American Psychoanalytic Association*, 41(S): 209–243.

Main, M., & Solomon, J. (1990). Procedures for identifying infants as disorganized/disoriented during the Ainsworth Stranger Situation. In: M. T. Greenberg, D. Cicchetti, & E. M. Cummings (Eds.), *Attachment in the Preschool Years: Theory, Research, and Intervention* (pp. 121–160). Chicago, IL: University of Chicago Press.

Makari, G. (2008). *Revolution in Mind: The Creation of Psychoanalysis*. New York: HarperCollins.

Mark, D. (2009). Waking dreams. *Psychoanalytic Dialogues*, 19: 405–414.

Marks, J. (1993). *The Hidden Children: The Secret Survivors of the Holocaust*. New York: Fawcett Columbine.

Marmer, S. S. (1980). Psychoanalysis of multiple personality. *International Journal of Psychoanalysis*, 61: 439–459.

Marmer, S. S. (1991). Multiple personality: a psychoanalytic perspective. *Psychiatric Clinics of North America*, 14: 677–693.

Marten, K., & Psarakos, S. (1995). Evidence of self-awareness in the bottle-nose dolphin (*Tursiops truncates*). In: S. T. Parker, R. W. Mitchell, & M. L. Boccia (Eds.), *Self-Awareness in Animals and Humans: Developmental Perspectives* (pp. 361–379). New York: Cambridge University Press.

Masson, J. M. (Ed. & Trans.) (1985). *The Complete Letters of Sigmund Freud to Wilhelm Fleiss 1887–1904*. Cambridge, MD: Belknap Press of Harvard University Press, 1985.

Mayer, E. L. (2007). *Extraordinary Knowing: Science, Skepticism, and the Inexplicable Powers of the Human Mind*. New York: Bantam Books.

Mayer, J. (2011). The secret sharer: is Thomas Drake an enemy of the state? *The New Yorker*, 23 May: 46–57.

McDougall, J. (1992). *Plea for a Measure of Abnormality*. New York: Brunner/Mazel.

McDougall, W. (1926). *An Outline of Abnormal Psychology*. London: Methuen.

Mellor, D. J., Diesch, T. J., Gunn, A. J., & Bennet, L. (2005). The importance of "awareness" for understanding fetal pain. *Brain Research Reviews, 49*: 455–471.

Mintz, I. (1975). Parapraxis and the mother–child relationship. *Psychoanalytic Quarterly, 44*: 460–461.

Morris, B. (1999). *Righteous Victims: A History of the Zionist-Arab Conflict, 1881–2001*. New York: Vintage Books

Moses, R. (1978). Adult psychic trauma: the question of early predisposition and some detailed mechanisms. *International Journal of Psycho-Analysis, 59*: 353–363.

Moskowitz, S. (1983). *Love Despite Hate: Child Survivors of the Holocaust and Their Adult Lives*. New York: Schocken Books.

Neumann, E. (1954). *The Origins and History of Consciousness*, R. F. C. Hull (Trans.). Princeton, NJ: Princeton University Press, 1993.

Niederland, W. G. (1961). The problem of the survivor. *Journal of the Hillside Hospital, 10*: 223–247.

Nir, Y. (1989). *The Lost Childhood: A Memoir*. New York: Berkeley Books.

Nunberg, H. (1955). *Principles of Psychoanalysis*. New York: International Universities Press.

Ogawa, J. R., Srolfe, L. A., Weinfield, N. S., Carlson, E. A., & Egeland, B. (1977). Development and the fragmented self: Longitudinal study of dissociative symptomatology in a nonclinical sample. *Development and Psychopathology, 9*: 855–879.

Ogden, T. H. (1986). *The Matrix of the Mind: Object Relations and the Psychoanalytic Mind*. Northvale, NJ: Jason Aronson.

Ogden, T. H. (1994). The analytic third: working with intersubjective clinical facts. *International Journal of Psychoanalysis, 75*: 3–19.

Oliner, M. (1996). External reality: the elusive dimension of psychoanalysis. *Psychoanalytic Quarterly, 65*: 267–300.

Oren, A. (1995). Amir assassin? *The New Republic*, 25 December, 1995, pp. 11–12.

Orne, M. T., Dinges, D. F., & Orne, E. C. (1984). On the differential diagnosis of multiple personality disorder in the forensic context. *International Journal of Clinical and Experimental Hypnosis, 32*: 118–169.

Ornstein, A. (1986). The Holocaust: reconstruction and the establishment of psychic continuity. In: A. Rothstein (Ed.), *The Reconstruction of Trauma: Its Significance in Clinical Work* (pp. 171–191). Madison, CT: International Universities Press.

Ostow, M. (1989). Sigmund and Jacob Freud and the Philippson Bible. *International Review of Psychoanalysis, 16*: 483–492.

Oxnam, R. B. (2005). *A Fractured Mind*. New York: Hyperion.

Parens, H. (2004). *Renewal of Life: Healing from the Holocaust*. Rockville, MD: Schreiber Publishing.

Person, E. S., & Klar, H. (1994). Establishing trauma: the difficulty distinguishing between memories and fantasies. *Journal of the American Psychoanalytic Association, 42*: 1055–1081.

Piaget, J., & Inhelder, B. (1969). *The Psychology of the Child*. New York: Basic Books.

Pierce, M. (2006). Intergenerational transmission of trauma: what we have learned from our work with mother and infants affected by the trauma of 9/11. *International Journal of Psychoanalysis, 87*: 555–557.

Pirandello, L. (1921). *Right You Are! (If You Think So): A Parable in Three Acts*, A. Livingston (Trans.). In: *Three Plays*. New York: E. P. Dutton, 1922.

Plotnik, J. M., de Waal, F. B. M., & Reiss, D. (2006). Self-recognition in an Asian elephant. *Proceedings of the Natural Academy of Sciences, 103*: 17053–17057.

Poe, E. A. (1845). The raven. In: *Great Tales and Poems of Edgar Allan Poe: 21 Short Story Masterpieces Plus 34 Narrative and Lyric Poems* (p. 378). New York: Pocket Books, 1951.

Pruyser, P. W. (1975). What splits in "splitting"? A scrutiny of the concept of splitting in psychoanalysis and psychiatry. *Bulletin of the Menninger Clinic, 39*: 1–46.

Pulver, S. E. (2003). On the astonishing clinical irrelevance of neuroscience. *Journal of the American Psychoanalytic Association, 51*: 755–772.

Putnam, E. (1989). *Diagnosis and Treatment of Multiple Personality Disorder*. New York: Guilford Press.

Racker, H. (1953). A contribution to the problem of counter-transference. *International Journal of Psychoanalysis, 34*: 313–324.

Racker, H. (1957). The meanings and uses of countertransference. *Psychoanalytic Quarterly*, 26: 303–357.

Rapaport, D. (1949). *Emotions and Memory*. The Menninger Clinic Monograph Series No. 2. Baltimore, MD: Williams & Wilkins.

Reik, T. (1911). Fusion of sex and death: "The ring that is sexual guilt and formed by coming into being and punishing, by Eros and Thanatos". In: H. Nunberg & E. Federn (Eds.), *Minutes of the Vienna Psychoanalytic Society* (4 vols). New York: International Universities Press, 1962–1975.

Reis, B. E. (1995). Time as the missing dimension in traumatic memory and dissociation subjectivity. In: J. L. Alpert (Ed.), *Sexual Abuse Recalled: Treating Trauma in the Era of the Recovered Memory Debate* (pp. 215–233). Northvale, NJ: Jason Aronson.

Reiser, M. F. (1994). *Memory in Mind and Brain*. New Haven, CT: Yale University Press.

Rizzuto, A. M. (1998). *Why Did Freud Reject God?* New Haven, CT: Yale University Press.

Roith, E. (2006). Ishmael and Isaac: an enduring conflict. In: P. Coles (Ed.), *Sibling Relationships* (pp. 49–74). London: Karnac.

Rosenbaum, M. (1980). The role of the term schizophrenia in the decline of the diagnosis of multiple personality. *Archives of General Psychiatry*, 37: 1383–1385.

Ross, C. (1989). *Multiple Personality Disorder: Diagnosis, Clinical Features, and Treatment*. New York: John Wiley.

Rothschild, D. (2009). On becoming one-self: reflections on the concept of integration as seen through a case of dissociative identity disorder. *Psychoanalytic Dialogues*, 19: 175–187.

Rumi (2006). Childhood friends. In: C. Barks (Ed.), *A Year With Rumi: Daily Readings*. San Francisco, CA: HarperSanFrancisco.

Sachs, O. (1967). Distinction between fantasy and reality elements in memory and reconstruction. *International Journal of Psychoanalysis*, 48: 416–423.

Sandler, J. (1960). The background of safety. In: *From Safety to Superego: Selected Papers of Joseph Sandler* (pp. 1–8). New York: Guilford Press, 1987.

Schafer, R. (1968). *Aspects of Internalization*. New York: International Universities Press.

Schafer, R. (1973). Action: its place in psychoanalytic interpretation and theory. *Annual of Psychoanalysis*, 1: 159–195.

Schafer, R. (1983). *The Analytic Attitude*. New York: Basic Books.

Schilder, P. (1950). *The Image and Appearance of the Human Body*. New York: International Universities Press.

Schmemann, S. (1996). Arafat's Police Hunt Bombers, Pushed Hard by Israelis. *The New York Times,* 28 February, 1996.

Schwartz, P. G. (1988). A case of concurrent multiple personality disorder and transsexualism. *Dissociation, 1*: 48–51.

Science Daily (2012). Are we closing in on dark matter? 18 December.

Segev, T. (1993). *The Seven Million—The Israelis and the Holocaust,* H. Watzman (Trans.). New York: Hill and Wang.

Sender, R. M. (1986). *The Cage.* New York: MacMillan.

Shakespeare, W. (1593). *Love's Labour's Lost.* In: A. L. Rowse (Ed.), *Annotated Shakespeare, Volume I* (pp. 179–229). New York: Clarkson N. Potter, 1978.

Shakespeare, W. (1598). *As You Like It.* In: A. L. Rowse (Ed.), *Annotated Shakespeare, Volume I* (pp. 340–389). New York: Clarkson N. Potter, 1978.

Shakespeare, W. (1600–1601). *Hamlet.* In: A. L. Rowse (Ed.), *Annotated Shakespeare, Volume III* (pp. 195–267). New York: Clarkson N. Potter, 1978.

Shengold, L. (1967). The effects of overstimulation: rat people. *International Journal of Psychoanalysis, 48*: 403–415.

Shengold, L. (1989). *Soul Murder: Effects of Child Abuse and Deprivation.* New Haven, CT: Yale University Press.

Shirer, W. L. (1984). *The Nightmare Years: 1930–1940, Vol. 2.* New York: Little, Brown.

Silber, A. (1970). Functional phenomenon: historical concept, contemporary defense. *Journal of the American Psychoanalytic Association, 18*: 519–538.

Silber, A. (1979). Childhood seduction, parental pathology and hysterical symptomatology: the genesis of an altered state of consciousness. *International Journal of Psychoanalysis, 60*: 109–116.

Silberer, H. (1909). Report on a method of eliciting and observing certain symbolic hallucination-phenomena. In: D. Rapaport (Ed.), *Organization and Pathology of Thought* (pp. 195–207). New York: Columbia University Press, 1957.

Simon, B. (2010). Review. *Therapy After Terror: 9/11, Psychotherapists, and Mental Health.* By Karen M. Seeley. New York: Cambridge University Press, 2008, 242 pp., $35.00. *Journal of the American Psychoanalytic Association, 58*: 169–175.

Slap, J. W., & Slap-Shelton, L. (1991). *The Schema in Clinical Psychoanalysis.* Hillsdale, NJ: Analytic Press.

Slap, J. W., & Trunnell, E. E. (1987). Reflections on the self state dream. *Psychoanalytic Quarterly, 56*: 251–262.

Slipp, S. (1984). *Object Relations: A Dynamic Bridge Between Individual and Family Treatment*. New York: Jason Aronson.

Socarides, C. (1992). Discussion of Brenner's "Dissociative Character". Annual Meeting, American Psychiatric Association, Washington, DC, May.

Solomon, Z., Kotler, M., & Mikulincer, M. (1988). Combat-related post-traumatic stress disorder among second generation Holocaust survivors: preliminary findings. *American Journal of Psychiatry, 145*: 865–868.

Spezzano, C. (2007). A home for the mind. *Psychoanalytic Quarterly, 76*: 1563–1583.

Spiegelman, A. (1986). *Maus I: A Survivor's Tale: My Father Bleeds History*. New York: Pantheon Books.

Spiegelman, A. (1991). *Maus II: A Survivor's Tale: And Here My Troubles Began*. New York: Pantheon Books.

Spielrein, S. (1912). Die Destruktion als Ursache des Werdens. *Jahrbuch für psychoanalytische und psychopathologische Forschungen, Vol. 4*. Leipzig & Vienna. English edn: Destruction as a cause of coming into being. *Journal of Analytical Psychology, 39*(1944): 155–186.

Steele, B. F. (1970). Parental abuse of infants and small children. In: E. J. Anthony & T. Benedek (Eds.), *Parenthood: Its Psychology and Psychopathology* (pp. 449–477). Boston: Little, Brown.

Stekel, W. (1911). *Sex and Dreams: The Language of Dreams*, J. S. Van-Teslaar (Trans.). Boston, MA: Gorman Press, 1922.

Sterba, R. (1934). The fate of the ego in analytic therapy. *International Journal of Psychoanalysis, 15*: 117–126.

Stern, D. B. (1997). *Unformulated Experience: From Dissociation to Imagination in Psychoanalysis*. Hillsdale, NJ: Analytic Press.

Stern, D. N. (1985). *Interpersonal World of the Infant: A View From Psychoanalysis and Developmental Psychology*. New York: Basic Books.

Stern, D. N., Sander, L. W., Nahum, J. P., Harrison, A. M., Lyons-Ruth, K., Morgan, A. C., Bruschweilerstern, N., & Tronick, E. Z. (1998). Non-interpretative mechanisms in psychoanalytic theory: The "something more" than interpretation. *International Journal of Psycho-Analysis, 79*: 903–921.

Stevenson, R. L. (1886). *Strange Case of Dr. Jekyll and Mr. Hyde* (p. 109). London: Longmans, Green.

Stone, L. (1954). The widening scope of indications for psychoanalysis. *Journal of the American Psychoanalytic Association, 2*: 567–594.

Strachey, J. (1934). The nature of the therapeutic action of psychoanalysis. *International Journal of Psychoanalysis, 15*: 127–159.

Strenger, C. (1989). The classic and the romantic vision in psychoanalysis. *International Journal of Psychoanalysis, 70*: 593–610.

Styron, W. (1979). *Sophie's Choice*. New York: Random House.

Szalai, A. (1934). "Infectious" parapraxes. *International Journal of Psychoanalysis, 15*: 187–190.

Szwajger, A. B. (1990). *I Remember Nothing More: The Warsaw Children's Hospital and the Jewish Resistance*, T. Darowska & D. Stok (Trans.). New York: Pantheon.

Taylor, W. S., & Martin, M. F. (1944). Multiple personality. *Journal of Abnormal and Social Psychology, 39*: 281–300.

The Brothers Grimm (1812). *Grimm's Fairy Tales*. In: C.W. Eliot (Ed.), *The Harvard Classics Shelf of Fiction, Volume 17* (p. 162). New York: P. F. Collier & Son, 1917.

The Who (1969). *Tommy*. Decca Records/MCA.

Thomson, J. A. (2003). Killer apes on American Airlines, or: how religion was the main hijacker on September 11. In: S. Varvin & V. D. Volkan (Eds.), *Violence or Dialogue? Psychoanalytic Insights on Terror and Terrorism* (pp. 73–84). London: International Psychoanalytical Association.

Tolstoy, L. (1877). *Anna Karenin*. In: C. W. Eliot (Ed.), *The Harvard Classics Shelf of Fiction, Volume 16*. New York: P. F. Collier & Son, 1917.

Van der Kolk, B. A., & Kadish, W. (1987). Amnesia, dissociation, and the return of the repressed. In: B. A. Van der Kolk (Ed.), *Psychological Trauma* (pp.173–190). Washington, DC: American Psychiatric Press.

Van IJzendoorn, M. H., Fridman, A., Bakermans-Kranenburg, M., & Sagi-Schwartz, A. (2013). Aftermath of genocide: Holocaust survivors' dissociation moderates offspring level of cortisol. *Journal of Loss and Trauma, 18:* 64–80.

Varvin, S., & Volkan, V. D. (Eds.) (2003). *Violence or Dialogue? Psychoanalytic Insights on Terror and Terrorism*. London: International Psychoanalytic Association.

Venters, B. J., & Pugh, B. F. (2013). Genomic organization of human transcription initiation complexes. *Nature* (Online), 18 September.

Volavková, H. (Ed.) (1993). *. . . I Never Saw Another Butterfly . . .: Children's Drawings and Poems from Terezin Concentration Camp 1942–1944*. New York: Schocken Books.

Volkan, V. D. (1981). *Linking Objects and Linking Phenomena: A Study of the Forms, Symptoms, Metapsychology, and Therapy of Complicated Mourning*. New York: International Universities Press.

Volkan, V. D. (1996). Intergenerational transmission and "chosen" traumas: a link between the psychology of the individual and that of an ethnic group. In: L. Rangell & R. Moses-Hrnshovski (Eds.), *Psychoanalysis at the Political Border: Essays In Honor of Rafael Moses* (pp. 251–276). Madison, CT: International Universities Press.

Volkan, V. D. (1997). *Bloodlines: From Ethnic Pride to Ethnic Terrorism*. New York: Farrar, Straus and Giroux.

Volkan, V. D. (2002). September 11 and societal regression. *Group Analysis, 35*: 456–483.

Volkan, V. D. (2004). *Blind Trust: Large Groups and Their Leaders in Time of Crisis and Terror*. Charlottesville, VA: Pitchstone.

Volkan, V. D. (2006). *Killing in the Name of Identity: A Study of Bloody Conflicts*. Charlottesville, VA: Pitchstone.

Volkan, V. D., Ast, G., & Greer, W. F. (2002). *The Third Reich in the Unconscious: Transgenerational Transmission and Its Consequences*. New York: Brunner/Routledge.

Wälder, R. (1933). The psychoanalytic theory of play. *Psychoanalytic Quarterly, 2*: 208–224.

Wälder, R. (1936). The principle of multiple function: observations on over-determination. *Psychoanalytic Quarterly, 5*: 45–62.

Wardi, D. (1992). *Memorial Candles: Children of the Holocaust*. New York: Routledge.

Watkins, H. H., & Watkins, J. G. (1997). *Ego States: Theory and Therapy*. New York: W. W. Norton.

Watkins, J. G., & Watkins, H. H. (1979). Ego states and hidden observers. *Journal of Altered States of Consciousness, 5*: 3–18.

Weil, A. P. (1970). The basic core. *Psychoanalytic Study of the Child, 25*: 442–460.

Whitmer, G. (2001). On the nature of dissociation. *Psychoanalytic Quarterly, 70*: 807–837.

Wholey, C. C. (1926). Moving picture demonstration of transition states in a state of multiple personality. *Psychoanalytic Review, 13*: 343–346.

Winnicott, D. W. (1935). The manic defence. In: *Collected Papers: Through Paediatrics to Psycho-Analysis* (pp. 129–144). London: Basic Books, 1958.

Winnicott, D. W. (1942). Why children play. In: *The Child and the Outside World: Studies in Developing Relationships* (pp. 149–152). London: Tavistock, 1957.

Winnicott, D. W. (1945). Primitive emotional development. *International Journal of Psychoanalysis, 26*: 137–143.

Winnicott, D. W. (1953). Transitional objects and transitional phenomena. *International Journal of Psychoanalysis, 34*: 89–97.

Winnicott, D. W. (1955). Metapsychological and clinical aspects of regression within the psycho-analytical set-up. *International Journal of Psychoanalysis, 36*: 16–26.

Winnicott, D. W. (1960). Ego distortion in terms of true self and false self. In: *The Maturational Processes and the Facilitating Environment: Studies in the Theory of Emotional Development* (pp. 140–152). New York: International Universities Press, 1965.

Winnicott, D. W. (1971). *Playing and Reality*. London: Penguin Books.

Winnicott, D. W. (1974). Fear of breakdown. *International Review of Psycho-Analysis, 1*: 103–107.

Winnicott, D. W. (1988). *Human Nature*. New York: Schocken Books.

Wurmser, L. (2004). Psychoanalytic reflections on 9/11, terrorism, and genocidal prejudice. *Journal of the American Psychoanalytic Association, 52*: 911–926.

Yehuda, R. (1999). Parental PTSD as a risk factor for PTSD. In: R. Yehuda (Ed.), *Risk Factors for Posttraumatic Stress Disorder* (pp. 93–123). Washington, DC: American Psychiatric Press.

Yerushalmi, Y. H. (1991). *Freud's Moses: Judaism Terminable and Interminable*. New Haven, CT: Yale University Press.

INDEX